AF506267

Socioeconomic Change and Land Use in Africa

Socioeconomic Change and Land Use in Africa

The Transformation of Property Rights in Maasailand

Esther Mwangi

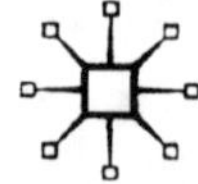

SOCIOECONOMIC CHANGE AND LAND USE IN AFRICA
Copyright © Esther Mwangi, 2007.

First published in 2007 by
PALGRAVE MACMILLAN™
175 Fifth Avenue, New York, N.Y. 10010 and
Houndmills, Basingstoke, Hampshire, England RG21 6XS
Companies and representatives throughout the world.

PALGRAVE MACMILLAN is the global academic imprint of the Palgrave Macmillan division of St. Martin's Press, LLC and of Palgrave Macmillan Ltd. Macmillan® is a registered trademark in the United States, United Kingdom and other countries. Palgrave is a registered trademark in the European Union and other countries.

ISBN-13: 978–1–4039–8005–2
ISBN-10: 1–4039–8005–5

Library of Congress Cataloging-in-Publication Data is available from the Library of Congress.

A catalogue record for this book is available from the British Library.

Design by Newgen Imaging Systems (P) Ltd., Chennai, India.

First edition: September 2007

10 9 8 7 6 5 4 3 2 1

Printed in the United States of America.

To the memory of my father, to my mother, brothers, and sisters

You are the wind beneath my wings

Contents

LIST OF TABLES

List of Illustrations

Acknowledgments

This book comes out of my dissertation research at Indiana University. I owe a tremendous debt of gratitude to my dissertation committee: Elinor Ostrom, Kathryn Firmin-Sellers, Clark Gibson, Mike McGinnis, and J. C. Randolph. I will always think of them as the best dissertation committee for their encouragement, engagement, energy, and enthusiasm. Lin Ostrom pushed me to get this book done. To this group of people, *Thank You* hardly says it all! I am responsible for any errors and omissions.

I am particularly grateful to the American Association of University Women, the Compton Foundation, the Institute for the Study of World Politics, and the National Science Foundation for their generous support of the research. Indiana University's Elinor Ostrom-Johan Skytte fellowship helped me finish writing the dissertation, an earlier version of this book.

The Indiana Workshop in Political Theory and Policy Analysis provided a wonderful home for the entire duration of my student life. Many thanks to all the staff for making it a warm and friendly place to work in. Vincent Ostrom, Amos Sawyer, and Amy Poteete were a great source of inspiration to this work. The Workshop's colloquium participants freely shared their ideas.

My gratitude also goes to my field researchers who remain very dear to me. Lucas Anduga, Peter Ndirangu, and Timothy Tonkei traversed many a dusty/muddy/nonexistent road with me. They gave selflessly of their time and their humor sustained me during the not-too-easy stretches of fieldwork. Asante sana!

In the Kajiado District Headquarters, the District Commissioner John Abduba, the District Land Adjudication Officer, Josiah Lessan, the District Livestock Officer Mwangi Kihiu, and Imke van der Horning and Lydia Naserian of the Netherlands Semi-Arid Development Project, all provided invaluable information and logistical support. Father Mol and Father Declan of the Catholic Diocese of Kajiado allowed the use of their extensive library and other facilities. In Nairobi, the Registrar of Group Ranches Suzy Kidemi was most supportive to this work. I thank you all. Life is dynamic, including Kenya's administration system, and the individuals mentioned here have since moved on to other positions in other places.

My peers in the program at Indiana, Anjali Bhat, Krister Andersson, Salvador Espinosa, Derek Kauneckis, Kunle Ooyerinde, Angelica Toniolo, and Nathan Vogt all played a part in encouraging me to the "phinishing" line and to get this book written. For this I am very grateful.

Because life is so dynamic, I finished the dissertation and I am currently working with a brilliant program on collective action and property rights. Ruth Meinzen-Dick pushed me to get this story "writ." Chelo Abrenilla, Stephan Dohrn, Helen Markelova, and Nancy McCarthy are wonderful colleagues. These CAPRi folk have read bits and pieces of this book and have all contributed in interesting and significant ways in getting it done and I thank them.

Finally, I am forever indebted to the children, women, and men of Enkaroni, Meto, Nentanai, and Torosei for the welcome, the warmth, and the friendship that was extended me during my stay, and continues to be extended to this time. This book is about you and for you. I hope it is a genuine reflection of your concerns. *Ashe OLENG!*

Foreword

Ruth Meinzen-Dick and Elinor Ostrom

Because of the fundamental importance of land for human identity as well as livelihoods, enormous debates have occurred over the best property rights system for land in Africa as well as in most developing countries and the developed world. The debates range from government ownership is best to private ownership is best, and recently community management is best. Those of us who have studied multiple governance and property rights systems on the ground have never found one broad type of property rights to be best. While each can generate a plausible narrative, simple "cure-all" proposals unfortunately overlook the many complexities of ecology and power relations that shape the property rights landscape.

Long ago, Robert Netting (1972, 1976) showed that when well-endowed peasants with substantial autonomy to devise their own rules used land in two ecological zones that they developed two different types of property rights systems. Swiss peasants used private property arrangements for their individual farm plots in the valleys of the Swiss Alps. The same individuals, however, crafted a variety of common property arrangements to manage their pastoral territories located in the patchy and not as productive highlands of the Swiss Alps. Netting's work three decades ago stressed the importance of devising property rights dependent on the conditions of the ecological systems and the importance of recognizing that indigenous peoples who had lived in regions for long periods of time were not automatically primitive peoples who did not know how to manage their land effectively.

In this book, Esther Mwangi brings her own background as an ecologist together with her advanced training in public policy to examine the adaptation of land tenure among the pastoral Maasai in Kenya. The study of the history of property rights changes and their results are extremely important in that it shows all of the governance systems in operation at some point in history. The British colonial powers presumed that the Maasai people were primitive and that they should be held responsible for the sparse vegetation occurring along the large extent of Southwestern Kenya. The colonial powers consistently took land away from the Maasai and either made it national parks under government ownership or turned large chunks over to those with strong connections to the colonial powers. The early independent government of Kenya continued the same practices. Government ownership, however, did not solve the problem of resource scarcity.

After independence, the government of Kenya created artificially bounded group ranches so that the Maasai would be comanaging much smaller chunks of land than had been in their initial distribution. This form of imposed, top-down comanagement did not work either. More recently, these group ranches have been subdivided into individual holdings. But privatization did not increase tenure security for many; youths and women in particular lost their customary rights to land.

This study demonstrates that none of the top-down, policy prescriptions were effective in terms of supporting better ecological conditions. All of them involved elite capture and a distribution of spoils.

A particularly important contribution of this study is that it gives a very detailed and important overview of how the process of privatization may lead to grossly unequal allocations that are also ecologically unviable. To understand these outcomes requires an analysis that includes attention to the linkage between ecological systems and the institutional, economic, social, and political environment that affect the incentives of resource users as well as relevant officials. Mwangi not only provides a cutting-edge theoretical analysis but backs this up with extensive field research drawing on multiple methods.

In 2005, the dissertation that forms an initial foundation for this book won the American Political Science Association's Harold Lasswell Prize for best dissertation in the field of public policy.

This book should be on the must reading list for all scholars and policy analysts recommending cure-alls for complex ecological systems. The fads and fashions of current policy prescriptions should not dominate serious, hard theoretical, and empirical research showing a wide diversity of property rights systems working relatively well in the diversity of ecological conditions that cover our earth. Hopefully, Esther Mwangi's book will be read by many policy makers before they continue the erroneous path that she demonstrates so vividly with her rigorous and careful research in Kenya.

CHAPTER ONE

THE POLICY PROBLEM: GROUP RANCH SUBDIVISION IN SEMIARID MAASAILAND

The transformation of property rights in land from "communal" rights based on indigenous systems to more formal, legally enforced individual rights has been a defining characteristic of agrarian development in many parts of sub-Saharan Africa (Okoth-Ogendo, 1993). Many African governments working closely with international development agencies anticipated that individual, private ownership would create incentives that would lead to increased agricultural production and greater environmental care. Consequently, they expended tremendous effort in transforming indigenous tenure systems in the late 1960s through to the early 1980s.

This book explores the process of property rights transformation from collectively held group ranches to individual, titled parcels among Maasai pastoralists in Kajiado district of Southwestern Kenya. It seeks to answer the following questions: What motivates group ranch members to subdivide their collective holdings into individual parcels? How is this transition process organized and conducted? What are the outcomes of subdivision? The Maasai have for a long time practiced transhumant pastoralism. Livestock forms the basis of their economic livelihoods, is the focus of their social relations, and is a critical element of their ethnic self-definition. Prior to major transformational changes, the Maasai sociopolitical structure comprised an age-set system, collective use of natural resources, and an "egalitarian" distribution of the means of production. The Maasai are administratively located in Kajiado and Narok districts of Southwestern Kenya.

I argue that while efficiency (or anticipated benefits of subdivision) is an important factor motivating group ranch members' support of subdivision, distributional concerns (how costs and benefits are distributed among actors) are dominant, both in the current and over time. The process of land allocation was marked by exclusion, conflict and competition, and an unequal distribution of wealth. Ecological outcomes of subdivision are ambiguous, but parcel reaggregation after subdivision suggests that landholdings are inappropriate to ecological conditions and also strengthens the argument that subdivision is a defensive strategy aimed at securing legitimate claims against unsanctioned appropriation.

The Maasai Group Ranches

Early experiments with land tenure reforms in Kenya's rangelands were group ranches in Maasai territory in the late 1960s and 1970s. A group ranch is land that has been demarcated and legally allocated to a group (Kenya, Republic of, 1968a) such as a tribe, a clan, section, family or other group of persons. The group ranch comprises a body of members to whom legal title has been jointly awarded and a management committee that is elected by this body. The committee is responsible for coordinating and implementing development projects on the group ranch. Although land is held in common by all group members, certain property rights, such a residency rights, are assigned to individuals. The group as a corporate body also retains some rights such as control over grazing rights, tillage, and water resources.

Group ranches were introduced in an attempt to control environmental degradation and to increase herd productivity. The British colonial government, as early as the 1950s, proposed the subdivision of Maasai communal land into privately owned parcels. According to the colonial authorities, indigenous systems of land management resulted in severe land degradation because they encouraged pastoralists to keep excessively large numbers of cattle that exceeded the environment's "carrying capacity." Colonial authorities thought that such systems provided inadequate incentives for groups or individuals to invest in conserving the land resource. Privatization was expected to create incentives that would lead individuals to adopt better resource management practice.

Initial efforts at privatization did not divide the range into individually owned units but rather sought to maintain legally titled group-held units, in keeping with the Maasai communal sociocultural structure. Upon Kenya's independence in 1963, successive governments continued to pursue the policies that had been proposed by colonial authorities. Although some group ranches were subdivided into individual units barely five years after their registration, most remained group-owned parcels until the mid-1980s. There is evidence that subdivision of group ranches into individual units is gaining momentum (Kimani and Pickard, 1998; Galaty, 1994a).

Viewed against the backdrop of Maasai pastoral livelihoods that have evolved in conditions of climatic variability and resource heterogeneity, the decision to subdivide is puzzling. Rainfall over most of Kajiado district is low, between 400 and 500 millimeters (about 16–20 inches) each year, and variably distributed across space and time. The mobility of Maasai herds allows for maximum and equitable exploitation of patchily distributed water and pasture. Mobility is also a crucial aspect of the reproduction of the social structure, structures that represent the dominant means of accumulating livestock and for investing herd capital (Kituyi, 1990). In most regions of the world where such conditions of variability persist the dominant land use is nomadic or transhumant pastoralism (Galaty and Johnson, 1990; Khazanov, 1984).

Subdivision of collective holdings into parcels and subsequent distribution among individuals may impede mobility, a vital component of livestock production systems under variable conditions (Bruce and Mearns, 2002; Niamir-Fuller, 1999; Behnke and Scoones, 1993; Sandford, 1983). Reduced mobility will increase vulnerability to drought and may jeopardize the viability of the livestock enterprise upon which pastoral livelihoods are dependent (Van der Brink et al., 1995). In the long run, it may also undermine the reproduction of the pastoral culture. No doubt the Maasai are aware of this.

But then *why* do they still pursue the subdivision of group ranches? How is this decision arrived at? Who participates? How is the transition organized? Unlike previous division of land in this area, when donor-sponsored, government-driven initiatives carved out group and individual ranches from the open, undivided Maasai range, the clamor for subdivision and individualization of these past two decades has emerged from within the Maasai community itself (Southgate and Hulme, 2000; Kimani and Pickard, 1998; Woodhouse, 1997; Blewett, 1995; Galaty, 1994a, 1994b; Rutten, 1992; Kituyi, 1990). Further, what are the environmental implications of this transition from group-owned land to individual units in a semiarid environment that is periodically ravaged by drought? This is a concern shared by many scholars who investigate why seemingly perverse property rights persist in the face of what would appear to be obvious alternatives.

The importance of land property rights as a policy issue cannot be overemphasized. In much of sub-Saharan Africa land is a crucial resource serving economic, cultural, and symbolic functions. Access to land is a key means to livelihood and survival. The institutions that define how land is held and distributed also determine social relations. These institutions range from constitutional provisions, statutes, and judicial rulings to norms, conventions, and customs regarding the allocation and use of property. Because property rights assign "ownership" to valuable assets and designate the distribution of the benefits and costs of resource use, they structure incentives for economic behavior (Libecap, 1989). Indeed, changes in property rights have been noted to affect macroeconomic performance and may result in economic growth or stagnation (Eggertsson, 1990; North, 1990).

The policy relevance of this study is broad. Land tenure reform is once again high on the development agenda (World Bank, 2003). Donors and governments of developing countries are seeking new avenues to invigorate economic growth and reduce poverty. Secure land rights for the rural and urban poor and foreign direct investment are viewed as important elements for growth and poverty reduction. Hernando de Soto's recent work in Peru, Egypt, Haiti, and the Philippines (de Soto, 2000) has refocused and animated the land reform debate. De Soto argues that because the assets and transactions of the poor in many developing and transition economies are informal, they lack formal, legal protection and consequently cannot be used to generate capital, one of the reasons why economic growth has stagnated in the developing countries, unlike the developed economies of the West. The absence of formal title to land and housing, for example, means that these assets cannot be used as collateral to support investment. Moreover informality increases the vulnerability of the poor to corruption and extortion by opportunistic groups and individuals, including government officials and politicians.

These arguments are not new but acquire force when the global figures of dead capital due to lack of titles in urban and rural areas is quantified as slightly over 9 trillion dollars. The study has been criticized on methodological grounds, not least because it assumes away the generally dismal performance of formalization efforts in Africa, Asia, and Latin America over the past five decades. The outcomes of some of these early privatization efforts are outlined later in the book. Interestingly, even in the United States, formalization of Native American land stifled individual entrepreneurship, increased litigation, and limited the value of land as collateral (Rodriguez et al., 2006). Nonetheless, de Soto's work has inspired the development community to act. Governments such as Tanzania, with support from Norway, are starting a major reform program to formalize the assets of the poor in both rural and urban areas. The Norwegian government has also formed a High Level Commission for the Legal Empowerment of the Poor, which views formalization of property ownership as a means to fight poverty.

This transition among the Maasai of Kajiado district represents the outcome of forces that will likely influence development throughout the arid and semiarid lands of Kenya, which account for approximately 80 percent of Kenya's terrestrial landmass. In many of these areas land is still collectively held as group ranches or as grazing schemes, and some following the Maasai example have started to privatize (Lesorogol, 2005, 2003). Similar processes may also be anticipated in different parts of Africa's rangelands, where group ranches and other forms of enclosures were implemented as part of rangeland development policy with donor support. The Kenyan group ranch was the forerunner of similar projects that were started in later periods in Rwanda, East Senegal, Niger, and Bostwana (Sandford, 1981). Broader land reforms aimed at restoring agricultural decline and as part of a wider process of democratic governance are gaining currency in different parts of Africa (Cotula et al., 2004; Toulmin and Quan, 2002). These reforms are legal in character, and scholars are troubled at the disconnect between local-level processes and macro-level policy (Wily, 2002). This research provides micro-level insights into the dynamics of how land resources are acquired and contested in order to inform these macro-scale legal reform processes.

Increasing democratization of former socialist regimes in central and eastern Europe and Asia in the early 1990s has seen extensive privatization of state and collective farmlands, while Mexico in Latin America continues to grapple with the challenges of redistributing land carved from the *ejidos* among its members (Banks, 2003; Fernandez-Gimenez, 2002; Munoz-Pina et al., 2003; Swinnen, 2001; Cungu and Swinnen, 2001; Doucha et al., 2001; Williams, 1996). All these countries are faced with the challenge of managing difficult transitions in property rights structures that will influence people's access to land and productive resources with ultimate implications for livelihoods, agricultural productivity, and environmental sustainability.

Group Ranch Subdivision in Kajiado District: Some Answers from Previous Research

There have been substantial efforts by scholars and practitioners to document and understand the process and implications of privatizing Maasai land. Earliest commentaries on group ranches expressed considerable concern over the organizational structure and ecological viability of group ranches. Davis (1970) envisioned that group ranch management committees would face severe challenges in enforcing livestock and grazing quotas and in dividing power within itself.[1] He also questioned the ecological and sociocultural basis of group ranches. Several years later Halderman's (1972) work in the Kaputiei region of northeastern Kajiado, where the first group ranches in Kajiado district were established, began to confirm the ecological challenge to group ranch viability. Because each group ranch did not include the complement of wet and dry season grazing, residents continued with their seminomadic practices. Group ranch boundaries were rapidly losing relevance particularly in times of stress. This undermines the primary intent of creating group ranches—to be able to exclude nonmembers as a way of creating incentives for members to manage their resources more carefully.

Njoka (1979) analyzing vegetation data over a 10-year period between 1969 and 1978 in 13 Kaputiei group ranches finds a decline in desirable grass species and an increase of undesired species, largely the result of higher grazing intensities. Investigation into livestock productivity, however, showed that group ranches were just as efficient, if not more efficient than the individual ranches that were created at about the same time (Bekure et al., 1991; Onchoke, 1986; Evangelou, 1984; White and Meadows, 1981). Increasing commoditization of livestock and livestock products seems to severely constrain women's access to and decision making over such resources (Kipury, 1989; Talle, 1988). The economic gap between Maasai men and women has widened.

Barely 10 years after their creation, group ranches begun to contemplate subdividing. A new set of closely related issues emerged. Halderman's (1985) continued work among the Kaputiei cautioned against the individualization of group land as the semiarid to arid nature of most land in Kajiado district required large land units to compensate for fluctuating water and grazing. Nonetheless, group ranches continued to subdivide, those in Kaputiei having begun as early as the late 1970s and early 1980s. Demands for subdivision in other parts of the Kajiado district increased between 1984 and 1996. By 1996, titles had been issued in 22 group ranches as compared to seven in 1984; 11 other group ranches were in various stages of subdivision (Kimani and Pickard, 1998). My field findings indicate that by 2000, 31 group ranches had subdivided and had titles issued, 14 had resolved to subdivide and were being surveyed, and only 12 have resisted subdivision.

What fueled these increased demands for individualization? Many of the earlier subdivisions were conducted in the Kaputiei and Keekonyokie areas of northeastern and northern areas of the districts that are relatively closer to Nairobi, Kenya's capital city, than other group ranches in the district. Both are also located in areas of significantly higher rainfall than the bulk of Kajiado district. Galaty (1993) characterizes the demand for subdivision as "overdetermined"; all individuals, both rich and poor were in favor, hence the overwhelming decision to subdivide. Three reasons seem to drive this overwhelming support for subdivision.

Group ranch members seem to anticipate "development" once individuals receive land titles. They would then use these titles as collateral against loans that they would invest in productivity-enhancing technologies (Galaty, 1999a, 1999b; Kimani and Pickard, 1998; Rutten, 1992; Grandin, 1987b). The success of the early individual ranchers, who had obtained loans from the Agricultural Finance Corporation and installed dips, water tanks, bought grade cattle, built permanent houses, and bought cars, was instrumental in fueling the desire. Most of these studies were conducted in the Kaputiei group ranches, with the exception of Kimani and Pickard (1998) who studied 10 group ranches in different parts of Kajiado district, across different rainfall zones and Maasai sections.

Individual's preferences for subdivision were also shaped by an increasing sense of uncertainty and dissatisfaction with the group ranch structure as a suitable mechanism of securing their land needs. Population increase within individual group ranches and the automatic registration of successive age sets increased the number of individuals entitled to a share in a limited land resource (Galaty, 1999a, 1999b, 1994a, 1994b; Kimani and Pickard, 1998). This sense of insecurity was heightened when outsiders or individuals with no legitimate claim to group ranch land were registered and allocated parcels (Galaty, 1992; Rutten, 1992). In some instances, parts of group ranch land were carved out and issued as individual ranches to those with the ability to influence the management committee (Galaty, 1994a, 1992). This last problem was particularly intense in Loodariak and Olchorro-Onyori group ranches in Keekonyokie section. Here, officials from the Ministry of Lands and some of their spouses were allocated group ranch land (Ole Simel, 1999). In Loodariak, for example, a total of 345 outsiders were registered and allocated a total of 20,000 hectares at the expense of 2,000 rightful owners.

In the more arid areas of Loitokitok division in southern Kajiado district, where the Ilkisongo reside, demands for subdivision are closely tied to the development of commercialized agriculture (Southgate and Hulme, 2000; Woodhouse, 1997). The success of irrigated cultivation by Kikuyu and Kamba immigrants has led to increasing calls for the subdivision of the Kimana group ranch.[2]

Thus there is a mix of motivations underlying individuals' decisions to support subdivision. But how has this process of subdivision played itself out? How were decisions made, and what were the outcomes? Few authors have tackled this question in much detail. In Elangata Wuas group ranch of the Ilodookilani section, the decision to subdivide was taken amidst great tensions between the Iseuri age set and their "sons" who feared exclusion (Galaty, 1994a). In Embolioi and Olkinos group ranches, a highly skewed distribution of land resources followed subdivision (Rutten, 1992).

Ole Simel (1999) provides a clearer illustration of the intensely controversial and political nature of subdivision. In Ewaso-Kedong, for example, large parcels were distributed to the committee members and to individuals with close ties to the committee. Sometimes these individuals were awarded more than one parcel. The extent of concentration was such that about 40,000 acres of group land were distributed among 400 individuals, leaving the remaining 800 members to share 12,000 acres. Individuals who were openly opposed to this inequitable distribution of holdings were allocated small parcels or parcels of lower productivity land as punishment. The previously cited case of Loodariak is yet another example. In order to silence dissension, the group ranch committee in collaboration with local government administration used threats and bribery. The Loodariak case is still under review by the courts. Ole Simel (1999) thus provides some valuable insights into the nature of interactions that shaped the transition from group ranches to individual parcels. Interactions that have far-reaching consequences on access to and distribution of land resources to different segments of the community.

These findings reveal crucial features of the process of subdivision, and generate more questions. If some members supported subdivision, such as the Iseuri elders of Elangata Wuas, while others did not, such as their "sons," then how was the transition implemented? How does social differentiation within the group ranch affect members' preferences for subdivision? What were the decision rules and how did they affect outcomes? Who were excluded and why? Because the bulk of the cited studies were conducted mainly in the Keekonyokie and Kaputiei areas, would the same results be found in the more drier regions of Kajiado district that are less close to Nairobi city? What was the role of different institutions, both "formal" and customary, in structuring the process, in creating accountability, and in mediating conflict? Clearly, a closer look at actors, their incentives, the institutions, and the varied interactions that determined the outcome of subdivision might deepen our understandings of this critical process.

The Evolution of Property Rights: Theoretical Perspectives

The property rights approach provides a set of theories that can be used to explain the Maasai's radical departure from the extensive pastoralism they have practiced for generations. The approach to property rights followed in this book is one out of a set of potential explanations for why and how property rights change. Marxist and dependency scholars, for example, tend to homogenize the preferences and incentives of differentiated actors, offer inadequate explanations of how collective outcomes are achieved, and ascribe to the state a dominant role that may not be borne out empirically (Gibson, 1999; North, 1997; Firmin-Sellers, 1996). Neoclassical analyses on the other hand overlook power asymmetries in society and the possibility that elite individuals and groups can work to block change. This book also adopts the foundational premise of the new institutionalism, which views individuals as goal-oriented actors who pursue strategies they believe will lead to their most preferred outcome/s, and uses the institutional analysis and development framework for organizing inquiry (Ostrom, 2005, 1990).[3] An institutional analysis that recognizes the role of politics and the possibility that economic actors will actively seek to improve their outcomes can provide greater insights into how specific property arrangements are changed or sustained.

What Motivates the Individualization of Property Rights to Resources?

Efficiency Arguments

Problems with sustainable and efficient use of resources have long been identified in scholarly literature. Hardin's (1968) tragedy thesis suggests that individually rational behavior in collective, interdependent settings may prevent the securing of socially desirable outcomes. Privatization and/or nationalization were Hardin's solutions, which have been criticized. He confuses common property with open access situations (Ciriacy-Wantrup and Bishop, 1975), disempowers the human agent (Ostrom et al., 1999), and leaves unaccounted-for situations in diverse geographical and historical settings, in which local populations have successfully used and managed communal resources (Ostrom, 2005; Ostrom, 1990; McCay and Acheson, 1987). Hardin's (1968) argument has had tremendous influence in justifying tenure reforms in favor of land privatization in much of sub-Saharan Africa. Government support for the early enclosure of the Maasai commons in the late 1960s in Kenya was based on tragedy-like arguments.

Hardin's call for privatization resonated among a group of property rights scholars engaged in understanding the emergence and evolution of property rights. According to these scholars, the development of exclusive property rights over land and related natural resources is triggered by changes in the economy such as technological innovation, changes in relative factor scarcities, and the creation of new markets (North and Thomas, 1973; Alchian and Demsetz, 1972; Demsetz, 1967). These changes in the external economy will cause the benefits of claiming rights in the new and privatized situation to exceed the costs of negotiating and enforcing those rights. Individuals will seek to adjust property rights to capture these new opportunities.

In a study of the introduction of private ownership of beavers among Indian hunters in eastern Canada, Demsetz (1967) demonstrates that due to the development of the commercial fur trade, hunting of beavers increased and individual hunters introduced exclusive rights in order to foster sustainable use and an increase in community wealth. North and Thomas (1973) provide a historical account of changing property rights in the Middle Ages. They show that plentiful land and scarce labor during the ninth century led to the feudal/manorial system, which institutionalized property rights over labor services. By the twelfth century, a growing population led to a change in the relative factor scarcities, resulting in a shift of property rights toward land instead of labor. The result was the beginning of the enclosure movement. These two case studies exemplify the basic arguments of the early property rights scholars: when a resource becomes scarce, for example, due to increasing population, it increases the value of a resource, which in turn increases the gains from privatization. The gains from privatization are enhanced because the governance costs of collective regimes are eliminated.

Demsetz et al. have also defined the incentive structures that emerge with privatization (Alchian and Demsetz, 1972). The ability to exclude others encourages individuals to invest in the quality of the resource because the person who bears the costs also reaps the rewards. Also, the transferability of rights under private property arrangements is supposed to ensure that resources end up with the most productive users. Privatization is thus expected to increase land or agricultural productivity and the wise use and conservation of resources. These preceding arguments crystalize around the notion of efficiency. Private, individual property rights to land are considered to be efficient, and institutions will always evolve toward greater efficiency. Property regimes other than private property for land are considered by many economists to be inefficient and prone to overuse.

Distributional Arguments
The economic theory of the origins and evolution of property rights based on efficiency is incomplete. It focuses exclusively on the "demand" side of a much wider property rights equation (Platteau, 2000; Eggerttsson, 1990; Libecap, 1998, 1989; Feeny, 1993; Thomson et al., 1992; North, 1990; Ostrom, 1990). Economic gains on their own are not necessary or sufficient to induce the implementation of alternative property rights arrangements. Instead, distributional conflicts and political intervention are crucial determinants of the path of institutional change. Indeed, institutions are not always created to be socially efficient; they may sometimes be created to serve specialized interests, particularly of those who have the power to devise new rules. Thus a more complete theory of property rights must address politics. State interventions, as well as the distributional consequences of private property, are neglected by the proponents of efficiency.

A wide diversity of property regimes exist in the real world, apart from private, individualized rights. Knight (1992) suggests that what discriminates institutions from each other is how they distribute benefits in society, rather than whether or not they are beneficial. Distribution refers to how wealth and political power will be assigned among individuals in society as a consequence of implementing the new property rights structure (Libecap, 1989). Understanding the origins of property rights and their transformations entails understanding the nature of conflicts over distribution and of the way in which these conflicts are resolved. This means that we need to identify the winners and losers of institutional change and their interactions within the political arena (Firmin-Sellers, 1996; Libecap, 1989).

Conflict over distribution is shaped by the formula used to allocate assets during privatization (Libecap, 1989). There are several ways of distributing assets (Platteau, 2000): rents can be divided among customary users in proportion to their respective rates of use in the status quo arrangement, or they can be divided equally among existing rights holders, or, alternatively, after first excluding those who do not meet predetermined criteria, rights can be allocated by equal distribution among those who conform to the predetermined criteria. Proportional division seems to be more common in the Western Hemisphere (Libecap, 1989; Roemer, 1989), while exclusion, followed by equal subdivision is typical of much of sub-Saharan Africa (Platteau, 2000; Baland and Platteau, 1998). The determination of how to distribute benefits is, however, an empirical matter that depends on social norms of equity and fairness that prevail within a community (Ensminger, 1992).

Because different allocation mechanisms distribute assets in different ways, actors will attempt to influence the process of institutional change in ways that accord them maximum advantages. Those likely to be disadvantaged will organize to oppose change. Those likely to benefit under the new arrangement will support the change. Each of the actors will engage those political institutions, both formal-legal and customary, that they perceive will be responsive to and best articulate their claims. Conflict will be less and change more likely where the anticipated aggregate benefits are large, where interests are more homogenous, and where the distribution of wealth under the proposed change is equalized (Libecap, 1989). Change may be slowed and even blocked where the distribution of benefits is concentrated.

In order to end conflict and implement new property arrangements some actors may invoke the authority of the state (Firmin-Sellers, 1996). Alternatively, powerful actors with a relative bargaining advantage may constrain others to comply with new institutional rules (Knight, 1992). Due to the resources they have, powerful actors make for credible commitments during bargaining and indeed may threaten retaliation. Weaker parties may thus be pressured to accept a less-preferred alternative.

The inclusion of distributional issues greatly enriches the analysis of property rights transformations. By acknowledging and extending the notion of individual benefit-cost calculus, distributional arguments capture the heterogeneity of societal actors and the asymmetries among variously endowed individuals with diverse interests and stakes in the outcome of institutional change. Thus an analysis that includes distributional issues may help explain institutional diversity but also significantly may help account for the implementation and existence of seemingly "irrational" property regimes, where more "efficient" alternatives are feasible. This is relevant in explaining the puzzle of why group ranch members in Kajiado district would support the subdivision of their land into smaller, individualized units. Group ranches seem better suited to the environmental conditions, make for greater compatibility with the Maasai cultural practice of extensive pastoralism, and allow for economies of scale in the provision of infrastructure.

Despite these significant inroads, property rights scholars are yet to more fully incorporate the role of the state and the impact of social capital (Baland and Platteau, 1998).

Alternative Mechanisms for Assigning Property Rights

The State

The market is not the only way in which property rights are allocated. Institutional change also depends on the capability and willingness of the political order to provide new arrangements, the "supply" side of institutions (Feeny, 1993; Thompson et al., 1992; Ostrom, 1990). When government officials in Thailand anticipated benefits from public investments, they met the demands for exclusive rights, yet declined to do so when institutional interventions would have been harmful to the interests of influential officials. Rulers, such as the paramount chief of Akyem Abuakwa of Ghana, have also manipulated political institutions to meet their own individual objectives (Firmin-Sellers, 1996, 1995). The supply of institutions, and in particular the political and economic costs and benefits to the ruling elites, is key to explaining the nature and scope of change.

In its pursuit of promoting its policy objectives in agriculture, political stabilization, political control, resource management, and land redistribution the African states in Ethiopia, Nigeria, Tanzania, and even South Africa have at various points in their histories attempted to extinguish or suppress private property to pave way for collectivization or national ownership (Okoth-Ogendo, 1993). Similarly, colonial Kenya privatized parts of the settler-occupied highlands to induce agricultural production. The end of the colonial era saw the same state encouraging land privatization in the African reserves to defuse escalating political tensions due to landlessness. Thus apart from supplying enforcement, registration, survey, and titles within a market-based framework of institutional change, the state directly influences change through its policy choices. This has been evident not only in Africa but in other parts of the world as well (Sanberg, 1993; Jodha, 1992, 1987).

Cultural Institutions

The market and the state are just a part of a diverse complex of systems for the creation of rights and access to land. In many parts of Africa indigenous forms of rights to land still persist. Land under customary tenure currently comprises about 60 percent of all of Africa's land (Bruce, 1998, 1988).

Having evolved in particular environments among specific ethnic or linguistic groups, such systems accordingly exhibit a wide range of diversity. Nonetheless, certain commonalities exist. Attributes such as ethnic identity and kinship in concert with status, gender, seniority, and residence feature prominently in the determination of access and use rights (Bruce, 1998; Shipton and Goheen, 1992; Berry, 1989; Bruce and Migot-Adholla, 1994). Group control over land is fairly common. The group may be an extended family, a lineage, a clan, a village, or a tribe, defined either by common descent, common residence, or both. Membership in the group often determines the nature, volume, and strength of rights. Rights over land are allocated for the relatively exclusive use of individuals or families in the group; such rights are not dissimilar to private ownership. The rights are allocated and administered by a local, indigenous authority, such as lineage elders, tribal chiefs, or land priests. Rights are held in trust for future generations by the local authorities, and the only rights possible are use rights; land transfers are rarely allowed. Rights may be allocated to nonmembers if they are affiliated to the group through residence or marriage and are granted temporary use rights subject to relatively strict controls. Thus the rights of use, transfer, allocation, and control and administration lie in different hands, while the negotiability of social identities introduces fluidity in indigenous land rights that can result in insecure rights.

Costs and Benefits of Private and Common Property Regimes

Each property rights structure has costs and benefits, which are not completely independent of the nature of the resource under investigation or of the technology that determines the use of the resource (Ostrom, 2001b; Kirk, 1999; Bromley, 1991a; Dahlman, 1980).

Three types of costs have been identified for communal ownership: costs of establishment and protection, internal governance costs, and the costs of excluding nonmembers. Governance costs include costs of decision making with respect to resource use, the costs of establishing organizations to facilitate production and exchange, and the costs of monitoring use. Governance costs are likely to vary with group size and heterogeneity (Platteau, 2000; Baland and Platteau,1996; Ostrom, 1990; Libecap, 1989; Field, 1986; Olson, 1965). They increase when rights holders violate or circumvent collective decisions on resource use. Governance costs also increase with population increase. By increasing the number of users, population pressure increases both the likelihood of externalities as well as their magnitude. Because population pressure increases the scarcity value of resources, it also induces a corresponding increase in the aggregate losses from collective exploitation. Under these circumstances, private property appears beneficial as it internalizes these externalities without involving any governance costs.

The creation and maintenance of individual property is not without cost either. These include the costs of boundary demarcation, recording and transferring titles, and fencing (Bromley, 1989). Where there are economies of scale that can be realized by maintaining collective ownership but ownership is individualized, several costs emerge. In the case of hunting or grazing, for instance, owners will need to reach a joint decision on keeping the range open and accessible (Platteau, 2000; Dahlman, 1980). This decision increases transactions costs in two ways. First, it needs considerable interaction among individuals, to either negotiate compensation for each others' use of grazing or for the damage of each others' property. Second, since each individual owns a geographically defined piece of soil, some may acquire a strong bargaining position and threaten withdrawal. Under conditions of economies of scale collective rights in grazing save on transactions costs. When the hidden costs of privatization are incorporated into the theory the costs of privatization may be far greater than that of communal ownership.

The previous review of the benefit-cost structure of different property arrangements compels a more careful reflection on the relationship between biophysical aspects of resources and the property regime. It is here that notions of sustainability, economic productivity, and the applicability of institutions to environmental and cultural contexts become relevant. These are issues that have only incompletely been addressed in the property rights debate (Ostrom, 2001a, 1990; Nugent and Sanchez, 1998; Bromley, 1991a; Dahlman, 1980). The existence of a wide diversity of property arrangements, sometimes even within the same cultural and socioeconomic community, begs questions that are not necessarily answered by a strict consideration of economic calculations on their own.

Studies, particularly in the high mountainous regions of the world, draw attention to the complexity of factors influencing the choice of property regimes. In Torbel in the Swiss Alps, for example, where population, technology, and political factors remained relatively stable for close to five centuries, the patchiness of high alpine pastures and the labor economies of collective herding necessitated a communal structure to access and management (Netting, 1976). By contrast, lower altitude pastures, grain fields, and vineyards, that is, resources of dependable productivity that can be improved in different ways and may be exploited by individual or family labor, were held under individual tenure. A similar situation, in which both communal and private property exist within the same vicinity and is practiced by the same people, occurs in the central Andean Alps (Guillet, 1981). Communal control, which is strongly correlated with pasture, is found at higher altitudes. Private, individual control is found in lower altitudes where continuous irrigated agriculture and specialized horticulture are practiced. The vertical gradient imposes constraints to land intensification, such as irrigation and ox-drawn ploughs. Stevenson (1991), working in the Bernese Alps finds that areas with better soil, fewer swampy spots, better grass quality, and better exposure to the sun are more likely to be individual property. But areas with poor precipitation conditions, strong prevailing winds, and poor exposure to the sun discourage individual ownership. These results are reiterated by Mendes (1988) working in the Moroccan Alps.

This relationship between environmental conditions and institutional choice is just as clear in the arid and semiarid regions of the tropics, which though culturally distinct share commonalities in supporting pastoral modes of land use and in which property regimes, at least over land, are more often than not collective in nature (Khazanov, 1984; Galaty and Johnson 1990; Sandford, 1983). But there are exceptions. Among the Shahsevan of Iranian Aberzaijan, individual households are allocated specific parcels for winter and summer pastures (Tapper, 1979, 1985, cited in Nugent and Sanchez, 1991). These are inheritable and transferable. The weather patterns here are unusually stable with little variation.

A more indicative example of interactions between institutions and environment is found among the Arabs occupying the Bukhara region of northeastern Afghanistan (Barfield, 1981; Kraler, 1955, cited in Nugent and Sanchez, 1991). Pasture rights among these herders were privately held until the mid-nineteenth century. Though highly seasonal, the weather here was regular and dependable. Later in the century this region came under Russian control, sending the Arabs into the Qataghan region of Afghanistan. In this malaria-infested area, pasture quality was low and the rainfall was highly variable interanually and spatially. This favored collective landholding and a decentralized, transhumant practice that was nomadic in character. After the First World War, the same herders were once again moved to better and more dependable pastures. Here, use rights were distributed to individual households and could be sold or rented. Due to the low risk involved, there was little advantage in large grazing grounds for communal grazing.

Clearly, not all land is the same, not all uses of the land are the same, and not all uses of the land are year round. The examples outlined above indicate that common property might have certain distinct advantages over private, individual property in certain biophysical situations. These advantages are related to minimizing risk in highly variable environments, promoting equitability of variable resources, and minimizing production and transactions costs (Niamir-Fuller, 1999, 1998; Scoones, 1995; Galaty and Johnson, 1990; Sandford, 1983; Dahlman, 1980).

In the alpine environment, for instance, a high variability of yields in different spaces, the dangers of avalanches and landslides destroying buildings, fences, grazing areas, paths, and roads impose considerable risk. Common property arrangements spread these risks, and they serve as an insurance against individuals incurring frequent financial expenses to mitigate/alleviate the consequences of environmental variability (Picht, 1987). In addition, not only does common property allow a more equitable distribution of a variable, though critical resource for Swiss peasants, but it is also associated with considerable savings on transactions and production costs. In risky environments, fencing costs are lower where individuals combine efforts as opposed to having a private owner fence a larger area. Economies of scale in herding, path, and building construction are also important. The Swiss grazing commons have for a long time been characterized by a well-defined community of users who are able to exclude outsiders. Consequently, the costs of establishing and protecting their collective rights are much lower than the costs of establishing rights for a large number of individually owned parcels. In the latter situation, each individual would have to find and transact with each other individual owner for every issue that arises. In addition, where facilities are unevenly distributed those disadvantaged will need to be compensated. In extreme cases even if most individuals can agree to cooperate, a few may follow a hold-out strategy, undermining the effort at reinstituting collective enterprise.

Similar arguments have been made for African rangelands. Here, rainfall variability is more important than the traditional determinants of property rights such as population density. Productivity is marginal and variable, and the costs of privatization may far exceed the benefits. Collective rights to land and land resources are a more equitable way of distributing variable resources and minimizing risk.

Thus the emergence and evolution of property rights occurs within a complex interplay of ecological, economic, political, and cultural conditions and are often designed to match the characteristics of the resource being exploited and the people who do the exploiting.

Privatization: Some Empirical Outcomes

The evolution of land rights in various parts of the world at different times lends considerable support for predictions by property rights scholars. From the pastoral Borana of southern Ethiopia (Kamara et al., 2004) to the pastoral Maasai areas of Amboseli in southern Kajiado (Woodhouse, 1997), to the frontier areas of the Brazilian Amazon (Alston et al., 1995), to colonial Kenya (Ault and Rutman, 1993); among the Orma pastoralists of Kenya (Ensminger, 1992); in Thailand (Feder and Feeny, 1991); and among the pastoralists of southern Sudan (Behnke, 1985a), exclusive property rights have emerged in response to increased commercialization and to changes in relative prices. In earlier times, the English parliamentary enclosures of 1790–1850, the highland clearances of Scotland of 1750–1855, and the fencing of the open range in North America from 1870 to 1890 bear historical testimony to insights of the property rights school (Richards, 1982; Dahlman, 1980; Yelling, 1977; Osgood, 1970; Mingay, 1968). In all these cases changes in the system of land allocation were initiated by economic forces.

But what have been the outcomes of privatization? Privatized, individual tenures do not automatically result in increased land productivity in cultivating regions of Kenya, Rwanda, Uganda, and Ghana (Bruce and Migot-Adholla, 1994; Migot-Adholla et al., 1991). In pastoral areas, though systematic studies are few, privatization programs have neither resulted in substantial increases in pastoral (livestock) productivity nor in decreased land degradation. In Kenya's Maasailand, for example, group ranches experienced higher net returns to land, labor, and livestock than private, individualized ranches (Onchoke, 1986). Other studies show that economic output rates between the two are barely different (Evangelou, 1984; White and Meadows, 1981). Land privatization here does not seem to be a sufficient condition for enhancing livestock productivity. Similar conclusions have been drawn in Botswana (de Ridder and Wagenaar, 1984) and in Angola (de Carvalho, 1974).

With regard to the environment and its wise use following privatization, studies in Botswana (Dahlberg, 2000), Senegal (Thebaud et al., 1995), New Zealand, Kenya (Rutten, 1992; Njoka, 1979), and Mongolia (Sheehy, 1993; Williams, 1996) point to instances of degradation following the privatization of formerly extensive pastoral resources. In fact overstocking and environmental deterioration appear to be just as common and serious in areas of rangeland in parts of the United States of America and Australia where both land and livestock are individually owned (Sandford, 1983). However, one recent study based on the assumption that herd migration is a way of conserving the environment suggests that privatization in Kajiado district enhances environmental conservation (Kabubuo-Mariara, 2005).

Apart from failing to meet empirical expectations in certain parts of the world under certain conditions, privatization may result in new externalities (Platteau, 1995). Property rights, and in particular rights to land, comprise a bundle of related rights, with each stick in the bundle representing a stream of benefits that accrue to the rights holder (Schlager and Ostrom, 1992; Bromley, 1991a). Yet in the interpretation of private property rights, some economists tend to focus more narrowly on alienation rights. In many parts of the world different people may hold different rights, at different times, to the same resource. Commentators on African tenure systems indicate that indigenous systems allow for multiple overlapping rights and claims (Bruce and Migot-Adholla, 1994; Berry, 1993; Okoth-Ogendo, 1989). Consequently, even where rights to resources may be tending toward greater exclusivity, some community members may, for example, have primary rights that are concurrent and/or sequential with secondary rights that permit entry or the collection of certain resources such as firewood, or construction materials, or even the grazing of livestock on the stubble remaining after crop harvesting. The rights to access, to manage, to exclude others from a resource, or to transmit or alienate a resource must all be considered (Schlager and Ostrom, 1992). Thus property rights, including private, individual property are not absolute but instead seem to be a function of what society is willing to acknowledge, defend, and enforce.

Resource privatization and land reforms conducted in many parts of the developing world disregarded the multiple overlapping rights to resources, denying individuals and groups their long-established access to critical resources (Wiebe and Meinzen-Dick, 1998; Meinzen-Dick et al., 1997; Rocheleau and Edmunds, 1997; Seabright, 1993; Coldham, 1978). Women are particularly disadvantaged because their rights to land are often dependent on a male relative (Lastarria-Cornhiel, 1997).

A concentration of land wealth is yet another externality that has been widely documented. Quite clearly the virtues of privatizing property rights to land have not been realized in all cases.

Path Dependence: Linking Choices across Time

In their efforts to achieve a deeper understanding of institutional change scholars are continuously faced with the dilemma of whether current changes are unique and separable from long-run processes. Some argue that institutional change is incremental; any change occurs within the parameters of existing or prior institutions (Libecap, 1998, 1989; North, 1990; Ostrom, 1990). History thus has a role in the explanation of institutional transformation. In order to understand today's choices, we need to track the incremental evolution of institutions. Path dependence is a common phenomenon in evolving systems such as biological systems or ecosystems and is an important feature in the development of social and political institutions.

How does history matter? North (1990) provides the conceptual foundation for a path-dependent framework. He suggests that actors are faced with making choices, both political and economic, at each point in the development of institutions. Although these choices may provide alternatives, previously viable options may, however, be foreclosed due to positive feedbacks within an existing institutional pattern. Thus change and/or reform may be difficult to achieve. Positive feedbacks may be sustained by actors' subjective models derived from past learning or where individuals are advantaged by existing institutional frameworks; they will have an interest in perpetuating the system (North, 1990; Libecap, 1989). These self-reinforcing (also referred to as positive feedback or increasing returns) properties of institutions are particularly potent in politics due to an absence of efficiency-enhancing mechanisms such as competition, the shorter time horizons of political actors, and the strong status quo bias built into political institutions (Pierson, 2000a). Policy reversal becomes even more difficult.

Recent attempts to specify the logic of path dependence more carefully identify three sequential and interrelated processes (Thelen, 2003, 1999; Mahoney, 2000; Pierson, 2000b). These comprise a critical juncture in which events trigger a move onto the path. This is followed by a period in which positive feedback or increasing returns reinforce movement along that path, maintaining a given institutional pattern. An end to the path occurs when new events dislodge the long-standing equilibrium.

The period prior to a critical juncture seems a reasonable time to specify the beginning of a sequence (Mahoney, 2001, 2000). During this time different institutional arrangements are available for selection, one of which ends up getting selected during the critical juncture. What is analytically significant at this moment is that the outcome of the critical juncture should be only stochastically related to the initial, precritical juncture conditions. It should be unpredictable, thereby qualifying a critical juncture as a point in time when an unpredictable, contingent outcome sets in motion a (somewhat) irreversible set of events.

How are critical junctures translated into lasting legacies? What are the mechanisms of reproduction of a given institutional path over time? How does a given institutional pattern get "locked-in"? Four mechanisms have been identified (Mahoney, 2000). Rational actors may choose to reproduce institutions, including suboptimal ones, as the costs of transformation outweigh the benefits. Or institutions may persist because they serve certain beneficial functions within the context in which they are embedded. Or actors may perpetuate institutions based on their subjective understandings and beliefs of appropriateness and morality. Most crucially, however, institutions are not neutral, and they distribute benefits and costs unevenly across society. In this final mechanism then, differentially endowed actors will have conflicting interests with regard to the reproduction of institutions. An institution may persist if the benefiting elites have sufficient strength to support its reproduction. Consequently, it is important to establish who has invested in particular institutional arrangements, how this investment is sustained over time, and how those who have not invested in the institutions are kept out (Thelen, 1999).

Each institutional path then is characterized by a set of constraints and incentives, which in turn generate characteristic strategies and shared decision rules that produce a pattern of behavior among actors. Changes in institutions that preserve these elements of the path's preexisting logic constitute a path of bounded innovation, and actors' decisions thus become linked across time. Consequently, a narrow focus on current outcomes alone is at best incomplete and sometimes misleading, because the necessary conditions for current outcomes may have occurred in the past. Specifying these longer-run mechanisms of reproduction and feedback is key to understanding institutional evolution and change.

While this notion of increasing returns is useful in explaining why institutions may follow a set pattern, some authors acknowledge that even though lock-in may occur, it is not necessarily irrevocable because further choice points may exist (Thelen, 2003). Those disadvantaged by prevailing institutions do not necessarily disappear. They may bide their time as conditions change or may even work within existing frameworks in pursuit of goals different from or even subversive to those of the institution's crafters.

The current subdivision of group ranches in Kajiado district cannot be considered in isolation of the historical relations and processes that have characterized land policy and politics in Maasailand and in Kenya more generally. Path dependence provides a fertile set of ideas to explore the relatedness of actors' decisions across the rich history of land-related interventions in Maasailand in colonial and postcolonial times.

Vegetation-Environment Relations: A Framework

The determination of generalized differences in vegetation by environmental factors is accepted as self-evident. While it is uncertain how far the smallest differences between vegetation samples are environmentally determined and how far they are matters of chance, it seems quite certain that intermediate degrees of differences between vegetation can commonly be related to differences in environmental factors (Greig-Smith, 1983). Thus differences in soil, topography, and climate are the major determinants of the kind and amount of vegetation that can be produced on a given piece of land.

In addition to carbon, oxygen, and hydrogen, the main components of air and water, plants need large quantities of nitrogen, phosphorous, and sulfur for constructing tissues and smaller quantities of such elements as iron, magnesium, manganese, zinc, copper, boron, and molybdenum for enzyme manufacture. Most of these elements originate from the soil (Bell, 1982; Pratt and Gwynne, 1977). Cation exchange capacity and pH are also useful indicators as they influence plant uptake of these micro- and macronutrients.

The factors determining the status of savanna vegetation have long been a matter of debate. Climatic fluctuations, fire, grazing pressure, grazing history, edaphic conditions, and geomorphology seem to constitute the core forces that shape the characteristics of savanna ecosystems (Cole, 1986; Bourliere, 1983; Huntley and Walker, 1982; Tinley, 1982). These factors determine the density of the tree layer, system productivity, and the rates of nutrient and water flow through the system (Solbrig et al., 1996).

Water is by far the most important variable (Solbrig, 1993, 1991). Several things affect soil moisture regimes: (1) the distribution of rainfall and the proportion of this water that enters the soil; (2) the water-holding capacity of the soil, which is a function of texture and depth; and (3) the amount of evapotranspiration, which is related in complex ways to climate, soil texture, soil surface characteristics, and the type of vegetation. The height and spacing of savanna components, that is, the relative proportions of trees, shrubs, and grasses is influenced mainly by soil moisture conditions (Cole, 1986, 1982). In East Africa, for example, studies in the Maasai Mara and Serengeti areas of Southwestern Kenya and Northeastern Tanzania show that moisture is the prime factor limiting plant productivity (van Wijngaarden, 1985; Belsky, 1983).

In addition to moisture, the level of plant-available nutrients is also a prime determinant. Data, also from the Serengeti, demonstrate that there is substantial local variation in plant-available nutrients (McNaughton and Banyikwa, 1995). This variation can produce considerable local patchiness in grass growth, with high growth rates in patches where mineralization rates are high, and low rates in nearby patches. Belsky (1988) found that subsurface soil concentrations of sodium had the greatest positive influence on the amount and intensity of grassland patterns in the Serengeti. More generally, Cole (1986, 1982) notes that though transition between the different savannah variants such as between savannah woodlands, shrub savannah, savannah grassland is partly related to aridity, the species composition within each category varies with nutrient status.

In the hierarchical arrangement of determinants the availability of water and soil nutrients is regarded as a primary determinant, whereas other effects such as grazing and fire have been identified as important modifiers. This ordering of effects has, however, not gone uncontested. Conventional range management as practiced in dryland Africa, drawing extensively from the experiences of American range ecologists, emphasizes the role of livestock grazing pressure in affecting range condition (Stoddart et al., 1975; Pratt and Gwynne, 1977). This, premised on notions of climax vegetation under equilibrium conditions, is most often characterized by the standing mass and species composition of range vegetation. The "new thinking" in range ecology, drawn from the lived experiences of African livestock herders, views range ecosystem processes as disequilibrial in nature and strongly emphasizes the role played by rainfall in influencing interannual variations in the productivity and species composition of range vegetation (Ellis and Swift, 1988; Westoby et al., 1989; Behnke and Scoones, 1993). Rainfall variability influences both livestock and vegetation densities. This notwithstanding, grazing, even within a highly variable physical condition, has been found to significantly affect plant species composition, abundance, and distribution, as demonstrated below.

The contribution of grazing to savanna composition and structure is variable (Pratt and Gwynne, 1977). Although grazing could lead to the evolution of grass species favored by grazers, it could also lead to species with hard unpalatable herbage. Nevertheless, it is widely documented that as a result of increased herbivore grazing, less palatable plants increase at the expense of more palatable ones (Ellison, 1960; Thurow and Hussein, 1989; Curry and Hacker, 1990). Similarly, studies from grasslands in different parts of the world show that pasture use can change overall plant group composition, with a shift toward a higher incidence of forbs and annual grasses and a decline of perennial grasses (O'Connor and Roux, 1995; Li et al., 1993; Tserendash and Erdenbataar, 1993; Mwalyosi, 1992). Light to moderate grazing also increases species richness, which subsequently declines sharply at very heavy grazing pressure (Mwendera et al., 1997). In the Mediterranean grasslands Noy-Meir et al. (1989) find that in protected/enclosed areas perennial species were more frequent and their total cover greater than in grazed areas. However, under light to moderate grazing their cover decreased to the benefit of annuals of a wide range of forms and families. Of those under heavy grazing, small and prostate annuals, rosette crucifers, and thistles remained abundant.

It is now also generally accepted that all of the open country in East Africa, with the exception of some edaphic grasslands, have been induced by a past history of natural and man-made fire (Pratt and Gwynne, 1977). Many of the climatic bushland and woodland savannah types would have attained thicket status were it not for fire. Fire per se favors the development and maintenance of a predominantly grassland vegetation by destroying the juvenile trees and shrubs and by preventing the development of more mature plants to a taller, fire-resistant stage (Trollope, 1982).

The history of vegetation is also crucial as correlations between present environmental differences and present vegetation may be confounded by past changes in environment and vegetation, so that the determining factors are primarily historical ones. Consequently, for a complete understanding of the vegetation, it is necessary to consider the past as well as the present, for each sample vegetation has a history and a background of plant colonization and succession (Pratt and Gwynne, 1977). Determining the effects of history is, however, difficult, and some authors suggest that the evidence of historical factors is often assumed, especially where measured environmental factors do not seem to influence the vegetation (Greig-Smith, 1983). Some authors have succeeded in separating out the effects of history. In the Sahel, for example, recent grazing/defoliation history has been found to have relatively little effect on species composition (Turner, 1999). Instead, nineteenth-century grazing by Fulani herders in Mali around ephemeral water pans has been found to have a greater influence on grass species composition and abundances. Medina (1996) suggests that conducting comparisons between communities in the same or in closely related geographical areas may help in minimizing the effects of history on vegetation.

Thus a complex of factors, interacting across time and space, influence vegetation dynamics in the semiarid rangelands.

Conclusion

This book is an attempt to understand the process of land property rights transformation in Kenya's Maasailand. It is concerned with explaining *why* group ranch members support the subdivision of their collective holdings, *how* this process of subdividing the group ranch is organized, and *what* outcomes have been realized. This chapter has laid out the policy issues and demands around property rights. It has surveyed the range of prior research on privatization in Maasailand and found that there are some additional questions for investigation. It has also laid out a theoretical framework that draws heavily from property rights approaches and grounded that in the new institutionalism. From the property rights literature, privatization occurs in response to changes in relative prices, and distributional questions drive the shift between the status quo and alternative arrangements. Further, transformation is part of a wider process that is embedded within concrete historical circumstances, and it has consequences too. Because transformation occurs within a given set of physical-ecological conditions, a feature that is only marginally explicated in current writing, transformation will have implications for the sustainability and use of resources.

The rest of the book is organized as follows: Chapter two presents the biophysical and sociocultural context of Kajiado district. Chapter three presents the research design. Chapter four is a historical analysis of the recent evolution of land property rights in Maasailand, while chapters five and six discuss the motivations underlying subdivision and the processes and outcomes of land allocation. Chapter seven explores the implications of the property rights transition on vegetation structure. Chapter eight summarizes key issues from earlier chapters and discusses their policy implications.

CHAPTER TWO
BACKGROUND TO KAJIADO DISTRICT, KENYA

This chapter presents a summary of the administrative, physical, and social conditions of Kajiado district that form the backdrop against which land and property relations were transformed.[1] Maps and tables illustrate the various biophysical and social attributes of the district, while the sociocultural and political organization of the Maasai is described.

Location and Size of Kajiado District

Kajiado district is located on the southern tip of the Rift Valley province, one of Kenya's eight provinces. A province is part of the country's administrative system and is further divided into districts, divisions, locations, and sublocations. Kajiado district is situated between longitudes 36°5' and 37°55' East and between latitudes 1°10' and 3°10' South (map 2.1). It covers an area of 21,105 square kilometers, which is 3.5 percent of Kenya's total area. It is the ninth largest district in Kenya and second largest in the Rift Valley province after Turkana district. It is bordered by the Republic of Tanzania to the southwest; Taita Taveta district to the southeast; Machakos district to the east; Narok to the west; and Nairobi, Kiambu, and Nakuru to the north.

The district is divided into seven administrative divisions: Ngong, Magadi, Isenya, Central, Namanga, Mashuru, and Loitokitok, which are further divided into 47 locations and 120 sublocations. Central division is the largest in the district and hosts the district headquarters Kajiado town. Two of the four group ranches that were investigated in this study—Enkaroni and Torosei—are located in Central division and each comprises an administrative location. The other two, that is Meto and Nentanai, are in Namanga division. Meto is an administrative location; Nentanai is part

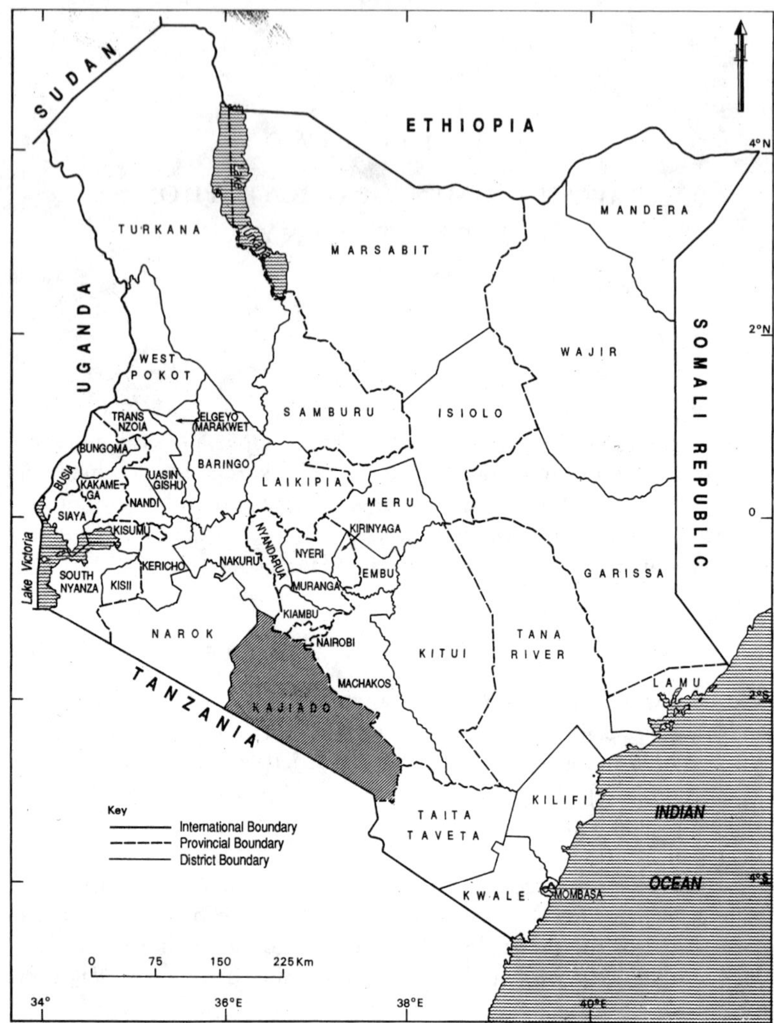

Map 2.1   Location of Kajiado District in Kenya

Source: Kenya, Republic of, 1990.

of the Bissil location. Politically, the district is divided into three parliamentary constituencies: Kajiado North, Kajiado Central, and Kajiado South. These do not coincide with administrative boundaries. All four group ranches are in the Kajiado central constituency.

Topography

The district is divided into four topographical areas: the Rift Valley, the Kaputiei Plains (Athi-Kapiti), the Central Broken Ground, and the Amboseli Plains.

The Rift Valley, part of the Great East African Rift that stretches from north of the Red Sea to Mozambique, forms a low depression on the western side of the district. Running across in a north-south direction, this area varies in altitude between 600 and 1,740 meters (1,968–5,708 feet) above sea level. Some of the important features in this system are the Kedong Valley, Mt. Suswa (2,357 meters or 7,732 feet), Oloolkesalie Hills, Lake Magadi, and Lake Natron.

The Central Broken Ground comprises a wide stretch of 20–70 kilometers (13–43 miles) that runs from the northeastern border across the district to the southwest. The eastern margin of this belt is occupied by the Machakos Hills, while its central parts have several hills such as Enkorika, Maparasha, Ilaingarrunyoni, and Ilemelepo Hills. On the extreme southern part of this topographical region are found the Nkiito and Oldoinyo Orok Hills. The Chyulu Hills and part of the slopes of Mt. Kilimanjaro form the southeastern part of the region. There are no permanent water sources in this area; it is characterized by numerous dry river beds that are an important source of sand for the construction industry. The altitude here ranges from 1,220 to 2,073 meters (4,002–6,801 feet) above sea level. Enkaroni, Nentanai, Meto, and Torosei group ranches fall under this topographical region. Torosei is on the southwestern section of this area and is bordered by the Magadi group ranch that is within the Rift Valley topographical area. Torosei thus represents a transition zone between the central broken grounds topographical zone and the bottom of the Rift Valley at Magadi. Enkaroni is close to the southern tip of the Ilemelepo Hills; Meto is close to the Nkiito Hills; and Nentanai is fairly close to the Maparasha Hills.

The Amboseli Plains are characterized by flat to gently undulating rolling slopes within a basin that is surrounded by Oldoinyo Orok and Ilaingarrunyoni Hills and the slopes of Mt. Kilimanjaro. The plains surround Lake Amboseli. Altitude ranges between 850 meters and 1,340 meters (2,788–4,396 feet) above sea level.

Climate

The district has a bimodal rainfall pattern. The short rains fall between October and December and the long rains between March and May. Annual rainfall in the district is strongly influenced by altitude. Loitokitok, on the foothills of Mt. Kilimanjaro in the south, has the highest average rainfall of about 1,250 millimeters (49 inches) per annum (map 2.2).

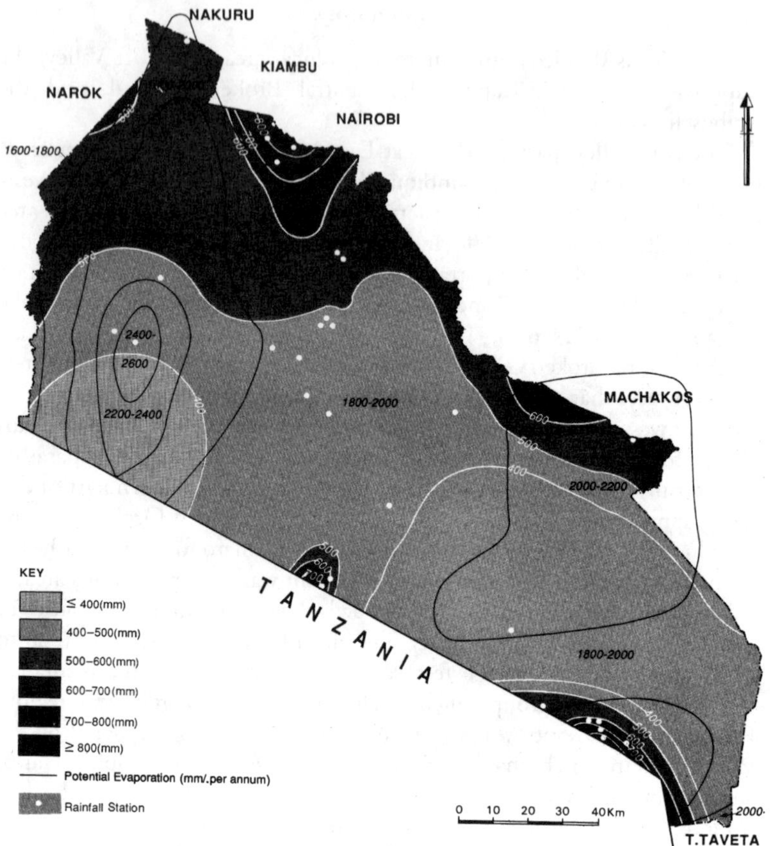

Map 2.2   Mean Annual Rainfall in Kajiado District
Source: Kenya, Republic of, 1990.

Lakes Magadi and Amboseli, the lowest points in the district, have the lowest average rainfall of less than 500 millimeters (20 inches) per annum. Heavy rains also occur around Ngong Hills, Chyulu Hills, the Nguruman escarpment, and the slopes of Mt. Kilimanjaro. For most areas, about 50 percent of the rainfall is received in the March–May season, while just about 30 percent is received in the October–December short rains. This pattern is, however, reversed in the Mt. Kilimanjaro area, with the December rains accounting for about 45 percent of the annual totals and March–May for about 30 percent of total annual rainfall. Apart from being low, the rainfall is highly variable from year to year.

Temperatures in the district also vary with altitude and season. The highest temperature of about 34 degrees centigrade (93 degrees Fahrenheit) is recorded around Lake Magadi, while the lowest minimum of about 10 degrees centigrade (50 degrees Fahrenheit) is experienced at Loitokitok on the eastern slopes of Mt. Kilimanjaro. Mean maximum of Loitokitok is about 22 degrees centigrade (71 degrees Fahrenheit). The coolest period is between July and August; the hottest is from November to April.

Based on these rainfall and temperature regimes, Kajiado district can be divided into five agroclimatic zones with varying ecological potentials (map 2.3). Fifty-five percent of the district falls under agroclimatic zone V

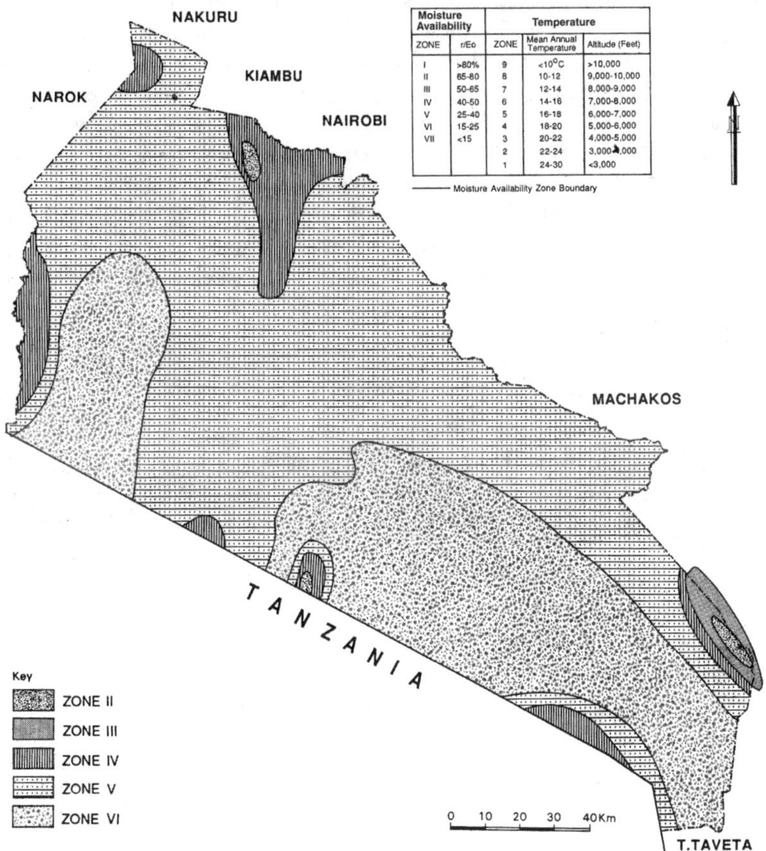

Moisture Availability		Temperature		
ZONE	r/Eo	ZONE	Mean Annual Temperature	Altitude (Feet)
I	>80%	9	<10°C	>10,000
II	65-80	8	10-12	9,000-10,000
III	50-65	7	12-14	8,000-9,000
IV	40-50	6	14-16	7,000-8,000
V	25-40	5	16-18	6,000-7,000
VI	15-25	4	18-20	5,000-6,000
VII	<15	3	20-22	4,000-5,000
		2	22-24	3,000-4,000
		1	24-30	<3,000

Map 2.3 Ecoclimatic Zones of Kajiado District
Source: Kenya, Republic of, 1990.

and 37 percent under agroclimatic zone VI. This makes Kajiado district part of the arid and semiarid lands of Kenya. Ranching forms the appropriate land use in ASAL (arid and semiarad lands) areas. Rain-fed agricultural potential, however, exists in agroecological zones II and III and parts of zone IV, mainly on the slopes of Mt. Kilimanjaro, Chyulu Hills, Namanga, Ngong Hills, Nguruman escarpment, and the flood plains of the Ewaso Ng'iro River. These areas comprise not more than 8 percent of the district.

Water Resources

Most of the district is drained by seasonal streams and rivers. It is thus more dependent on groundwater reserves. Major rivers in the district are Athi in the north, Ewaso Ng'iro in the west, Olekejuado in the central parts, and Nooltureishi in the south. These rivers run in both wet and dry seasons. In the central part the major watercourse is the seasonal Kiboko River, which is made up of the Olkejuado and Eselenkei tributaries. Shallow wells are dug along the water course of both rivers. Most group ranches are demarcated to include such areas. Group ranch members who are able to invest in the digging of the wells are granted permission by the committee to do so. However, they are under obligation to allow access to other members, often on a family basis on condition that those using the shallow well participate in its maintenance and observe the watering rules.

Vegetation

Vegetation in the district is influenced by altitude, soil type, human occupation, and utilization of the land. The main vegetation types consist of wooded grassland, open grassland, and semidesert bushland and scrub. Dominant species associations in these vegetation types are presented in table 2.1.

In the low rainfall Rift Valley topographical region of Kajiado district, vegetation comprises thorn bushes and sparsely distributed grass. Here, the main woody species in the northern reaches is *Tarchonanthus camphoratus*, while *Themeda triandra* is the dominant grass. The southern reaches are dominated by *Acacia* species. The Athi Plains comprise mainly grasslands and wooded grassland physiognomic types typically found around Ngong area. *Themeda triandra* and *Acacia drepanolobium* form the main association here. The Amboseli Plains comprise largely of bushlands interspersed with open grasslands. *Acacia* and *Commiphora* are the dominant species here. Swampy areas can also be found at the foot slopes of Mt. Kilimanjaro. The central broken grounds, where our study sites are located, comprise wooded bushlands dominated by species of *Acacia*.

Table 2.1 Species Associations in Main Vegetation Types

Zone and Type	*Vegetation Association*
Wooded grassland	*Digitaria macroblephara* *Cymbopogon pospischilli* *Combretum zeyheri* *Balanites aegyptiaca*
Wooded and bushed grassland	*Pennisetum mezianum* *Lintonia nutans* *Commiphora africanus*
Woodland	*Chloris roxburghiana* *Themeda triandra* *Commiphora africanus*
Grassland and woodland	*Digitaria macroblephara* *Cymbopogon pospischilli* *Combretun zeyheri* *Balanites aegyptiaca* *Acacia seyal* *Acacia xanthophloea* *Acacia drepanolobium* *Commiphora africanus* *Cynodon dactylon*
Bushland and woodland	*Pennisetum strammineum* *Cenchrus ciliaris* *Acacia nubica* *Acacia tortilis* *Commiphora africanus*
Bushland	*Pennisetum strammineum* *Cynodon plectostachyus* *Acacia mellifera* *Balanites aegyptiaca* *Commiphora africanus*
Grassland	*Digitaria macroblephara* *Sporobolus fibriatus* *Ipomoea kituensis* *(an invader in species common degraded areas)*

Source: Kenya, Republic of, 1990.

The vegetation over much of Kajiado is undergoing rapid modification. Clearance for agriculture in both the relatively higher potential areas and more marginal ones is one reason for this modification. Also in areas that have been undergoing or have undergone subdivision, trees are cut down for charcoal to feed demands in Nairobi. *Acacia tortilis* seems to the species of preference. The areas between Meto and Ilbissel, such as around Ilpartimaru group ranch, seem to be the worst hit. Bush encroachment of predominantly *Acacia mellifera* seems to be underway in Meto and Nentanai areas. Weedy species such as *Ipomeoa kituensis* are rapidly invading degraded areas.

Population Structure and Composition

Kajiado district has one of the highest population growth rates in Kenya. The population here has increased steadily from 22,000 in 1948 to 86,000 in 1969, to 149,005 in 1979, to 258,659 in 1989, and to 406,054 in 1999. Between 1989 and 1999 alone the population increased by 57 percent. While the population is predominantly Maasai, the district is also occupied by non-Maasai groups such as the Kikuyu, Kamba, Luo, and Somali. A significant portion of the district's population increase can be attributed to the influx of the non-Maasai groups primarily Kikuyu and Kamba cultivators moving away from the overcrowding in the central highlands. Only about half or even less is due to natural growth among the Maasai themselves. The Kikuyu and Kamba are found in the higher potential areas of the district such as in Ngong, Loitokitok, and in the foot slopes of the Namanga Hills. Luos are found around Kiserian, Ongata Rongai, and Ngong, while Luhyas settle predominantly in the Nguruman area. Other ethnic groups such as Somalis are found in the urban centers. Table 2.2 presents Kajiado district's ethnic composition.

Average population density has also increased over the years, from 4 to 7, to 12, to 19 persons per square kilometer from 1969, 1979, 1989, 1999, respectively. Though the district is on average sparsely populated, its distribution is highly uneven. Densities range from 41 persons per square kilometer in parts of Ngong division to a low of four to 7.6 persons per square kilometer in some locations such as Torosei in Central division, Oldoinyo Nyokie in Magadi division, and Lenkism in Loitokitok. The sparsely

Table 2.2   Kajiado District Population: Ethnic Composition

Ethnic Group	1969		1989		Increase (1969–1989) (%)	Annual Growth
	Number	*% of Total*	*Number*	*% of Total*		
Maasai	58,961	68.6	146,268	56.55	148.1	4.9
Kikuyu	16,258	18.9	61,446	23.96	277.9	7.2
Kamba	4,321	5.0	20,755	8.02	380.3	8.6
Luo	1,612	2.0	8,084	3.13	401.5	8.9
Luhyia	1,166	1.3	5,416	2.09	364.5	8.4
Others	3,585	4.2	16,710	6.25	366.1	8.4
Total	85,903	100	258,679	100	201.1	6.0

Source: SNV/SARDEP, 1999.

populated areas are much more arid than the rest. High densities in the Ngong division are largely due to its proximity to Nairobi and also immigration by cultivating communities.

Kajiado district's population is generally characterized as youthful. In 1969, those aged 15 years and below accounted for about 48 percent of the total population. By 1979, the proportion of children had increased to 49.4 percent. The 1989 census indicates that the proportion of population that is under 20 years is about 60 percent of the district's total population.

Socioeconomic Development

About 92 percent of the district is used as rangeland. It is dominated by pastoral economic activities. It also supports a significant portion of the country's wildlife population. Livestock continues to be the main source of subsistence. Milk, meat, and blood form the major diet among the Maasai. Livestock production is centered on movement between wet and dry season grazing areas. The historical confinement of the Maasai plus the recent immigration of cultivators has slowly reduced the wet season grazing areas. Movement is thus confined within the more marginal areas.

The dominant livestock production units are individual and group ranches, and grazing systems have been modeled on the traditional transhumant system. Map 2.4 presents the distribution of group and individual ranches within the district. Most group ranches range from 3,000 hectares to 151,000 hectares in size, while individual ranches are on average 800 hectares. The number of group ranches is steadily diminishing as group ranch members begin to subdivide and distribute among themselves.

Map 2.4 highlights the location of the group ranches that I studied. Meto and Torosei are neighboring group ranches both located on Kenya's border with Tanzania. Meto is 65 kilometers from Bissel, the main livestock market in the area, while Torosei is about 56 kilometers. Enkaroni, only about 8 kilometers from Bissel is located almost in the middle of Kajiado district, while Nentanai is 18 kilometers to the southeast of Enkaroni and Bissel. Enkaroni, Meto, and Nentanai have subdivided and issued land titles to members, while Torosei is still in the process of subdividing.

Sociocultural and Political Organization

The Maasai are a pastoral people with livestock as the basis of their economic livelihood, the focus of social relations, and a critical element of ethnic self-definition. Pastoralism was traditionally considered to be the only worthy pursuit, and tilling the earth was regarded as a degrading enterprise. This often-quoted "pure" form of pastoralism is rapidly changing as Maasai

Map 2.4   Distribution of Group and Individual Ranches in Kajiado District
Source: Kenya, Republic of, 1990.

confront formal markets, state intervention, immigrants, and land pressure. Maasai are now increasingly engaged in agriculture, trade, and formal employment (Kituyi, 1990). Nonetheless, they have retained some herd mobility and "being people of cattle" is still core to their self-identification. They are still pastoralists.

Throughout history under difficult circumstances such as drought or disease, some Maasai periodically fell out of the pastoral enterprise; some became cultivators, hunter gatherers, or even sought employment with the colonial administration (Waller, 1993). These individuals would switch to the pastoral mode as soon as they rebuilt their herds.

In this section I describe the social, political, and economic organization of the Maasai. This has been extensively documented by prior scholars. I draw heavily from the following works: Spencer (1997, 1993, 1988); Mol (1996); Galaty (1989, 1981); Ingule (1980); Berntsen (1979a); Baxter and Almagor (1978); Jacobs (1965); Bernadi (1952); and from two anonymous and undated articles, probably written by colonial administrators during the 1940s, which I found in the library of the Catholic Diocese of Kajiado.

Territorial Organization

The Maasai were (and still are) divided into sections (*iloshon*, singular = *olosho*), sometimes referred to as tribes or subtribes, each occupying a specified territory and having an autonomous political structure that is based on an age-grade system. There are 12 sections of the Maasai. The areas I studied were inhabited by three—the Loodokilani (of Torosei), Matapato (of Meto and Nentanai), and Purko (of Enkaroni). Figure 2.1 provides a schema of the different levels of territorial organization among the Maasai, which I also describe in this section.

The *olosho* is the highest level of territorial unity and is the basis of organizational authority in the hands of age-set leaders, elders' councils, and sectional leadership. Individual male heads of polygynous families secure rights to common grazing and water within their sectional boundaries by initiation into a specific age set. Each section is associated with recognized boundaries that are defended against unauthorized intrusion by the warrior age set (*ilmurran*); access by nonmembers has to be negotiated. In periods of drought or famine there was institutionalized sharing of each others resources. Pastoral producers defined their rights to resources in the context of their membership in *olosho*. Maasai relations were pursued in the context of the *olosho*. The *olosho* constituted the context within which social organization and the pursuit of economic resources were realized.

Most *olosho* contain areas of widely different ecological character, from high potential forest to low potential semiarid scrubland, and members of *olosho* coordinate the use of the range. Some of this coordination was achieved by mutual agreement to reserve highland pasture for dry seasons and areas in closest proximity to each settlement for young and old stock. In times of environmental stress herds were moved freely from any region within the *olosho* with accessible pastures, if not across *olosho* boundaries to exploit grazing elsewhere. Relations among members of *olosho* were generated and sustained by ideological and social practices such as ritual and ceremony as well as by reciprocity.

Each *olosho* is divided into localities (*inkutot*, singular = *enkutoto*). The locality is the basis of the Maasai transhumant herding system, which

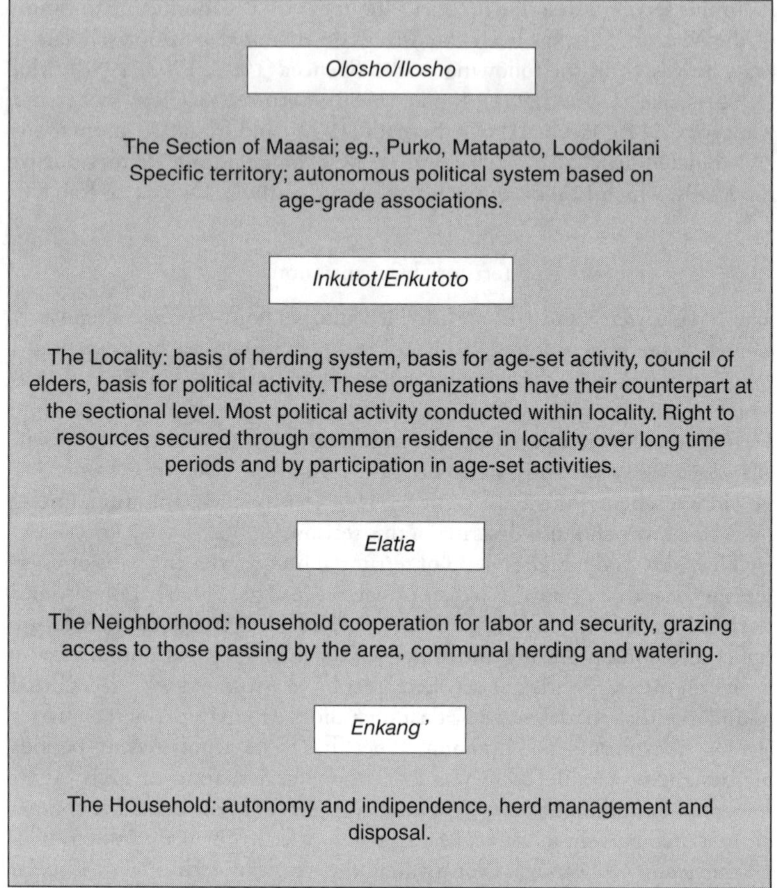

Figure 2.1 Maasai Sociopolitical and Territorial Organization

Note: Maasai are also divided into sublocation, location, constituencies, and districts. This is another level of authority due to incorporation into Kenyan territory. The changes that led to the formation of group and individual ranches between 1970s and 1990s brought about another layer of authority at variance with traditional structure.

involves herd and family movements from permanent, high potential, dry season pasture reserves based on permanent river, well, or spring water supplies to temporary, outlying, low potential, wet season grazing areas based on rain ponds and other temporary surface water supplies. Local organization ensured that Maasai stock had access to both types of pasture for grazing and conservation purposes. They helped guarantee that various traditional management techniques were employed, such as the regular burning of portions of grassland to help regenerate new grass growth and the judicious grazing of goats to prevent destruction of grass roots. Under traditional herd management practices and other self-regulatory mechanisms exhaustion of pasture was temporary and probably not serious since the pastoralists had more opportunity to move their herds elsewhere. The locality was also the basis for age-set activities (see section on age sets, "Maasai Age Sets," this chapter). Each locality had its own age-set spokesman and its own council of elders to settle disputes and enforce customary law. These bodies had their counterparts on the sectional level, which met to decide on intersectional disputes and to organize intersectional age-set activities. However, the bulk of political activities were organized and carried out by local age sets without recourse to the approval of the sectional council.

The locality is the most important unit within Maasai society in which authority structures are embedded. Individual families secured rights to communal resources only by common residence within the same locality over long periods of time and by regular participation in local age-set activities. Each locality was further subdivided into progressively smaller units, the most basic being the individual household where control over livestock and labor occurred. It is still unclear how this concept of locality can be translated under the group ranch system and even now that group ranches are undergoing subdivision.

At the most micro level, nested within the locality, the most relevant unit of cooperation was the grouping of a number of individual households into a common residential site (*elatia*) in which membership was optional. Cooperation between different neighborhoods took the form of granting grazing access to herders who were temporarily passing through the area. There were also neighborhood controls on grazing. Each neighborhood, for example, had two types of dry season grazing, one to be used in the early to middle dry season and the other to be used in the late dry season. Collective sanctions would be imposed against any individual herding prematurely. Elders decided the opening date for each of these reserves and disallowed the construction of permanent settlements in these areas. Indeed, specific areas were designated for homesteads, preventing individual families from selectively appropriating the best areas of pasture, as well as keeping structures from being scattered across the countryside, which would otherwise interfere with the grazing of other herders. Large-scale transhumance, determined consensually and enforced through community sanctions, involved coordination by different herding groups who adjusted their movement in response to the presence and trajectory of one another.

Jacobs (1980) points out that past traditional localities seemed to have been stable, with adequate quantities of both wet and dry season pastures, and considerable mobility between the two. The absence of surface water, periodic droughts, and livestock disease limited livestock production and maintained the balance of the human-ecological system.

The settlement presented a convenient locus for combining labor and providing security, but herd management was individualized. Each household is autonomous and regulates its affairs independently. However, in the common interest herds were pastured and watered communally and corralled at night in the open places for security against predators. Elders met to discuss herd movements and to determine whose sons will act as herd boys and which elders will supervise them.

Some scholars argue that the presentation of an "egalitarian" ethos among the communal Maasai obscures real and lived inequalities among individuals, families, and households over access to and control of resources. While information on wealth differentials is scanty, especially for the precolonial period, scholars are increasingly acknowledging that the notion of Maasai "egalitarianism" may well be a myth (Waller, personal communication) and that there existed and continue to exist differentials among pastoral communities (Mulder and Sellen, 1994). Indeed, an edited volume has been dedicated to the analysis of poverty and pastoralism in eastern Africa (Anderson and Broch-Due, 1999).

Earliest recorded evidence of Maasai wealth differentials result from the enumeration of livestock distribution in 1912–1913 during the movement of Purko Maasai from the northern Maasai Reserve in Laikipia (the Maasai moves are discussed in chapter four). Statistics from these records indicate that the wealthiest 20 percent of the community accounted for about 54 percent of the Purko stock, while the bottom 25 percent held just about 4 percent of the cattle (Waller, 1999). These differential endowments persisted even six decades later, with 33 percent of total households owning 66 percent of the cattle in Kiboko and Olkarkar group ranches on the eastern part of Kajiado district (Jahnke et al., 1972). Similar trends were noted for Elangata Wuas group ranch (Bill and Anderson, 1980) and for Olkarkar, Merueshi, and Mbirikani group ranches (Bekure et al., 1991). In this last case about 50 percent of households owned only 10 percent of the entire herds, while the richest 20 percent controlled 60 percent of the cattle. This wealth disparity is not unique to the Maasai of Kajiado, similar cases have been documented among the Ariaal (Fratkin and Smith, 1994; Fratkin and Roth, 1990), the Mukogodo (Herren, 1990), the Datoga of Tanzania (Mulder, 1991; Tomikawa, 1979), and among Asian pastoralists (Bradburn, 1982).

These inequalities have persisted in spite of intermittent and stochastic events such as drought, disease epidemics, and cattle raiding. They have also persisted in spite of the Maasai's sustained traditional practice of distributing livestock among friends and family. It is a common feature of Maasai pastoralism for individuals to distribute parts of their herds to friends and relatives who have better access to good grazing or for livestock-poor individuals to be assisted by friends and/or family through loans or gifts of livestock (Ndagala, 1991; Hedlund, 1971). Sometimes up to 30–40 percent of an individual's herds may be distributed in this way. Such transfers of cattle, including through marriage, strengthens social ties and creates reciprocal roles, rights, and obligations. Individuals whose livestock have been decimated by epidemics may, for example, call upon such obligations to rebuild their herds. Those with large herds, on the other hand, are able to widely disperse their herds as a way of spreading risk.

Mulder and Sellen (1994) suggest that stochastic events and herd redistributive strategies are insufficient to obliterate inequalities. Stochastic events for one are more likely to place poor families below minimum subsistence levels, leaving them less able to recover from such losses in the long term. By contrast, the wealthy have greater resources and better developed social networks, and the incremental impact of crises can strengthen their position and increase differentiation (Waller, 1999). In any case, even if inequalities are reduced, it does not mean that all players remain in the game.

The important point, however, is that with free access to land there was enormous opportunity for individuals to rise from poverty to wealth; mobility and wide access to resources were the mainstay of poor herders (Waller, 1999; Halderman, 1989). Each Maasai recognized that the achievement of wealth was as much a possibility as the descent into poverty, through luck, misfortune, good or bad management. Poverty was not a permanent condition for all herders at all times. Though material resources were unequal, there was relative equality of opportunity.

Similar inequalities have been documented with regard to access to prime grazing resources among families living in specific locales (Little, 1985), to seasonally available forage (Ellis and Swift, 1988), to the use of preferred settlement sites (Grandin, 1988; Western and Dunne, 1979), and to control over key water resources.

Maasai pastoralism allowed for various kinds of accommodations with the agricultural communities living in the region such as the Kikuyu. Through marital exchange the Maasai solidified bonds of friendship and adoption. Such relations were important and had implications for complementarities across modes of subsistence. Market exchanges also took place such as between Maasai and their farming neighbors, from whom Maasai sought agricultural produce in exchange for livestock. The Maasai also sought the supply of superior steers from mainly Boran pastoralists of northern Kenya and southern Ethiopia. Maasai gave away products not required for the reproduction of their pastoral adaptation and received prestige goods and food. Maasai dependence on trade only rose at times of crisis such as drought or epidemics and receded during good years.

Maasai Age Sets

The age set is a central institution in Maasai social and political organization. It comprises initiates of the same period who have been formally integrated as a corporate group. Maasai conceive of their age system as passing through four named stages of the male life cycle: boyhood (*ilaiyok*), warriorhood (*ilmurran*), elderhood (*ilmoruak*), and ancient elderhood (*ildasati*). Women are not grouped into corporate sets but are attached to male age sets by association. They tend to be identified with the male age sets with whom they danced as young, unmarried maidens and later, through marriage, adopt the age sets of their husbands. Political action among the Maasai occurred and still occurs within the age-set system under the leadership of men selected from the age set. Through membership in age sets, men participate in political affairs, cooperate in political action, and acquire political power and influence.

Until he is circumcised a man is not part of any age set. An age set consists of males circumcised within a specific 10–14-year period. Usually the initiates were 12–15 years old, though the first boys circumcised into a new age set might be a few years older. Among most Maasai sections, this 14-year period is divided into two shorter periods of about seven years each. The men of the first seven-year period are the right hand circumcision group while those of the second seven-year period are the left hand circumcision. These two groups are usually identified by separate names until their joining in the *olng'esherr* ceremony described below.

After circumcision, the boys become junior warriors. During the second or third year of junior warriorhood, age mates from one or more localities group together in a warrior village called a *manyatta*. These *manyattas* comprise individuals drawn from within the same section but whose locality may vary. During my fieldwork, it appeared that warrior villages are created in each group ranch area, with an age-set sponsor providing the ground upon which the *manyatta* would be constructed. The location of the *manyatta* would be shifted several times before the *ilmurran* are shaved. When this time nears, each section consolidates it warriors in one *manyatta* to await the shaving ceremony described below. Within the warrior villages bonds are created and strengthened among the age mates. These villages also serve as educational institutions in which the young men learn the traditions and expectations of social life. The villages also serve as a forum through which the young men develop oratory and debating skills necessary for community administration. In the past, individual warriors and whole age sets earned praise and respect by successfully raiding cattle, which increased their individual wealth and that of their grazing unit. These *manyattas* are usually inhabited for a continuous period of three to four years before being permanently abandoned. Today, this period is rapidly growing shorter because some of the young men go to school. In some parts of Maasailand, local politicians and administrators have actively discouraged the practice.

Roughly five years after the circumcision period is opened, when young men are 18–26 years of age, the most important ceremony of a section, the shaving of the warriors (*eunoto*) takes place. During this ceremony, the warriors' dreadlocks are shaved and they replace their spears with a stick. Such ceremonies are performed at the level of the section for the entire section. At this ceremony also, age-set leaders such as the speaker (*ol aiguenani*, plural = *il aiguenak*), the ritual leader (*ol aunoni*; *il aunok* or *ol otuno*, plural = *il otunok*), and the knot tier (*olobornkeene*) are vested with office. Men who emerge as leaders at this time remain as leaders in the age set and in society as a whole until they passed into official retirement. The shaving ceremony thus marks the apex of organization and unity for the warriors of a section. It also marks their transition into a new status, senior warriorhood.

Several years after the shaving ceremony of the right hand circumcision group, young uninitiated men band together in preparation for the formation of a left hand circumcision group. The right hand circumcision group precedes the left hand circumcision group in matters of ritual and political importance. The age sets of all sections maintain some temporal uniformity, even though each section has its own dynamism.

After about 14 years, the right and left hand groups are unified into an official age set during the *olng'esherr* ceremony and subsequently named. This becomes their official name. They now stop being senior warriors and graduate to junior elderhood. This ceremonial cycle is set off by the Ilkisonko section in southern Kajiado and all others follow suit. The name given to an age set by the Ilkisonko is adopted by all sections of the Maasai. This universal acceptance is significant. It demonstrates the unity of the age-set system throughout Maasailand and synchronizes age-set activity across the entire Maasailand.

As senior warriors are graduated to elderhood by performing the *olng'esherr* ceremony, each age set above them is automatically advanced in status, that is, junior elders become senior elders to make room for the new junior elders who were formerly senior warriors. And senior elders are retired from active political life. The principal role of junior and senior elders, who range in age from 28 to 56 years, is to maintain law and order in their locality. In conjunction with their local age-set spokesman they meet regularly in local elders' councils (*entiguana*) to settle disputes and make decisions for their locality as a whole. Although politico-judicial matters are shared between senior and junior elders and their respective spokesmen/ leaders, senior elders tend to dominate in the decision-making process while junior elders execute their decisions. Retired elders, usually above 65 years, are no longer considered legitimate participants in public affairs, though they are accorded great respect. Their only active social role is to give advice in matters of public ritual practices and to instill in their grandchildren a sense of traditional values. Table 2.3 presents Maasai age-set chronology between the late eighteenth century and 1985. Table 2.4 shows the age sets I encountered during my fieldwork and the approximate ages for each set across the Ilpurko, Ilmatapato, and Illodookilani sections.

This cyclic progression of corporate age sets through a fixed system of rank stages establishes a status hierarchy to which ideal modes of behavior and authority are attached. One age set is automatically senior to the next. One age set pays respect (*inkanyit*) to all groups senior to it and receives respect and deference from all those junior to it. Relations among members of the same age set are cordial, cooperative, and informal based on their status as coevals. However, the expected relations of deference and respect between adjacent age sets are complicated by rivalry and competition. Junior age sets are often eager to assume the roles of their seniors. Seniors are often reluctant to hand over power or share certain rights with their juniors. Alternate age sets, united by the *ol piron* bond, share special relations of solidarity and mutual support. During the circumcision of members of a new age set, the young elders of the alternate age set above them (i.e., the

Table 2.3   Maasai Age-Set Chronology

Age Set	Approximate Dates as Warriors
Iltiyioki	1791–1811
Ilmerishari	1806–1826
Ilkidotu	1821–1841
Iltuati I	1836–1856
Ilnyankusi I	1851–1871
Ilaimer	1866–1886
Iltalala	1881–1905
Iltuati II	1896–1917
Iltareto	1911–1929
Ilterito	1926–1948
Ilnyankusi II	1942–1959
Iseuri	1957–1975
Ilkiseyia (Ilkitoip)	1973–1985

Source: Mol, 1996.

Table 2.4 Ilpurko, Ilmatapato, Ilodookilani Age Sets

Group Ranch	Section	Retired Elders	Retired Elders	Senior Elders	Elders	Junior Elders	
Enkaroni	Ilpurko	Ilterito, >90	Ilnyankusi, 70–89	Iseuri, 57–68	Ilkiseyia, 45–54	Ilkingonde, 30–38	Ilkilaku, 18–25
Meto	Ilmatapato		Ilnyankusi [a]Ilkalikal, 75–90 [b]Ilkamanik, 65–75	Iseuri Ilkololik, 60–65 Ilepurulek, 55–60	Ilkitoip Ilkiseyia, 45–55 Irang Irang, 35–45	No Name Ilking'onde, 30–35 Ilmajeshi, 25–30	No Name Ilpaang'u, 18–25
Nentanai	Ilmatapato		Ilnyankusi Ilkalikal, 80–90 Ilkamanik, 75–80	Iseuri Ilkololik, 60–70 Leputulek, 50–60	Ilkitoip Ilkiseyia, 40–50 Ilng'orisho, 35–40		Ilpaang'u, 20–25
Torosei	Iloodokilani	Ilterito Ilkitatin, >100 Ilmadidani, 90–100	Ilnyankusi Ilkalikal, 80–90 Ilkamanek, 70–80	Iseuri Ilkololek, 60–70 Ilkisakara, 50–60	Ilkitoip Ilkiseyia, 45–50 Irang Irang, 40–45	No Name Ilkishili, 35–40 Ilmajeshi, 30–35	No Name Ilpaang'u, 20–30

Notes: [a] Right hand
[b] Left Hand.

Source: Own field work.

junior elders at the time) ceremoniously bring their age set into existence by lighting a fire for them with a fire stick. By "breathing life into" the ritual fire that symbolically "gives birth" to the new age set, the junior elders establish their position as the "fathers" of the new age set. They are the sponsoring elders (*il piron*) and are responsible for the education and "policing" of the young warriors. The *il piron* elders teach the warriors the values respected by society and levy punishments for their misdeeds.

In this cyclic system, changes of status entail changes in prestige and influence and hence in power and authority. An age set is at the lowest point of the power continuum at its first establishment and reaches the apex at senior elderhood. However, the differentiation of authority according to different spheres of activity together with the structural relationships between and among age sets brings to play a balance of power within the age-set system core to the maintenance of the Maasai decentralized political system. Kinship, lineage, and clans are of minor political significance. The cross-cutting nature of the age system unifies territorial and clan fragmentation.

The Maasai are now also divided into locations, sublocations, districts, and constituencies under Kenya's current administrative system. They are also part of a province through which they are territorially incorporated into the Kenyan system.

Chapter Three
Research Design

This chapter provides an outline of the method and design of the study. It discusses how study sites were selected, the techniques used for social and ecological data collection, and the methods of data analysis.

Selection of Study Sites

Earlier studies on subdivision in Kajiado district (see chapter one) were mainly conducted in the Keekonyokie and Kaputiei areas of northern and eastern Kajiado district, respectively. These areas of northern and eastern Kajiado district are generally closer to Nairobi, Kenya's capital city, are ethnically diverse, and receive higher annual rainfall relative to other parts of the district. They were among the first to subdivide. Individual ranches were carved out of these higher potential areas even prior to the creation of group ranches (see chapter four). Though distant from Nairobi city, the area around Loitokitok town, on the foot slopes of Mt. Kilimanjaro, also experiences similar conditions of ethnic diversity and high rainfalls. Land here was privatized fairly early on. Similarly, in areas around the Amboseli swamps such as the Kimana group ranch, which have several perennial streams from Mt. Kilimanjaro flowing along its borders, members have begun demanding for subdivision. In Kimana, land close to the rivers is irrigated by Kikuyu and Kamba lessees who practice vegetable farming for local commercial sale and for export to international markets. Kimana group ranch members have begun subdividing this productive part of the group ranch.

These cases suggest that closeness to major cities and towns, high populations of immigrant cultivating communities, and high agricultural potential are important conditions for the drive toward subdivision and increased privatization in Kajiado district. But what of the rest of Kajiado, where these conditions hardly hold and where there is still pressure to subdivide? The sites selected for this study are an attempt to represent conditions different from those in the above-mentioned cases, that is, conditions that are reflective of the situation over most of the district. The areas of Ngong, Kaputiei, and Loitokitok represent no more than 8–10 percent of the district. The larger part of the district is more arid, has negligible proportions of immigrant populations, and is fairly distant from large towns. Study site selection was also influenced by a need to ensure relative homogeneity of biophysical and ecological conditions to enable the assessment of ecological variation between subdivided and unsubdivided areas.

The central resource management area provided relative homogeneity and some control for the influence of environment. Recent resource assessments partitioned Kajiado district into areas of similar ecology and biophysical conditions, the so-called resource management areas (ETC East Africa, 1998). The central resource management area, which covers a large part of central Kajiado district including the entire Central administrative division and parts of Namanga division, is shown to have relatively unvarying vegetation, geology, and soils at a broader scale (see chapter two). Rainfall amounts and patterns in the central resource management area is similar, though significantly lower than in the higher potential areas of the district. In addition, individuals from other ethnic groups are mainly concentrated within the urban centers, primarily in Kajiado town. Selecting all four sites in one ecological zone provides some control for the impact of ecology on processes in the group ranch.

Within the central RMA (resource management area) of Kajiado, four sites or group ranch areas were selected: Enkaroni group ranch area, Meto

Table 3.1   Basic Information for Enkaroni, Meto, Nentanai, and Torosei

	Meaning	Year GR Incorporated	Size (Hectares)	Members	Agreed to Subdivide	Titles Issued by October 2002	Distance from Bissel (Kilometers)
Enkaroni	Place with no water.	April 1975	11,378	356	May 1988	310	8 (5 miles)
Meto	River originating from Tanzania.	December 1977	28,928	645	September 1989	400	65 (40 miles)
Nentanai	River. Also was warrior village for Ilmatapato warriors.	December 1977	3,696	57	March 1987	42	18 (11 miles)
Torosei	River flowing between gorges called Torosoit.	June 1977	45,445	300	September 1989	—	56 (35 miles)

Source: Own field work.

group ranch area, Nentanai group ranch area, and Torosei group ranch (see map 2.4). These were selected to include variations in size and location. Nentanai is the smallest group ranch, both in terms of size and membership, while Torosei is the largest (table 3.1). Enkaroni and Meto are intermediate in both regards. Bissel, the main livestock marketing center that serves these four areas, was selected as a reference point (Zaal, 1999a). Enkaroni is about 8 kilometers away from Bissel and Nentanai 18 kilometers, while Meto and Torosei are 65 kilometers and 56 kilometers away, respectively, each sharing a border with Tanzania (map 3.1). Meto and Torosei are

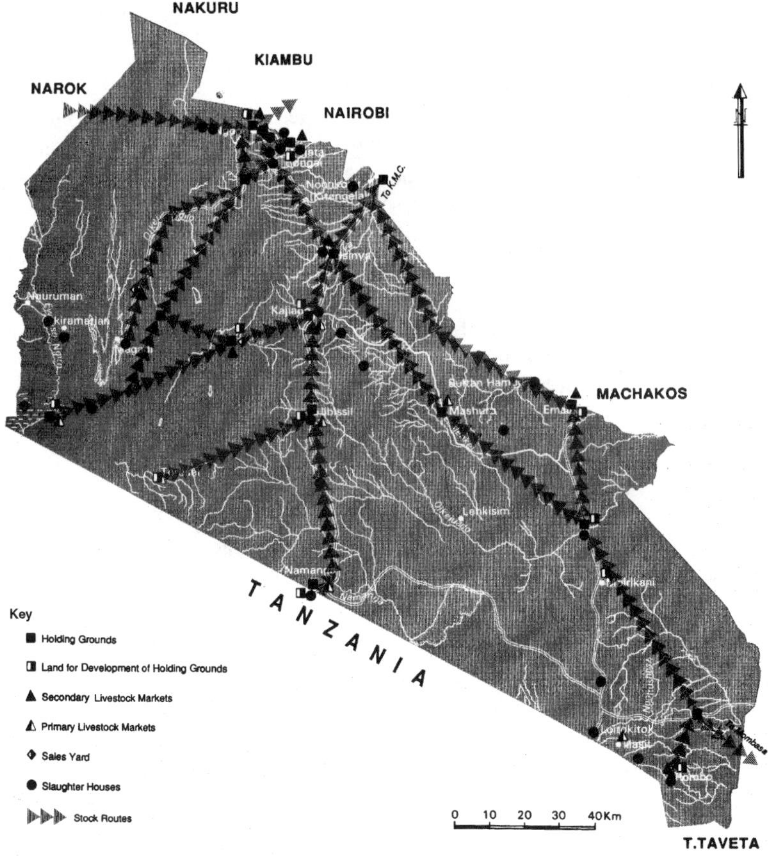

Map 3.1 Livestock Markets in Kajiado District
Source: Kenya, Republic of, 1990.

neighboring group ranches that are on different ends of the subdivision continuum. Meto, being the first to begin issuing titles to members, is the most advanced. Torosei has not been formally surveyed and thus no titles have been issued. Nentanai only began to issue titles in May 2001.

Unlike Enkaroni, Meto, and Nentanai, Torosei retains crucial elements of the group ranch structure. Members not only live in large homesteads, but shared grazing alternating between wet and dry season pastures in the plains and hills is still practiced.[1] In addition, the group ranches selected includes three sections of the Maasai: Ilpurko, Iloodokilani, and Ilmatapato. This was unplanned and not expected to influence results because difference among sections appear minimal, expressed primarily in minor differences in dressing and dialect.

Data Collection

Fieldwork was conducted over a one-year period from January 2001 to January 2002. A second phase of fieldwork was conducted from June to August of 2002. The first part of the 2001 fieldwork was focused on interviews. This was interrupted in April, a month after the onset of the long rains by a session of vegetation and soil data collection. The interviews resumed later in July. The switch from interviews to vegetation sampling and back again to interviews was designed to capture the period of maximum plant growth following the onset of rains that is accompanied by a flowering of grasses, to make it easier to identify grasses, herbs, and forbs. Starting with interviews was helpful in determining sites for vegetation and soil sampling.

Social Data

Archival Material

The purpose of collecting archival material was to obtain a historical perspective on land relations in Maasailand beyond that obtained from books and journals. Such "gray" literature would assist in indicating who the primary actors were, the principle or vested interests in land in Kajiado district over the years, and to help determine whether Maasai preferences were changing over time and insights as to why. This material was also expected to capture local and national debates that had a bearing on processes of land transformation. This was important in establishing the context of current processes and for identifying possible individuals and groups to interview.

Material consulted was from a wide diversity of sources. The Catholic Church library in Kajiado town holds newspaper articles and cuttings on land-related issues and debates in Maasailand from the 1950s. Much of this was perused, with some focus on the period from 1968, when the group ranches were created, to the present. The church also had a wide range of gray literature from visiting researchers, writers, and practitioners for a period of close to five decades.

Group ranch files were obtained from the Land Adjudication Department at the District Headquarters in Kajiado town. These files were of two types: meetings and disputes files. Meetings files contained minutes of group ranch annual general meetings, recorded and accepted changes in memberships, changes in group ranch management committees endorsed by group members, minutes of meetings of group ranch management committees, changes to the group ranch register such as due to deaths, replacements, new registrations and deletions, official communications from the Registrar of group ranches, and official communications from the Land Control Board. The disputes files held correspondence on group ranch boundary disputes, individual and group complaints over the conduct of subdivision, and minutes of arbitration meetings conducted by the District Commissioner's office.

As with the "gray" literature, group ranch files were examined to gain insights into the process of subdivision, to identify key actors and the controversies surrounding the process of subdivision and to identify the roles of the different arms of government administration in the process. Knowledge and information from this archival search fed into the questionnaire surveys, with continuous shifting between the two to cross-check and verify the validity of information. Archival search, however, was the first step to starting the fieldwork.

Questionnaire Survey

The semistructured survey was intended to obtain responses from individuals who were members and/or residing in the group ranches selected for study. Questions asked in the survey are discussed later in this section. The semistructured nature of the questionnaire provided opportunity for individuals to express alternative responses that may not have been anticipated in the structured responses. It also allowed respondents to explain their responses. Interviews were helpful in providing insights on how individuals viewed the process, what their concerns were, and the strategies they used in the process of subdivision. Though this survey was designed to capture some structured responses it relied more heavily on the unstructured text in explaining the process.

Research Assistants and Their Familiarization with the Study

Interviews were conducted with the help of three research assistants who have extensive knowledge and experience on land and other issues in

Kajiado district. Two of the assistants have lived and worked in Kajiado district ever since the late 1970s when they were employed as range officers in the Range Management Department of the Ministry of Agriculture and Livestock Development. They are not Maasai. The Range Management Department in collaboration with the Ministry of Water Development and the Land Adjudication were the key government actors in the development of group ranches. These two assistants were actively involved in the planning and management of group ranches throughout the 1980s, in appraising group and individual ranches for Agricultural Finance Corporation loan schemes and were involved in making ecological viability appraisals in the run-up to subdivision. After subdivision, they have been involved in livestock upgrade projects as well as in projects to diversify livestock breeds in different parts of the district.

Both individuals have a sound knowledge of the ecology, of ecological techniques and have had experience with interviewing both men and women in Kajiado district. In addition, they have a fair knowledge of the language and culture, and many individuals are familiar with them.

The third research assistant was born and raised in Enkorika group ranch, also in Central Division in Kajiado. He is employed in the Land Adjudication Department at the District Headquarters in Kajiado district, and he participated in the process of subdividing group ranches. Prior to joining the Department, in the late 1980s and in the early 1990s, this assistant worked with earlier investigators in Kajiado district, that is, Drs. Marcel Rutten and Chris Southgate.

Prior to the onset of fieldwork we discussed the purpose and goals of the research and held training sessions in early February. In the early months of data collection, we conducted the interviews as a foursome and later split into groups of two.

Selecting Respondents

Interviews were restricted to individuals who "belonged" to each of the group ranches. For example, an individual from Kimana residing in Torosei was not interviewed because he/she was not a member of Torosei and thus not a legitimate participant in decision making in Torosei. An individual who is a member of Nentanai though residing in Oldonyo Orok group ranch but still identifies himself as belonging to Nentanai was interviewed.

Respondents were selected to take into account variations in structural features in the group ranch that were anticipated to influence actors' preferences, positions, and their involvement in the transition (table 3.2). Male elders in the different age sets, from the retired, through senior to junior elders, were interviewed. The youth, many of whom were denied registration

Table 3.2 Interviews by Age Set and Gender

	Ilterito	Ilnyankusi	Iseuri	Ilkiseyia	IrangIrang	Ilkingonde Ilkishili	Ilmajeshi	Ilkilaku Iltakeri	Widows	Married Women
Enkaroni		4	11	20	8	12	2	1	3	17
Meto	1	6	17	22	13	22	—	1	15	12
Nentanai		5	10	6	4	1	—	—	6	6
Torosei		1	16	13	12	33	11	1	4	15
Total (334)	1	16	54	61	37	68	13	3	28	50
% of Total	0.30	4.79	16.17	18.26	10.78	20.36	3.89	0.90	8.38	14.97

Source: Own field work.

and excluded from the process of subdivision, were also interviewed. Women, both married and widowed, were interviewed as were committee members and local administrators such as the chiefs and/or their assistants.

Each of the group ranches was divided into more localized settlement areas that are known and recognized by the community, in order to gather views from individuals living in different parts of each group ranch. In each of these localized settlement areas the interviewers would move from homestead to homestead interviewing individuals, as far as was accessible. Some distant parts of Torosei such as those around Lake Kaponko on the border with Magadi could only be reached by a two-day's walk and thus excluded from the survey. To obtain the responses of individuals living in such distant areas, or those individuals who could not be found in their homesteads due to other engagements, the survey instrument was also administered in local trading centers within the group ranch and in Bissel town during market days.

Thus though the administration of the survey instrument was designed to interview individuals within their local settings, it was flexible enough to accommodate the varying availability of respondents. Because not all individuals, particularly the elderly, were conversant with Kiswahili, interpretations were conducted in Ki-Maasai. Interviewees were given the option of not answering any question they preferred not to and of terminating the interview at any point during the conversation. All respondents were assured anonymity.

The questions in the interview were designed to capture different themes in the broader process of subdivision. The first section was introductory and designed to secure the respondent's confidence by recording names, age set, education, fluency in Kiswahili, and area of residence, before proceeding to the sensitive questions of subdivision and land allocation. It also attempts to establish how far gone into subdivision the group ranches were, whether or

Table 3.3 Proportion of Group Ranch Members Interviewed

	No. of Members	No. of Members Interviewed	% Interviewed
Enkaroni	356	48	13
Meto	645	88	14
Nentanai	57	30	53
Torosei	300	64	21

not individuals had title, whether or not individuals had conducted "improvements" on their land, whether they allowed others to pass through their land, and so on.

The second section asked the question of why individuals opted for subdivision, whether they participated in the decision to subdivide, how parcel sizes and locations were determined and distributed, whether individuals contested allocations if unhappy, how they organized such protest and with what success. This section also obtained opinions on whom or which category of individuals were most or least in favor of subdivision and why. Other sections looked at the evolution of group ranch membership rules, at grazing management, at perceptions of ecological change following subdivision, and into issues of post-transitional collective behavior. For Torosei group ranch, which had not formally subdivided by the time of fieldwork, a slight variant of the original survey instrument included questions intended to reflect reasons why this group ranch delayed subdividing yet members resolved to subdivide about the same time as with the other group ranches of Enkaroni, Meto, and Nentanai.

A total of 334 interviews were conducted across different categories of elders, the youths, married women, and widows for all four study sites. Table 3.2 provides a breakdown of these respondents by group ranch and social category. The proportion of registered membership, interviewed in each group ranch is given above (table 3.3).

Unstructured, In-Depth Interviews

These were conducted individually with various politicians, retired civil servants, land adjudication officials, the district administration, and ministry officials in Nairobi. The purpose of these interviews was to gain insights into the issue of subdivision and to follow up on issues that emerged during the interview of local communities. Questions asked related primarily to the timing of subdivision, to official procedure and coordination, to the issue of disputes and their resolution, the role of the bureaucracy, the politicians' perspectives, and the role of the judiciary in the subdivision process.

A second set of unstructured in-depth interviews were conducted from June to August of 2002, following a preliminary review of the data that had been collected the previous year. In this second phase of interviews, individuals were selected to provide clarification and further insights into the process. Specific individuals who collectively or individually challenged outcomes were sought out. Individuals with parcels excessively larger than others were purposely sought, as were the leaders of groups of youth that protested the outcome of subdivision. In addition, the structure of the committee and the criteria for its election/selection was more closely investigated during this second period in the field. The puzzle of why the outcome turned out against members' expectations contrary to collective agreement was further probed.

Certain contrasts between group ranches were further examined in the second set of investigations. This included an investigation into why the members of Meto and Nentanai did not organize to contest outcomes, yet those in Enkaroni did; why the youth in Meto and Nentanai were unable to organize and/or sustain a challenge to their exclusion yet those in Enkaroni did. Table 3.4 provides a list of individuals who were interviewed in the in-depth interviews during both the first and second phases of fieldwork in 2001 and 2002, respectively.

Table 3.4　Individuals Selected for In-Depth Interviewing (2001)

Position
Registrar of Group Ranches
Chief Matapato location, 1970–1982. Covered all areas between Bissel and Namanga. Oversaw the allocation of individual ranches in Matapato location.
1980–1986, Clerk to Kajiado County Council
1987–1989, permanent secretary in the Civil Service
Group Ranch Education Program officer, Catholic Diocese of Ngong, 1976–1994; director, Neighborhood Initiative Alliance, 1994-to date
District land adjudication and settlement officer and assistant registrar of group ranches
Justice of the High Court of Kenya
District commissioner, Kajiado district
Catholic priest lived and worked in Narok and Kajiado districts for 40 years
Kajiado district surveyor, 1991–2000;
Currently a private surveyor based in Kajiado Town
Prominent Maasai and National Politician since colonial time
Was member of Parliament for Kajiado North Constituency
Private Surveyor
Range Management Department, Ministry of Livestock Development, 1968–1983
Implemented the Group (and Individual) Ranch Program

Source: Own field work.

Ecological Methods

The initial intent of this part of the study was to investigate ecological differences and/or similarities among group ranches that had been subdivided and individualized and those that had not. These pure categories hardly exist in the field. Most group ranches in Kajiado district are at different points of the transition toward complete individualization. Majority have had formal survey and mapping conducted, and titles had begun to be issued or were beginning to be issued. Those who have not advanced to this stage have been entangled in conflict over distribution. Few others in the more arid areas have resisted the move to subdivide and have retained the group ranch's communal structure for the use and management of resources. Three of the group ranches studied (Enkaroni, Meto, and Nentanai) fall under the first category, where land titles continue to be issued and individuals settled on their own parcels. The fourth group ranch (Torosei), located on the transition zone to the arid bottom of the Rift Valley, still waits to subdivide.

Although most group ranches have subdivided and individualized, it became obvious in the course of field interviews and observation that individuals in privatized areas follow diverse styles of resource and pasture management. Some, based on friendship and kinship ties or neighborhood considerations, reconsolidate their privately owned units to pursue a collectivized form of management with rotational grazing within this consolidated unit. Others, who are unable to accept the unequal distribution of livestock holdings, prefer to pursue individualized livestock management strategies. Of this latter category, some have relatively large land units and others relatively smaller ones. Yet others have large livestock holdings, which they graze on their small or large parcels. Some others still have few livestock, which they graze on their small or large parcels. Thus even within group ranches that have been privatized, diverse strategies, with diverse implications for ecology and sustainability, are pursued by herders.

These unexpected strategies formed the basis for the design of vegetation and soil sampling procedures. While it differs from a direct comparison of communal as against individual ownership, it draws attention to a more complex reality. This part of the study is thus exploratory in nature, intended to highlight the possible role of management strategies in sustainability and as a basis for generating further hypotheses that can be subjected to more rigorous investigation.

The group ranches were thus stratified according to five management regimes/strategies that were obtained by discussions with group ranch members and also from personal observation (table 3.5). The management strategies included communal as against individualized. Under the "communal" strategies, individuals, on the basis of neighborhood, kinship,

Table 3.5 Pasture Management Regimes and Livestock Concentration

	Large Parcel, Many Livestock	Large Parcel, Few Livestock	Small-Many	Small-Few	Communal
Enkaroni	Size: 134 hectares Livestock: 260 cattle (15 plots)	Size: 111.5 hectares Livestock: 80 cows, 200 shoats (15 plots)	Size: 26.5 hectares Livestock: 80 cows, 80 sheep, 120 goats (15 plots)	Size: 40 hectares Livestock: 23 cattle, 22 sheep, 29 goats (15 plots)	(30 Plots)
Meto	Size: 114.5 hectares Livestock: 100 cows, 200 goats, 60 sheep (15 plots)	Size: 116.14 hectares Livestock: 50 cows, 100 goats (15 plots)	Size: 40.31 hectares Livestock: 80 cows, 25 sheep, 125 goats (15 plots)	Size: 27.33 hectares Livestock: 36 goats, 4 sheep (15 plots)	(15 Plots)
Nentanai	Size: 152.44 hectares Livestock: 200 cows, 100 sheep, 100 goats (15 plots)	Size: 126.73 hectares Livestock: 50 cows, 60 sheep, 20 goats (12 plots)	Size: Livestock: 70 cows, 40 sheep, 100 goats (12 plots)	Size: 41 hectares Livestock: 8 cows, 15 goats, 5 sheep (15 plots)	(30 Plots)
Torosei	—	—	—	—	(36 Plots)

Source: Own field work.

or friendship ties consolidated their parcels for the purpose of grazing and livestock management. Under the individualized strategies, parcel owners wary of the uneven distribution of livestock holdings among each other preferred to pursue livestock and pasture management individually. They actively excluded others from grazing their livestock in their parcels both through fencing and active monitoring of parcel boundaries. In this latter category, I varied the parcel between "large" and "small." I also varied the livestock holdings between "few" and "many." These categories of small, large, few, and many were not obtained by any "objective" measurement but through conversations with Maasai herders. The form of stratification described here and categories I have delineated were only possible in Enkaroni, Meto, and Nentanai, which had formally subdivided.

The Torosei group ranch has not been formally subdivided. Though group ranch members seem to have a general sense of the likely locations of their assigned parcels, they are still pursuing a coordinated strategy of livestock movement between the plains areas in the wet season and the hilly areas in the dry season. Many are still residing in large, extended homesteads comprising both family and friends. Both the hill and plains areas of Torosei were sampled and subsequently coded under the communal/reassociation category. Most vegetation sampling was conducted between April and June 2001, and part of it was conducted in July. This period was after the rains and corresponded with peak flowering periods for various plants for ease of identification.

Sampling plots were randomly located in each of the management areas indicated above. The herbaceous, shrubby, and tree layers were measured within a series of nested, variable size plots. For the herbaceous layer, visual estimates of aerial cover, plant heights, and species composition were recorded in a 1-meter-squared quadrant. The herbaceous layer was defined as any nonwoody plant material 1 meter or less in height. The shrubby layer, more than 1 meter in height, consisted of woody plants with multiple stems and branching fairly close to the ground. Shrubs were measured in a circular plot defined by a 5-meter radius. Species composition, height, and cover were also measured.

Aerial cover for each shrub was measured by recording the extent of the foliage in two perpendicular dimensions. A tree was defined as any single-stemmed woody species having a diameter at breast height (about 1.3 meters above ground) that is greater than 10 centimeters. Tree cover was measured by recording tree girth at 1.3 meters above ground level. All tree species in the plot were recorded.

In each sample plot, soil was extracted from two depths, 0–10 centimeters and 10–20 centimeters where feasible, using a soil augur. All soil samples were stored in paper bags and transported to the National Agricultural Laboratories (NARL) and the Kenya Soil Survey (KSS), both departments within the Kenya Agricultural Research Institute. NARL conducted the soil chemical analysis, while KSS conducted the physical analysis. Each sample was analyzed for percent nitrogen, organic carbon, and for available potassium, calcium, magnesium, manganese, and sodium. Soil pH and texture were also determined. All soil samples were analyzed according to KARI standard procedures (Hinga et al., 1980).

Percent slope was recorded for each plot by the use of a clinometer.

A total of 257 plots across the different management types in each of the group ranch areas were sampled. On average about 15 plots were sampled for each management type; this was doubled in the case of communal-type regimes. Each plot's location was referenced geographically by the use of a global positioning system.

Plant species were identified at the East African Herbarium in the National Museums of Kenya after the following authorities: Agnew and Agnew (1994); Beentje et al. (1994); Ibrahim and Kabuye (1988); Clayton et al. (1974); Clayton, 1970; Clayton and Renvoize, 1982.

A total of 137 species were identified; a complete species listing can be found in Mwangi (2003). Of these 23 are grasses, 42 nongrass herbs, 42 shrubs, and 30 trees. About seven species remained unidentified due to the poor quality of specimen collected. Of these four are grasses, one herb, and two shrubs.

Data Analysis

The analysis of the interview data is largely qualitative and interpretive. The choice of qualitative method was guided by the nature of the problem, which is an attempt to understand a profound and deeply puzzling phenomenon that represents a significant break away from established Maasai cultural practice. Obtaining details about opinions, events, and experiences of individuals and groups during the process of group ranch subdivision seems most meaningfully addressed through description of preferences, of actions and interactions.

The analysis disaggregates respondents according to gender, age set, age and marital status, whether rich or poor, and likewise outlines their preferences and motivations for supporting or opposing subdivision. Matrices are used to summarize and depict this. Analysis also comprises a focused reading of individuals' responses to identify cross-cutting or narrow emergent themes. The first theme that emerged had to do with motivations; the second theme that emerged had to do with the distribution and allocation of parcels. Within each of these themes, subthemes were identified, which considered the rules that determined action and interactions, the differing ability of individuals and groups to respond to their new situation, and how individuals and groups aligned or misaligned their actions and interactions. The themes were first integrated for each group ranch in the form of a summary memo. These memos were then integrated for all group ranches under the different thematic areas.

Descriptive statistics calculated proportions and were used to illustrate the distribution of various motivating factors for subdivision among different categories of individuals in each group ranch (chapter four). Similarly, the distribution of land parcels among individuals for each group ranch was summarized using arithmetic mean and standard deviation. All are measures of central tendency and were aimed at illustrating the extent of land concentration following subdivision (chapter five).

The analysis of ecological outcomes was quantified. Canonical Correspondence Analysis on PC-Ord, version 4.0 (McCune and Mefford, 1999) was used to explore the relationship between plant species cover and environmental variables. Default specifications were used, and Monte Carlo runs were to test the null hypothesis that there is no relationship between matrices. Separate analyses were run for herbaceous, shrubby, and tree species. Percentage cover values for the 10 highest-ranking herbaceous, shrub, and tree species were calculated.

Chapter Four
The Footprints of History

Introduction

The recent historical change of property rights to land in Kenya's Maasailand, and in Kenya more generally, is closely linked to the advent of British colonial administration at the close of the nineteenth century. This administration's objectives of political control, revenue generation, and economic development in first the East African Protectorate and later the Kenya Colony, were at the core of a series of land-based policy interventions, which are discussed in this chapter. The postcolonial administration in turn drew heavily from and gave expression to ideas and interventions crafted by its predecessor. These new institutional arrangements resulted in greater privatization of Maasailand and a fundamental reworking of land property rights systems and relations among the Maasai.

By grounding analysis within concrete temporal processes, this chapter seeks to provide a deeper understanding of current transformations in Kenya's Maasailand. It argues that historical processes are greatly relevant in shaping the broad direction of current processes of transformation. It suggests that the battery of closely related interventions and rules (see table 4.1 for summary of rules) that were crafted and implemented by the colonial and early postcolonial states in Kenya has served to constrain and focus institutional choice for the ordinary Maasai, to the extent that individualization of land rights now appears to be the most attractive option of those available.

As indicated in chapter one, theories of path dependence suggest that history constrains present and future options for change and that current phenomena cannot be adequately understood without knowledge of how they have been shaped by past events. This continuity between past and current decisions is thought to be fostered by the self-reinforcing character of institutions. Once an institutional path is adopted, it becomes more and more difficult to change it or to select previously available options even if those earlier alternatives would have been more efficient. This reinforcement

Table 4.1 Summary of Significant Interventions in Maasailand

Instrument	*Objective*	*Outcome*
Maasai treaties of 1904 and 1911 with the East African Protectorate.	Appropriation of Maasailand.	Maasai moved first into North and South reserves. 1911 resulted in all Maasai being moved and retained within southern reserve. Creation of the "white highlands."
The Kenya Land Commission, 1932.	Evaluating the land needs of Africans; evaluating African land claims over land alienated to nonnatives.	Communal rights in African reserves but strong preference for movement toward individual rights; alienated land not returned to Maasai, instead agricultural communities encouraged to help "develop" Maasai land; grazing schemes to encourage better land management amongst Maasai.
East African Royal Commission, 1952.	Evaluate the outcomes of the Kenya Land Commission; to recommend modifications in tribal tenure necessary for the development of land.	Communal tenure in pastoral areas be eliminated; customary rights inefficient and replaced with individual tenure; government policy to encourage individual tenure among Africans and to institute a system of registration of negotiable title.
The Swynnerton Plan, 1952.	Fast forwarding reform of traditional tenure and promoting commercialized production systems among Africans; soothe escalating political tensions.	Land Adjudication and Registration programs and individualization of tenure in African reserves.
The Group (Land Representatives) Act, 1968.	Tenure security for the Maasai; incentives for investment in commercialized systems of livestock production among the Maasai.	Creation of a management committee with immense discretion that was used to dole out land to their close associates, influential politicians, and government officials; insecurity of tenure among ordinary Maasai; subdivision of group ranches.

Source: Own work.

of one sequence across time may happen because those parties with a vested interest in the status quo will oppose institutional change unless they can be made better-off. Movement within a given path exhibits a distinct pattern of incentives and constraints. It is similarly associated with characteristic strategies and approaches to problems and decisions. These approaches, constraints, and incentives relive themselves when actors are confronted with new situations.

The beginning of each path is marked by a critical juncture during which a particular institutional alternative is selected out of a choice set and is reproduced in subsequent time periods. The adoption of an alternative during a critical juncture is a contingent event that is independent of the initial conditions. Similarly, the mechanism by which an adopted institution is perpetuated is also distinct from the critical juncture.

This chapter highlights historical events relevant to current institutional choices in Maasailand. It uses path dependence to analyze the continuities of diverse actors' choices and the outcomes of those choices across time.

The Precolonial Period

Very little is known of the early history of the Maasai. Linguistic evidence and the accounts of early writers suggest that the ancestors of the modern Maa-speakers originated from the region around southern Sudan that is inhabited by Nilotic-speaking peoples found also in adjacent parts of north-western Kenya and northern Uganda (Sommer and Vosen, 1993; Sandford, 1919). The Maasai separated and migrated southward across the Rift Valley in Kenya and into Tanzania. This southward movement occurred in two stages (Sutton, 1993). The first, about 300 years ago, saw the Maasai settle into an elevated stretch of Kenya's Rift Valley around the Nakuru area. The second stage was characterized by an outward radiation south-eastward to Ngong, across the Athi-Kaputiei Plains, and to the foothills of Mt. Kilimanjaro. Some Maasai also radiated southwestward across Loita, Mara, and into Serengeti.

The ancestors of the Maasai were originally agropastoralists, raising sorghum and millet along with cattle and small stock (Spear, 1993). Their southward territorial expansion is, however, thought to have involved a profound and rapid transformation of Maasai social, institutional, and ritual development toward a greater ethnic self-consciousness that is centered on the pastoral ideal (Sutton, 1993; Berntsen, 1979b). This happened mainly during the second southward expansion, which brought the Maasai into contact with other communities. The pastoral ideal and the emergence of a "pure" pastoral diet emerged via close interactions with the Sirikwa, a Kalenjin-speaking group that was resident in the elevated grasslands of the upper Rift Valley. The supposedly pure pastoral diet was supplemented by grain during periods of drought. This was obtained through relations with cultivating communities who farmed the fertile highlands surrounding the plains, for example, the Kikuyu, Chagga, Sonjo, and Nandi. Trade, intermarriage, and stock exchange were common between the Maasai and their neighbors (Spear, 1993). These associations were facilitated by shared cultural norms.

To sustain the pastoral economy, resources such as water, pasture, and salt licks had to be defended against incursions by other communities, both Maa-speakers and non-Maa. In times of drought, or when disease decimated herds, raiding was at times necessary to feed the community. Consequently, the Maasai developed and maintained a military organization with weapons and techniques for defense and attack. The age-set system, which defined the duties of age sets, their regular initiation, and their transition to power were formalized at this time (Sutton, 1993).

Pastoral resources were collectively held under the auspices of each Maasai section (these have been described in detail in chapter two). A section was and still is a territorially defined unit of the Maasai, under which is incorporated different units of production such as neighborhoods, camps, and households. The section occupied and used a defined geographical area with clearly defined boundaries, which was protected from other communities. Within each section, movement occurred between designated dry and wet season grazing areas, and particular rules and norms developed for the management and use of pasture resources. Upon request, families, camps, or neighborhoods would, for instance, grant access to herders temporarily passing the neighborhood. Under conditions of extreme drought, however, different sections came into contact with each other, often without conflict. Sectional alliances allowed for shared access to pasture outside the territory of each section. Under conditions of extreme environmental stress intersectional conflict over resources sometimes escalated into war. The *"Iloikop"* wars by which the Maasai gained control over much of the Rift Valley were fought over the control of strategic water and pastures (Galaty, 1993). Losers would either be assimilated or would drop out of the pastoral economy.

In the nineteenth century, prior to the entry of the colonial administrators, the territorial boundaries between the Maa-speaking communities, and between pastoralists and cultivators in the Rift Valley region were generally known. They were, however, permeable and constantly shifting and subject to continuous redefinition. Indeed, individuals and groups moved between different communities and economies, altering their identities as they did so. Communities were able to absorb and shed members easily and rapidly in response to changes in the availability of resources and the demand for labor (Waller, 1993).

The ecological status of Maasailand in precolonial time is primarily based on anecdotal information from early travelers and colonial administrators. Thomson's travels through Maasai land in 1883 depict a wide diversity of landscape and vegetation conditions (Thomson, 1885). From these accounts, the southern part of Maasailand comprises what he called the "Nyika dry savannah" that is devoid of much grass. Here water was scarce and rainfall so little that there was "hardly a blade of grass to be seen." These were areas of Maasailand surrounding the Maparasha Hills, Oldonyo Orok, and perhaps the Amboseli Plains. It is likely that Thomson's travels in this particular area coincided with a dry spell. Further north of Bissel area and into the Kaputiei Plains (present-day northeastern Kajiado district), Thomson stumbled upon a grand expanse of undulating country, the hollows of which were "knee-deep in rich and succulent pasture . . . ridges covered in trees of moderate size" (Thomson, 1885, 170).

Several years later, retired Governor Charles Eliot commenting on the pasturage potential of the East African Protectorate remarked on how areas of Maasailand would "afford excellent grass to cattle owned by both natives and Europeans" (Eliot, 1905, 170). The areas he mentioned of—Ngong, Laikipia, Naivasha, Kedong Valley, Endabibi Plains, north of Lake Elementaita, and north of Lake Nakuru—were all parts of the Rift Valley that were utilized by the Maasai and later appropriated for European settlement. Eliot further suggested that the quality of the pasturage may have been due to long periods of continuous grazing by native cattle.

The influence of traditional pastoralism on the historical development of ecological regimes in Maasai land has generated much controversy; however, the above accounts of the early writers does seem to suggest that Maasai pastoralism had some beneficial effects on resource productivity. It might also suggest that during those times herd mobility may well have enabled the achievement of a balance between pasture resources and livestock holdings.

The Colonial Period, 1895–1963

A Series of Treaties

Much of the historical literature on the precolonial extent of Maasai territory suggests that at the height of their power in the latter half of the nineteenth century, pastoral Maasai occupied a swathe of country measuring about 500 miles from North to South and about 200 miles from East to West at its widest points (Jacobs, 1965; Huntingford, 1953). This was roughly from the arid plains around Lake Baringo 1^0 North of the equator, down through the Rift Valley, to the edge of the wooded savannah slightly north of Central Tanganyika. This land may have amounted to about 10 million acres (Tignor, 1976).

When the British colonists entered Maasai territory toward the end of the nineteenth century, they encountered what they perceived to be vast, "unoccupied" lands. The drought of 1897, rinderpest, bovine pleuropneumonia, and small pox epidemics, and Maasai intersectional wars had decimated both the Maasai populations and their herds (Tignor, 1976; Sorrenson, 1968; Kenya Colony and Protectorate, 1934; Sandford, 1919). The Athi Plains, the Uasin Gishu, and Laikipia plateaus were, for example, only partially occupied by small groups of Maasai, while the rest of Maasai territory was even more sparsely populated. British administrators concluded that the Maasai had more land than they needed, much of which was not under any productive use. This mistaken notion of productive land lying idle together with the presentation of Maasai as a warlike predatory group that terrorized neighboring groups was used to justify Brutish annexation of Maasailand (Halderman, 1989; Kipury, 1989; Collet, 1987). Not only had the Massai "stolen from others," but having stolen it they did not even utilize it.

British interest in East Africa was prompted by a need to control the headwaters of the Nile (in Uganda) and to control trading routes to India. Consequently, a railway was constructed linking the East African coast and Lake Victoria in the interior in the years between 1895 and 1901. A large part of the railway traversed Maasai territory. In the period between 1902 and 1903, Maasai roamed freely on both sides of this railway from Molo to Naivasha in the Rift Valley and on the south side from Nairobi to Kiu (Sandford, 1919). The Protectorate government was, however, obliged to balance the budget to offset the costs of constructing and operating the railway. More generally the British wanted the East Africa Protectorate to pay for its own administration (Tignor, 1976). Agricultural exports appeared to be the solution and European settlers the most effective producers.

Settlers were thus encouraged to make applications for land on which they would farm.[1] The land most sought after by the settlers was that adjacent to the Uganda railway; many of the land grant applications would absorb the best and most favored grazing of the Maasai between Lakes Nakuru and Naivasha. This brought into focus the question of Maasai and in a more general sense of African land rights as opposed to that of the settlers who were intended to power economic development in the Protectorate.

In pondering the question of Maasai rights, the then high commissioner Sir Charles Eliot contended that two issues had been conflated by local Protectorate administrators and by administrators in the Foreign Office in London (Sandford, 1919). These were the rights of the Maasai to *inhabit* particular areas as opposed to their rights to *monopolize* particular areas to the exclusion of others. To Eliot the first right was undoubted but the second questionable. Wandering tribes had no right to keep out superior races just because they had acquired the habit of straggling over more land than they needed. Rights could be created to accommodate the European settlers.

Eliot duly considered possible arrangements that would accommodate both Maasai and Europeans. He flirted with the idea of Maasai coexistence in small villages among European farms, with Maasai serving as farm employees for the settlers. He ruled this out as it would aggravate tensions between the two groups. He instead recommended the creation of separate reserves for the Maasai. This option was also favored by the Secretary of State for foreign affairs who feared that conflict between Maasai and the settlers would erode Maasai customs and organization. The Maasai had to be moved. Land concessions were thus granted to several applicants notably the East African Syndicate[2] (320,000 acres), Lord Delamere (100,000 acres), and to Chamberlain and Flemmer who each received 32,000 acres (Tignor, 1976). The next step was to evict the Maasai. Some of Eliot's subordinates who had spoken with Maasai elders disfavored the eviction. Apparently though Maasai found the concession to the East African Syndicate acceptable, they were anxious to retain the rest of their Rift Valley estate.[3]

In 1904, colonial administrators signed a treaty with a Maasai "chief" they had installed. This treaty would see the Maasai vacate a large part of their territory in the Rift Valley for occupation by settlers. "Paramount Chief" Lenana and other Maasai leaders signed the treaty on behalf of the Maasai. The terms of this treaty specified that the Purko, Keekonyokie, Loita, and Damat sections would move northward into Laikipia, while the Kaputiei, Matapato, Loodokilani, and Sikirari would withdraw into the Southern Reserve (Tignor, 1976). The terms also specified that a 5 square mile area on Kinangop would be set aside for important ritual ceremonies and that a road linking the two Maasai reserves would be constructed. About 2,000 rupees would be paid to the Maasai in compensation, and the treaty would be in force for as long as the Maasai existed as a race.

This first move was not entirely successful because some Maasai refused to leave their homesteads, some warriors asserted they would rather die than move, while still others who were dissatisfied with the grazing in the north moved back to the Rift Valley.

Seven years later, in 1911, the British reversed the 1904 agreement and forced Maasai to move from the northern Laikipia reserve to a smaller and less fertile reserve in the south, the locations of Kajiado and Narok districts where the bulk of the Maasai currently reside. Once again the Maasai signed a treaty, but this time under considerable duress. Though Paramount Chief Lenana supposedly favored the move because he needed to amalgamate the Maasai from the various sections of the tribe under his authority, other Maasai leaders were hesitant (Sandford, 1919). Land in the south was dry, tick-infested, and already populated by other Maasai sections. Resistance to this second move ended in court proceedings brought against the government by the Maasai. The plaintiffs claimed that those who had signed the treaty had done so under duress and that their signatures did not bind the rest of the tribe. The case was heard by the East African Protectorate High Court and was dismissed on a technicality: the treaties were an act of state and thus not challengeable in a Protectorate court.

The land vacated by the Maasai, close to 2 million hectares, was renamed the "white highlands" and given to the settlement of Europeans, whose agricultural and other commercial activities were anticipated to power economic development in the new Kenya Colony. In response to settlers' demands, private, individually owned farms, and commercial ranches were formed in these areas.

In order to alienate the land, the administrators borrowed and applied Western notions of ownership, which they expediently entrenched in the law (Okoth-Ogendo, 1991, 1976; Halderman, 1989). According to them, Africans only "owned" land during the period it was actively occupied or cultivated. When they moved off the land it reverted to "wasteland." This convenient misreading of African land tenure institutions allowed the government to assert its claims to such waste and otherwise unoccupied land, which it then leased or outright sold to settlers. The Crown Lands Ordinance gave this interpretation legal force.

The years 1904 and 1911 represent the first wave of land alienation from the Maasai. In total out of about 31,000 square kilometers of European settled land (excluding forest reserves), 18,000 square kilometers were former Maasai lands (Rutten, 1995). Land in the Southern Reserve to which the Maasai were relocated was either too small or too arid to support transhumant pastoralism or just simply inhospitable. The northern boundary of this reserve was drawn to exclude the most valuable water supplies, which were included in the land alienated to the Europeans.

Of the 10 million acres of the reserve, 2 million acres was arid or semiarid, 800,000 infested with tsetse fly and 300,000 subject to East Coast Fever (Lewis, 1965, cited in Kipury, 1989).

The British were able to accomplish the eviction of the Maasai because they found them in a weakened state following the disasters of the late nineteenth century (Spencer, 1983). Survivors were preoccupied with recouping their recent losses and could not put up substantial resistance.

National Parks and Game Reserves

The passing of the National Parks Ordinance in 1945 paved the way for the second wave of land alienation. In order to promote wildlife conservation and tourism the colonial authority carved out parts of Maasailand for the development of national parks, game reserves, and game conservation areas. In 1946, Nairobi National Park was created (117 square kilometers) and Tsavo (21,000 square kilometers) designated a Game Reserve. In 1947, Amboseli National Park was gazetted (3,260 square kilometers), Ngong National Reserve (512 square kilometers) in 1949, West Chyulu Conservation Area (373 square kilometers) in 1961, and Kitengela Conservation Area (530 square kilometers) in 1965 (Kituyi, 1990). These areas are part of present-day Kajiado district. Once again most of the land expropriated from the Maasai constituted dry season highland or swamp-lands and salt licks that are strategic resources for the sustenance of Maasai livestock management systems.

Blaming the Victims: Colonial Administration
and Narratives of Degradation

Following the treaties of 1904 and 1911, the Maasai were confined in the Southern Reserve which was declared a "closed" district (Kipury, 1989; Sandford, 1919). Here restrictions on livestock movements via quarantine regulations were placed on Maasai herds. This was to prevent the mixing of Maasai herds with new breeds brought in from England, which did not have resistance to tropical disease. This restriction also blocked traditional trade relations and exchange between Maasai and the northern Somali and Borana pastoralists. These relations were also valued as a source of acquiring seed for improving Maasai stock.

Several authors argue that the ban placed on the movement of Maasai herds outside the reserve was intended to exclude Maasai from participating in the beef and dairy industries in order to eliminate any form of competition that such participation would give to the settler communities (Doornbos and Markakis, 1991; Kipury, 1989; Spencer, 1983; Raikes, 1981; James, 1939). During this time, nothing save for taxation was done to incorporate Maasai into the colonial economy. Taxation was largely conducted to meet the costs of the two world wars, as Maasai were thought to be wealthier and more self-sufficient than their cultivating neighbors. The lack of market off-take and the introduction of veterinary services within the reserve led to considerable herd proliferation within the confines of the Maasai reserve. Herd recovery was greatly aided by "authorized" raiding against the intransigent wa-Kamba, Kikuyu, and Nandi communities. British officers employed Maasai as mercenaries who were paid with captured cattle (Bridges, 1991; Halderman, 1989).

By 1932, colonial administrators were beginning to express concern about these large herds. Excessive herds were presumed to be responsible for soil erosion and land degradation in the reserve. The rinderpest epidemic of 1890 had greatly reduced livestock populations, such that by 1904 cattle were estimated at only 50,000 and sheep and goats at 600,000.[4] By 1914, Maasai cattle were 600,000 and sheep and goats over 1 million. In later years, possibly 1940s to 1950s, even after the droughts of 1933 and 1934, cattle had increased to 700,000 and shoats to 800,000, including a large number of donkeys.

Many colonial administrators were unable or reluctant, to connect Maasai herd proliferation and range degradation to the land alienation they had earlier suffered, and their confinement to a much smaller, less productive range. According to these administrators soil degradation in the Maasai reserve was the consequence of Maasai "irrationality."[5] The Maasai's "cattle complex," his psychological attachment to the beast (Herskovitz, 1926) led him to emphasize quantity over quality, leading him to overgraze and degrade the environment. This environmental destruction was also seen as a threat to the large herds of wildlife resident within the Maasai reserves. Even if the administrators had acknowledged the underlying cause of degradation, the range of possible remedies was constrained by the presence of privileged and politically influential settler communities. Treating the symptoms proved far much easier than curing the disease.

While there was consensus amongst government officials that Maasai held excessive cattle, there was disagreement on the extent to which overstocking contributed to soil erosion and degradation. The large populations of wild ungulates within the Maasai reserves and the variable climate may have as well been to blame (James, 1939). The Kajiado district veterinary officer, in response to a draft district development plan, questioned the validity of the degradation argument, suggesting that it may well be "exaggerated because of the prominence now given to soil deterioration in arable areas or unsuitable areas given over to arable farming."[6]

There was also marked disagreement on appropriate solutions. District planners recommended forced destocking and withdrawal of water supplies. The veterinary department, on the other hand, due to a better understanding of the logic of Maasai herding practice was less radical in its proposals. They acknowledged that drought insurance was at the core of Maasai herd accumulation, and that land scarcities and the influx of cultivators into the reserve were additional problems. These were problems that could not be delinked from earlier administrative decisions. Consequently the district veterinary officer suggested that the problem of reducing Maasai herds be approached gradually and indirectly in order to ensure greater "submission to control and development. . . . The answer must lie in control, control in its widest sense."[7] The Veterinary Department thus recommended the introduction of marketing outlets to reduce Maasai stocking levels. The department also recommended that more land be put under Maasai use by freeing the land from disease and by providing additional water.

In response to these signs of pressure on traditional land tenure systems and continuing protests over land alienation, the colonial administration mandated the Kenya Land Commission (KLC) in April 1932, also known as the Carter Commission after its chair, Sir William Morris Carter (Kenya Colony and Protectorate, 1934). The Carter Commission was charged with the work of evaluating the current and future land needs of the African population. It was required to make recommendations on whether land should be held in tribal or individual tenure, and whether it was feasible to set aside more land for communities or individual Africans of recognized tribes. It was also concerned with evaluating African land claims over land alienated to nonnatives.

The Kenya Land Commission, April 1932

The Kenya Land Commission, also known as the Carter Commission, comprised four members. The backgrounds of these commissioners have been extensively analyzed (Breen, 1979). The chair of the commission, Sir William Morris Carter, was a former chief justice in East Africa who had served in various land tenure commissions in Uganda. His most significant achievement was in chairing the Southern Rhodesia land commission in which he recommended territorial segregation. Rupert William Hemsted was a retired colonial administrator who became a settler, while Frank O'Brien Wilson, an ex-naval officer had also retired as a settler in Kamba country. Both were appointed to satisfy the colonial office's (in London) need for the participation of "local" men. Both however were highly compromised in their status as settlers. The secretary of the commission, S. H. Fazan, was Kiambu's District Commissioner whose interests lay in applied anthropology and the economics of African life.

Observing an immediate danger from overstocking of cattle, sheep, goats, and donkeys on African pastoral land, the commission recommended the culling of the stock, and that the government should unremittingly pursue a policy of controlling the cattle population within the limits of grazing capacities. With regard to land tenure, the commission recommended that each reserve be built on the basis of its native custom, but that it should progressively be guided toward private tenure, proceeding through the group, the family and toward the individual holding.

In their memorandum to the Kenya Land Commission, the Maasai complained that the area they inhabited in the Southern Reserve was without adequate resources to sustain their pastoral livelihoods and demanded that Laikipia be returned to them. The commissioners however, held that the Maasai occupied Kenya's best pastoral land, were Kenya's wealthiest tribe, and had sufficient land to meet their needs.[8] There was thus no need to revise the treaties of 1904 and 1911 to enable the Maasai to recover their northern grazing areas in the Laikipia plateau and elsewhere. In fact, because the Maasai were tying up too much land, they should be forced to give leases of land to other communities, particularly the cultivators, to "develop" their land. Leasing land to cultivating tribes would be useful in reducing the tsetse fly areas and bringing more vacant land into effective use. It would also be useful in relieving overcrowding in other African areas, particularly in the Kikuyu Reserve. Interestingly, even by the time of the commission's formation cultivation was already being practiced in the relatively better watered, northern most part of the Maasai reserve by Kikuyu women who were married to Maasai (James, 1939).

The Kenya Land Commission ended the theoretical security over land rights which the Treaty of 1911 gave to the Maasai. The recommendations of the Kenya Land Commission were accepted by His Majesty's government and by the Colony's legislature and subsequently given legal effect.

The issue of increasing cultivation in Maasai Reserve deserves special mention because, while the administration regarded the degradation in Maasai Reserve as originating from irrational herd accumulation by the Maasai, the Maasai themselves thought differently. According to Campbell (1993) Maasai perceptions of the origins of the problem was twofold. First, degradation was the consequence of constrained grazing following large-scale appropriations for European settlement. Second, it was also a consequence of losing the remaining good quality grazing to cultivation. Efforts to restrict Kikuyu and Kamba migrants to the Reserve began as early as 1927. The years 1947 and 1951 saw the institution of legal procedures to limit cultivation and to more strictly regulate land use in the district (Rutten, 1995; Campbell, 1993). These efforts were undermined by the fact that immigration of cultivators was based on marital and kinship ties. The declaration of Emergency in Kenya in 1952 resulted in the expulsion of Kikuyu from Kajiado and the problem of encroachment was temporarily relieved.

The Settlers' Influence on Public Policy

The large-scale appropriation of Maasailand for the benefit of European settlement and the continued protection of settler assets throughout the colonial period is a decisive indication of the settlers' influential position in the country's political arena. Much of what happened was sanctioned both by local administrators as well as the officials in the Foreign/Colonial Office in London. Promoting economic development within the East African

Protectorate and later in the Kenya Colony was of primary interest to administrators. Maasai/native land rights were dismissed as humanitarian sentiments.

Halderman (1989) provides an insightful analysis of how the settler community established and entrenched their political influence. He argues that while much of the settlers' influence may have originated from their claims to being essential for economic development, they were also skilled at political organization and at using personal contacts within the administration to achieve their goals. It also helped their cause that high-ranking officials including Protectorate commissioners and Colony governors were sympathetic to their cause.

Commissioner Charles Eliot for one was a vigorous proponent of settler rights and superiority. He succumbed to settler demands to prevent Indians from being awarded land grants in areas adjacent to the Uganda railway line. This decision was not taken in consultation with the Foreign Office in London. Similarly, he withdrew a set of stringent rules that the Commissioner of Lands had crafted for the development of settlers' holdings and instead replaced them with rules that were more acceptable to settlers' objectives. A good example was his authorization of rules for the leasing of pastoral lands, allowing leases of up to 10,000 acres at a cost of 1d per acre (Sorrenson, 1968). He also offered two South Africans—Robert Chamberlain and A. S. Flemmer—freehold grants of 10,000 acres each and to Lord Delamere, his close associate and friend a land award of 100,000 acres. Sir Charles Eliot was the architect of the first Maasai move of 1904. This treaty, which was supposed to last for as long as the Maasai endured as a race, was swiftly reversed several years later to create more room for settlers.

The settlers grounded their influence over land policy issues by first creating and then securing elected representation on the land board (Halderman, 1989). Under the auspices of their settler associations, they pressured the Governor in 1907 to appoint a land board. Though government officials initially controlled the land board, the Protectorate government, without consulting the Foreign Office in London, went ahead and gave settlers a large majority in the land board. All other groups, unlike the settler majority had minority representation and had to be nominated as opposed to being elected. Through this board, the settlers prevented Indians from acquiring land in the highlands, and influenced subsequent land policy such as the Kenya Land Commission. In 1915, they successfully pressed for the redefinition of the Crown Lands Ordinance. Crown Lands were consequently extended from just being waste/unoccupied lands to include all lands occupied by the natives of the Protectorate as well as all lands reserved for the use of these tribes. This empowered the Governor to withdraw land and sell it to outsiders if satisfied that it was no longer needed by Africans.

Leys (1923) recorded a disturbing incident which pointedly illustrates the unlimited influence, not only over policy, but over the conduct of administrative affairs that settlers held. Soon after the First World War, after Commissioner Hemsted had returned to England, some Maasai warriors resumed their proscribed raiding excursions. The government withdrew all its administrators from the Maasai reserve allowing Lord Delamere, a settler, to take full charge of the reserve for a fortnight. Lord Delamere was the recognized leader of the settlers and a long-standing mentor of previous governors such as Sir Charles Eliot, Sir Percy Girourd, and Sir Edward Northey. Through their agency he was able to direct the policy of making Kenya a colony governed by its European residents.

The political influence of the settlers dramatically increased following the Second World War because they were allowed to elect representatives to the Legislative Council; some were even appointed to the Executive Council. The outcome of this is that the colonial government consulted the elected Europeans before introducing any new legislation.

The Grazing Schemes: Treating the
Symptoms, Ignoring the Disease

An important outcome of the Kenya Land Commission was the grazing schemes implemented in the pastoral areas of Kenya. These grazing schemes were implemented under the auspices of the African Land Development Organization (ALDEV). The ALDEV was initially started with the objective of searching for new land for resettling native populations (Kenya, Republic of, 1962). But as it became increasingly clear to colonial administrators that the root problem that had to be subdued was land mismanagement rather than overpopulation, it switched emphasis to the reconditioning and reclaiming of existing African areas.[9] In order to achieve this objective ALDEV also invested effort in coordinating the activities of departments responsible for land use and development in African areas. Consequently, the Directors of Agriculture, of Veterinary Services, and the head of the Provincial Administration and/or their representatives constituted the ALDEV board. ALDEV had control of over 6 million sterling pounds for implementing its objectives.

Grazing schemes begun in the arid and semiarid areas of the country were part of ALDEV's plan for "reconditioning, reclamation and resettlement of African areas, leading on eventually after the battle to conserve the soil has been won, to the development of these areas by farming." The schemes were simply aimed at controlling grazing by providing permanent water supplies in ranch-like units and in the introduction of destocking systems. The British were ready to finance the grazing schemes because they thought that their veterinary innovations had created the problem of overstocking, which they were obligated to remedy.

The grazing scheme turned on the reduction of livestock numbers as a way of bringing grazing pressure to conform to the land's "carrying capacity." This system also provided water supplies, disease control, and it attempted to create special markets. Each scheme was administered by a livestock officer with the assistance of a grazing committee comprising 12 elders, who were also responsible for the enforcement of regulations. Livestock officers acted under special ordinances and bylaws that conferred broad powers upon them. They determined who could graze livestock in the scheme, number of animals each could graze, where they could graze, and they enforced fines for the violators. The bylaws had no provision for any appeal against the livestock officer's decisions.

In Kajiado district, grazing schemes were introduced at the level of the Maasai section. For each scheme a committee was created to assist in ascertaining seasonal livestock movements. But first, in 1946, a model ranch unit was set up in Konza in order "to demonstrate to the Maasai how a permanent water supply can be most beneficially used and the advantages of control grazing, that is relating the number of cattle to the carrying capacity of the land."[10] The Konza scheme was also aimed at demonstrating the improvement of stock breeding and selections, and to conduct experiments in pasture improvements. The first Maasai families, chosen by elders, took up residence in January 1949. Each agreed to weekly livestock dipping, to give prophylactic injections, to follow rotational grazing plans and to restrict livestock to prescribed numbers. A manager was resident from the start of the ranch until 1958.

Commentaries on the performance of the Konza demonstration scheme vary, indicating either administrative bias or biases arising out of the stage of the project's cycle at which such evaluations were made. One commentator saw the ranching scheme as an unqualified success: "Maasai are entirely satisfied with their new life. Throughout the two years of drought their cattle have flourished, while outside Konza they have witnessed the normal Maasai scene of practically no grazing and cattle dying and in poor condition" (Anonymous, Undated). Fallon (1962), a USAID range management advisor to Kenya's Ministry of Agriculture and Livestock Husbandry in the early 1960s, characterizes the scheme as a drastic failure almost 10 years into its implementation. Fencing fell into disrepair and did not prevent game animals; residents did not restrict livestock numbers; and the drought of 1959 forced residents out. Both commentators however regarded the schemes as having planted "the seeds of change" or having "brought home to the Maasai the advantages of being sedentary."

Apart from the Konza demonstration scheme, further efforts established the Ilkisonko grazing scheme in 1954 and the Loodokilani scheme in 1959. The Matapato scheme, though ready in 1957, was suspended due to opposition from local residents.

Like the Konza demonstration scheme, all of the other grazing schemes ran into difficulties and were eventually abandoned. Instead of decreasing livestock numbers, they increased these numbers. Schemes did not function during droughts. Owing to uncontrolled livestock increases, water development contributed to significant resource depletion (Fallon, 1962). Destocking proved particularly difficult for various reasons (Jahnke, 1978): many pastoral tribes were already living at submarginal levels and stock reduction only further reduced the supply of meat and milk for the household; culling programs did not fit into the traditional social patterns because many societies are built on an intricate system of human bonds established by lending, renting, exchanging, and gifting livestock for different reasons in different situations.

Despite the performance and outcome of grazing schemes, some authors view them as the precursors of latter-day group ranches (Ng'ethe, 1992; Ole Sadera, 1986). They helped in accumulating experience, ideas and exposure that was invaluable for modifying the design of future pastoral development initiatives.

The East Africa Royal Commission,
October 1952

About 20 years after the reporting of the Kenya Land Commission (KLC), in October 1952, the British government appointed the East Africa Royal Commission as a follow up. This commission, named after its Chair Sir Hugh Dow, was to evaluate the feasibility of economic development via the introduction of better farming methods, and to recommend adaptations and modifications in traditional tribal tenure necessary for the full development of land in the territory (Kenya, Government of, 1966). This commission comprised nine individuals: one being a woman and one, Kidaha Makwaia, an African native, and chief of Shinyanga region of Tanzania.

Though the Dow Commission regretted that the Kenya Land Commission's approach to land and development was narrow, focusing on the tribal perspective rather than from the generalized need of the population, the commissioners were fully in agreement with the KLCs recommendations regarding the Maasai. Like the KLC, the Dow Commission viewed Maasai "conservatism," exemplified by their communal ownership of resources and individual livestock ownership as well as their unreasonable clinging to custom as the cause of land degradation and decline. The commissioners suggested that communal tenure in combination with individual livestock ownership in pastoral areas be eliminated.

The Dow Commission recognized the possibility of collective rights in pastoral areas, with proper rotation and stock limits, but only as an intermediate stage toward individual ranching after the development of additional water supplies and with the availability of more land through the clearing of tsetse-infested areas. The commissioners proposed ranches, access to markets, better breeding practices, and commercialization of stock farming as solutions to the "pastoral problem." They also suggested that all land be individualized and customary rights be dispensed with as they are inefficient. They thought that transferability and disposal of individual property renders it more accessible for economic use. The Dow commissioners were particularly critical of the recommendations of the Kenya Land Commission. They took fault with it's emphasis on tribal exclusivity and a reliance on custom as the way to land tenure security. Such a security, they argued, could only achieve a subsistence and stagnant economy because land was not a negotiable asset.

The Kenya government accepted the general recommendations of the Royal commission, and a policy pronouncement on June 1956 stated, "[I]t is the policy of the government to encourage the emergence of individual land tenure amongst Africans where conditions are ripe for it, and in due course, to institute a system of registration of negotiable title" (Kenya, Government of, 1966). The stage was clearly set for a big drive to individual tenure. The tribal boundaries that had been frozen in place by the Kenya Land Commission were disintegrating.

The Swynnerton Plan, 1955: Fast
Track to Individual Property

The Swynnerton Plan (Kenya Colony and Protectorate, 1955), named after the Director of Agriculture who authored it, was commissioned by the Governor of the Kenya Colony to look into ways of dealing with the growing land pressures, mainly in the Kikuyu Reserve, that were threatening the colony's political stability. It was concerned with the reform of traditional tenure systems and with promoting cash crop production. It emphasized individual land tenure and individual enterprise, since development based on communal land tenures were deemed to have failed. It also recommended an increased commercialization of animal production.

For the livestock sector, the plan proposed remedies in the form of livestock marketing, controlled grazing, water supply, and tsetse and livestock disease eradication. The prime objective was to exploit the potential of Maasai stock to contribute to the national economy. But since the "result" of individualized tenure in central province was landlessness and political unrest, the colonial government chose a different path for the pastoral areas. Instead of individual holdings, the Swynnerton Plan concentrated effort in promoting schemes and "group ranches." The schemes were supposed to be managed according to "scientific principles," such as grazing rotations, water and veterinary facilities provided, and small-scale irrigation practiced. Environmental interventions such as soil conservation, afforestation, and rehabilitation were to be taken up to restore denuded areas. In order to ensure that these innovations were strictly followed the government was to impose strict measures such as "grazing guards," fines, and imprisonment for pastoralists who were lax in observing the rules.

The Swynnerton Plan, coming well at the end of the colonial era set much of the stage for agriculture and land development in the new nation.

Beyond the Colonial: 1963–Current

Kenya gained independence from Britain in December 1963. The newly formed Kenya administration followed the policies laid out in the Swynnerton Plan and the Dow Commission. This independent Government embarked on a zealous land reform initiative embodied in the Land Adjudication Act. Land adjudication was aimed at establishing freehold title to land and to promote long-term investment in former reserve land thought essential to restore and increase productivity. For this to occur security of tenure was considered paramount, and land registration accorded priority.

In the pastoral areas, and particularly in Maasailand, land adjudication was conducted with the expectation that Maasai would adjust their herd management strategies, destock, and conserve the resource base. Instead of attempting to directly control herders and their livestock management techniques, government changed tactics employing a less obvious though just as blunt a strategy.

The results of the Dow Commission and the Swynnerton Plan resulted in the establishment of individual ranches[11] in Maasailand. Because the individual ranchers were to be used as a model for the rest of the Maasai to emulate, conditions had to be created that would ensure their success. Low-interest credit for the purchase of superior breeds and the construction of on-farm infrastructure such as boreholes, water pans was availed through the Agricultural Finance Corporation. This was part of World Bank Financing to Kenya's Livestock sector under the Kenya Livestock Development Program. The individual ranchers also had support from livestock extension officers from the Ministry of Agriculture and Livestock Development.

Individual ranches were a tactical scheme in the broader plan to individualize land and to commercialize livestock production in Maasailand. They were anticipated to serve an invaluable demonstration function in a couple of crucial ways (Jahnke et al., 1972). First, they would showcase the beneficial effects of innovation. Second, the individual rancher is easier to persuade to adopt innovations and easier to supervise in their execution as opposed to a whole group.

The first individual ranch was established as early as 1954 (Campbell, 1993). By 1963, 24 individual ranches had been created (Rutten, 1992). In 1965, 28 more individual ranches were established in the Kaputiei area to the east of Kajiado district (Hedlund, 1971). These took up about seven percent of the entire land held territorially by the Kaputiei Maasai. Adjudication first began in higher potential and better watered areas of Kajiado district such as Ngong division in the north and Loitikotok to the south on the foothills of Mt Kilimanjaro. In Ngong, between 1964 and 1968, the 8,000 hectares under individual units increased to 10,000 hectares (Rutten, 1992). The first owners of individual ranches were all Maasai, but "Maasai with a difference" (Simpson, 1973). They included politicians, local chiefs, local store keepers, government officials as well as cattle traders, that is, wealthy and/or influential individuals with ties to the administration. They were the elite Maasai. They, having acquired their large individual ranches, in their turn sold off portions to Kikuyu cultivators for agricultural and speculation purposes.

This progressive development of individual ranches, each averaging between 300–800 hectares (Grandin, 1987a, 1987b) raised several concerns amongst administrators. They feared a land grab by the wealthy and influential Maasai at the expense of the majority. They also saw an increasing insecurity with individualized holdings as land was easily transferred through sales to the hands of non-Maasai. Ordinary Maasai on their part were alarmed that the creation of individual ranches together with sales to non-Maasai might create a situation of landlessness, or result in remaining land being too small to be viable.

These concerns were expressed in the Lawrence report of 1965–1966 (Kenya, Republic of, 1966), which recommended the establishment of group ranches as opposed to individual ranches in Narok and Kajiado districts. Group ranches were envisaged as an alternative way of realizing the same goals of accelerating agricultural and pastoral development as under individualized holdings but with the added advantage of safeguarding against alienation to non-Maasai. Such an institutional arrangement was also regarded favorably by both commercial banks and the World Bank as the registered group ranches would create ownership among a collective of individuals, who would then be able to borrow against the security of their collective title.

The educated Maasai of both Narok and Kajiado were, however, hostile to the recommendations of the Lawrence report. They felt that an endorsement of group ranching would jeopardize their own individual holdings, which by that time had not been legalized and were being allocated by the local district councils (Doherty, 1987). They wanted to have their holdings legalized so that they could receive loans for development of wheat farms in Narok, and to upgrade their cattle technology. They thus argued that land ownership in Maasailand should not be differentiated from that in the rest of the country which was under rapid transition to individual holdings. This active opposition to the group ranch concept by influential members of the Maasai society was counteracted by granting them large individual ranches (Jahnke et al., 1972). A program of land adjudication was nonetheless undertaken in Kajiado and group ranches subsequently created.

The Creation of Group Ranches

Group ranches were created with the official expectation that they would provide tenure security, creating incentives for the Maasai to invest in range improvement and ultimately to reduce the tendency to over accumulate livestock. Group ranches would also act as collateral for loans to enable investment in range enhancement and livestock improvement. The program entailed a shift in land tenure and organization from one under which the range was under common ownership, to an abridged version of the original commons, variable in size and membership, but held under corporate title.

The Land Adjudication Act of June 1968, which provided for the recording of rights and interests in customary lands, and their assignment to their customary users, facilitated the creation of group ranches. Much of the description that follows draws from this document (Kenya, Republic of, 1968b). According to this Act, a "group" meant a tribe, clan, section, family, or other group of persons, whose land under recognized customary law belonged communally to the members of the group. In the adjudication of Kajiado district, such determinations were made by an adjudication committee that comprised officers from the Land Adjudication Department and elders from each section of the Maasai. After the group was recorded as having joint interests and thus ownership of the land, the land adjudication officer advised the group to apply for their group representatives to be incorporated under the Land (Group Representatives) Act of June 1968. This application was endorsed by the chairman of the Adjudication Committee and an authorized agent of the group. The Registrar of group ranches convened a meeting of the members of the group and adopted a constitution, elected not more than ten and not less than three persons to be group representatives of the group and elected officers of the group. Whereas the Land Adjudication Act provided for the creation of groups and group ranches, the Land (Group Representatives) Act provided for the governance and administration of group ranches.

Under the Land (Group Representatives) Act, every member of the group ranch is deemed to share in the ownership of group land in *equal, undivided shares*. And each is entitled to reside in group land with family and dependents (Kenya, Republic of, 1968a). The group representatives are expected to ensure that the rights of any person under recognized customary law are safeguarded in so far as that is *compatible with the operations of the group*. The group representatives are also authorized to hold property on behalf of, and to act on behalf of and for the collective benefit of all members of the group. They are required to fully and effectively consult group ranch members. The Act empowers the group to craft its own rules regarding the running of its own affairs such as procedures for the administration of its property, the registration of new members, and the disbursement of funds for group projects. Each group is required to hold a general meeting of its members every year. All group members are entitled to attend these meetings and to vote in them. No business should be transacted at a meeting of a group unless at least 60 percent of the members of the group are present at the meeting. A resolution of the group supported by the votes of not less than 60 percent of the members of the group present at the meeting is treated as the group's decision.

From the group representatives, a committee is to be elected by open ballot each year at the group's annual general meeting. The committee comprises a chair, vice chair, secretary, treasurer, and three other members of whom at least two are elected from the group representatives. The committee is required to assist and encourage members to manage the land or graze their stock in accordance with sound principles of land use, range management, animal husbandry, and commercial practice. The committee responsible for conducting group affairs has the responsibility of achieving "the greatest practicable social and economic benefits" for the members. It can raise credit and is involved in development planning. Every member is required to accept and comply with decisions of the committee regarding membership and the rights and obligations of any person in matters relating to the use of the group land and other assets. However any member aggrieved by a committee decision has the formal right to appeal to the group representatives, the Registrar of group representatives, or to a subordinate court having jurisdiction in the area.

The last item in the Act provides for group ranch dissolution. This can only occur after a written application signed by a majority of the group representatives, after a resolution passed by a 60 percent majority of the group in a special general meeting convened for that purpose. Subsequently, the affairs of the group may be wound up in a manner approved by the Registrar or failing that, in a manner directed by the High Court. The persons who were officers of the group immediately before the dissolution shall continue in office until after the completion of the proceedings.

One gains some insights into the philosophy and intent of the legislation as viewed from the side of government by reading Davis's (1970) conversations with government officials at the time, such as with F. M. Charnley who was the Commissioner of Lands, L. S. Sherif and S. J. Meadows, who were involved in the drafting of the legislation. According to these officials' interpretations, the Act was principally intended to foster the commercialization of Maasai livestock management systems and to transform land into an economic good subject to free buying and selling. The transformation was envisaged to be simpler, with lower costs and tax rates under a special new Act, than under corporate law. Group ranching was also envisaged to facilitate the commoditization of Maasai herds and lands without creating a large pool of landless individuals. Paradoxically, it was also envisioned to provide an evolutionary mode of transformation that would be based on the traditional ways of the Maasai.

To implement this development program, the Kenyan government sought loans and grants from international agencies such as the World Bank, USAID, the Swedish Aid agency, Canadian Development Agency, and the United Kingdom. The loans were granted under the auspices of the Kenya Livestock Development Program (KLDP). This program combined investment and extension services with the establishment of group ranches under a land adjudication and registration program.[12] The Department of Land Adjudication and Registrar of group representatives, both in the Ministry of Lands and Settlement, were extensively involved in the initial establishment of group ranches. The Range Management division of the Ministry of Agriculture played a key role in drawing up group ranch development plans. The Ministry of Water Development coordinated water development. The Agricultural Finance Corporation administered the loans provided by the donors.

The first group ranches to be adjudicated in Kajiado district were in the Kaputiei section of eastern Kajiado. Here, 14 ranches averaging 1,900 hectares, and about 100 families each were established in the latter part of the 1960s (Davis, 1970). In some northern areas of Kajiado district however, producers refused group ranches and were given individual tenure to holdings of usually less than 100 hectares (Grandin, 1987b). Group ranches were later adjudicated in other parts of the district.

Why Did the Kenya Government and the Ordinary Maasai Accept the Concept of Group Ranching?

The Kenya government needed to raise the low levels of productivity associated with subsistence pastoral practices in semiarid regions such as Maasailand in order to supply growing urban populations with reasonably priced meat. Group ranching schemes appeared to offer the most efficient means of utilizing development loan investments to bring pastoral regions into commercial production. Group-based schemes were expected to enjoy economies of scale for the provision of infrastructure such as livestock dips, water, and roads. For group ranches, capital costs per unit of ranch area were estimated to be only about one third of those for individual ranches (Grandin, 1986). Group ranches were already fully stocked by the members' privately owned cattle and there was no need to provide funds for ranch employees, such as in the case of individual ranching. The group ranch option also seemed to offer the possibility of developing pastoral lands without making pastoralists landless. This was a major concern since similar programs to individualize communal lands in the high potential Kikuyu areas resulted in landlessness and political unrest. Famine relief was also increasing becoming a burden and a political embarrassment to the Kenya government. Inputs through the project were anticipated to lower the need for famine relief activities (Jahnke et al., 1972), while stabilized ranching was expected to provide a better opportunity to control overgrazing.

And why did the ordinary Maasai accept group ranches? Many scholars agree that although the Maasai did not accept or even understand some features of the group ranch such as grazing quotas, boundary maintenance and the management committee they accepted the idea of group ranches primarily because it afforded them protection against further land appropriation from government, against the incursion of non-Maasai and from a land grab by the elite Maasai (Fratkin, 1994; Campbell, 1991; Goldschmidt, 1980; Hopcraft, 1980; Halderman, 1972; Hedlund, 1971). The earlier sections of this chapter demonstrated that the history of Maasailand since the late 1800s has been one of dispossession. More recently still, population pressures in the high potential areas of the country resulted in infiltration of immigrants into Maasailand.

For the Maasai, group ranch development also carried with it the promise of water development in the form of dams and boreholes, as well as the promise of improved livestock husbandry through introduction of dipping facilities and regular vaccination against prevalent animal diseases (Davis, 1970). Water is a crucial limiting factor in Maasai livestock husbandry. Any measure that promised to enhance herd survival and productivity was likely to engender Maasai support.

Some scholars contend that the memory of the 1961 drought may have been factored into Maasai decision making (Fratkin, 1994; Goldschmidt, 1980). It is not clear why this would have been a compelling reason for the Maasai as they have been confronted with similar situations previously. On the contrary this may have given the government an additional lever to justify the introduction of group ranches and individual ranches (Halderman, 1989). Nevertheless, what is important is that the Maasai accepted the government's imposition of group ranches because it emerged as the most expedient solution to a diverse set of threats that had dogged them throughout their century old history of relations with formal government administration and with "others."

Scholars were troubled by various aspects of the structure of group ranches. Davis (1970), for example, was skeptical about the committee's ability to coordinate livestock numbers and allocate grazing quotas amongst members of the group ranch. He was concerned that such allocations be made available to individuals most able to generate profits. Other issues that were anticipated to affect the smooth operation of group ranches included whether traditional authority structures would be able to deal with problems of estate management and commercial ranching. The ecological and social integrity of the adjudicated units was also a primary concern. These are all issues that in later years came to haunt group ranch implementation and may have played varying roles in group ranch disintegration and subdivision.

The Failure of Group Ranches

Group ranching as a policy was introduced with great optimism and enthusiasm among policy makers and planners. It is now widely accepted, however, that group ranches failed to meet their intended objectives. A consequence of this failure has been increasing demands for their dissolution and subsequent division into individual, titled units for distribution among their registered members. This disintegration began as early as the mid-1970s for the Kaputiei ranches, but gained momentum 10 to 15 years later in other parts of Kajiado district. By 1985, 22 group ranches had resolved to subdivide; seven went ahead and subdivided (Munei, 1987).

A variety of reasons have been proposed to account for the failure of group ranches. Some scholars note that group ranches were undermined by a lack of ecological viability (Kipury, 1989; Halderman, 1989, 1972; Hopcraft, 1980; Njoka, 1979). Because ranches were not sufficiently extensive to allow pastoralists to exploit the discontinuity and heterogeneity of resources within their environment adequately, group ranch boundaries were not respected, especially in times of drought. Maasai relied on movement across group ranches under traditional norms of reciprocity via kinship and friendship ties. The key argument levied here is that if ranch boundaries are not strictly observed, their logic is undermined. The incentive to invest in pasture management and stinting is undermined as those who did not invest effort would also benefit.

Munei (1987) however, dismissed these arguments as "ecologically deterministic." He states that ecology is merely a constraint and should not be used as a basis to judge operational viability. According to him the important issue is whether the group ranch was able to gather sufficient resources to enable the countering or alleviation of these constraints. This is an important point. Movement amongst Maasai across different sections and territory has occurred across time. While the enclosure of group ranches has served to intensify droughts and increase movement, this would have been less so if appropriate infrastructure had been developed within the ranch. Consequently, the lack of boundary integrity must be evaluated within the general framework of group ranch operations, and not presented as a prime reason for failure.

In evaluating the performance of group ranches, economists argue that it failed to alter the incentive structure that operated in the commons (Hopcraft, 1980). They conceptualize the group ranch as an abridged commons, which is beset with the same problems that afflicted the earlier commons, that is, individually rational behavior that leads to suboptimal social outcomes. Because the committee was not vested with sufficient authority to control livestock numbers and grazing patterns, group ranches experienced an overgrazing problem. While these arguments are fundamental to the current plight of group ranches, they must be further extended to increase their credibility. As we see in later chapters the concern was not so much with overgrazing as with the unequal stocking levels amongst group ranch members. The committee did not wield sufficient authority to mediate against an over accumulation of stock amongst group ranch members.

In several cases, the major credit institution, the Agricultural Finance Corporation, was reluctant to advance new credits to group ranches because group ranch land was deemed as ineffective collateral as it was held collectively (Migot-Adholla and Little, 1980). Difficulties were experienced in enforcing loan repayments but it was not easy to attach or foreclose the entire group ranch. Credit issued to individuals under individual ownership was deemed a more reliable form of security, which individual ranchers continued to enjoy. Group ranches were however locked out of their principal source of development funds. In addition, there were many instances in which loans acquired in the name of the group ranch were used for productive investments from which only a part of the membership benefited (Galaty, 1994b). Members were unwilling to repay such loans. The World Bank itself, as early as 1977, expressed frustration with the lack of increased off-take from group ranches and recommended that group ranches give way to more commercialized forms of production (Munei, 1987).

The above suite of reasons was provided by observers in the very early stages of group ranch disintegration and lacked the insights that came with later studies, which have been discussed in chapter one. These more recent studies indicate that carving of individual ranches out of existing group ranches and their allocation to influential community members served to create insecurities among ordinary group ranch members, who subsequently resolved to subdivide (Ole Simel, 1999; Galaty, 1994b, 1992). The addition of noncustomary rights holders into the register of members plus the gradual addition of newly matured men into the register as population increased was yet another reason why members clamored for subdivision (Davis, 2000; Galaty, 1992; Grandin, 1987b). Rutten (1992) draws attention to the unlawful and devious acquisition of public land in Kajiado by elites, which I illustrate in table 4.2 below. Such incidences were crucial in informing group ranch members' decisions to subdivide.

All of these events served to create a sense of tenure insecurity for group ranch members at several fronts. First, over how much would be left of the group ranch to be shared by an ever-growing population after carving out chunks of it and subsequently allocating to influential individuals; second, it created doubt about the effectiveness of the collective title under the group ranch structure to provide sufficient protection against predation by avaricious and influential local and national elites. Thus individuals saw it more beneficial to subdivide earlier rather than later. Grandin (1987a,b) also indicates that group ranch members were increasingly aware that access to loans was greatly facilitated through individual titles that could be used for collateral.

Table 4.2 indicates that group ranches did not offer absolute security for Maasai land. The group ranch committee, local and national elites, and government officials were able to remove land from the collective holding for individual gain.

Discussion

The preceding sections of this chapter have illustrated the historical origins and dynamics of formal land-related institutions in Kenya's Maasailand. Throughout the colonial time and in the run-up to Kenya's independence, formal property institutions were imposed on the Maasai (and other ethnic groups) through the agency of the state. These state-imposed rules subordinated Maasai interests and institutions while privileging and defending that of the settlers. The outcome of the imposed rules and policies was a shrunken resource base that only inadequately sustained Maasai systems of

Table 4.2 Some Land Grabbing in Maasailand in Recent Times

Source	Case
The Weekly Review, July 11, 1977	One thousand acres out of 6,000 acres of Rombo Group Ranch allegedly allocated to sons and supporters of politicians. Complaining elders feared that time lag and inadequate knowledge of the legal infrastructure may outpace their rights.
Daily Nation, September 17, 1981	Forty acres of land in Ololua allocated to two "big sharks" without authority from the Kajiado County Council. This area had been declared a green belt.
Daily Nation, February 5, 1983	County councilors allocated themselves public utility plots in North and South Kajiado Constituencies. The County Council Chairman grabbed 60.7 hectares and 100 acres. Parcel #31 (100 acres) of Elangata Wuas Group Ranch was allocated to a county councilor who in turn leased it to a quarrying firm.
Daily Nation, July 31, 1984	Four hundred and seventeen plots allocated to landless by Kajiado Plot Allocation Committee on order from President Moi.
Daily Nation, October 24, 1984	Some councilors of the Olekejuado County Council have been allocated the above plots. Genuine landless people have been ignored. Senior civil servants, councilors, and so on who had land elsewhere had been allocated.
Daily Nation, November 15, 1984	Above plot allocations suspended by Rift Valley provincial commissioner. Seventy-six squatters who should have been given priority during the allocations had been left out. Kajiado South Member of Parliament together with the Chairman Olkejuado County Council pleaded for the allocations to stand.
Daily Nation, December 29, 1984	District officer for Kajiado Central Division warned people against buying land in group ranches. Addressing members of the Kitengela Group Ranch, the district officer noted that some people had illegally purchased land from members way in excess of individual members' entitlement.
Daily Nation, August 15, 1986	District officer of Kajiado Central Division banned the selling of unsurveyed group ranch land.
Daily Nation, December 31, 1986	A clique of local politicians to include 50 councilors, administration officials, and businessmen have allegedly excised 2,500 acres from the Ewaso Kedong Group Ranch.

production and served to heighten a sense of tenure insecurity. Considerable suspicion and resentment of the state by the Maasai was an important outcome. These responses can be generalized to other ethnic communities such as the Kikuyu whose land losses were felt more acutely due to the small size of their reserve in relation to their large and rapidly expanding population.

Many of the policy interventions affecting access to land resources during the colonial time were directed toward enhancing private, individualized rights. This property rights structure successfully secured land that was thought necessary for economic production by the immigrant settler community. These settler rights, actively enforced by the state, were not reversed even against the backdrop of increasing Maasai discontent (see rulings of the Kenya Land Commission). Because private property seemed to confer broad security to land rights, local African populations demanded the same. Private property would protect their rights from encroachment by "others" and also from state appropriation. Demand for private property, fiercest in the Kikuyu reserve, was partly expressed in the emergence of the Mau Mau freedom fighter movement that threatened political security within the colony.

The colonial government was thus pressured to respond to native grievances through the Swynnerton Plan, which recommended individualization of the communal African reserves and set the foundations for an extensive land adjudication and registration program throughout the last few years of the colony in the late 1950s and early 1960s. One important outcome of this aggressive individualization campaign was the creation of massive individual ranches in Maasailand. These were issued to politicians and to the educated and economic elites of the Maasai. Administrators viewed the distribution of individual ranches to the Maasai elite as an opportunity that would temper their spirited opposition against the group ranch concept and that would pave the way for the creation and implementation of group ranches in Maasailand.

In response to concerns that individualizing the whole of Maasailand among its rightful owners would result in economically unviable production units, administrators in independent Kenya saw group ranches as a more economically attractive alternative. The Group (Land Representatives) Act was passed in 1968. It created exclusive land ownership and rights among groups of Maasai residing within an identified area in each territorial section of the Maasai. A land title was issued in the name of each group, thus formalizing collective rights. The creation of group ranches was very much in the spirit of privatizing Maasailand to secure it against further appropriations by the state and from losses to non-Maasai and/or the elite Maasai. Its endorsement by the general Maasai population was based on the need to protect their land against such threat. Only this time around, the institution was created to also take account of the variable nature of the resources that are at the core to Maasai economic production systems. Once again the state was expected to be the ultimate enforcer of these rights.

Path dependence is premised on the identification of a critical juncture during which time one out of several decision possibilities is selected; this then sets an institutional path going, which gets perpetuated over time because the feasibility of adopting other institutional alternatives gradually diminishes. This framework is relevant in explaining the gradual and focused privatization of Maasailand through time. Figure 4.1 provides a summary of this process.

In this account, the critical juncture was the decision by the Protectorate administrators and officials in the Foreign Office in England to encourage European immigrants to settle in Kenya. Their farming and other commercial production activities were anticipated to raise revenue that would cover the costs of constructing and operating the expensive Uganda railway. It would also contribute toward making the Protectorate pay for its administration. Admittedly, the range of options available for the administrators to achieve these goals may have been limited. However, there were several possibilities, for example, creating capacities among native communities to generate revenue, or using the extensive experience and outreach of the Imperial British East Africa Company to achieve the goals of revenue generation.

Once administrators selected the policy of encouraging a settler community, they had to create space for the settlers to occupy. They accomplished this through the enactment of the Crown Lands Act, which allowed the British Crown to appropriate land that was "unoccupied" and therefore without legitimate ownership. Following the settlers' demands, land given to them was converted to individual freehold even as Africans were relegated to reservations where shared land rights were accorded them by virtue of their membership within their respective communities. Subsequent attempts by Maasai and others to regain land appropriated by settlers through the Kenya Land Commission or court proceedings were unsuccessful as the state and its actors were solidly in support of settler rights. Rather than face up to the thorny issue of reversing rights allocated to the settler community, colony officials instead launched a vigorous program to combat supposed land degradation within the Maasai and other African reserve areas.

The settler themselves were well organized as members of associations through which they sought and established representation in land boards and even in the Colony's Legislative Council. They were thus able to establish and sustain political influence and ensure that their individual rights were privileged over all other native rights in the Colony. The institution of private property was thus anchored and well on its way to dominating

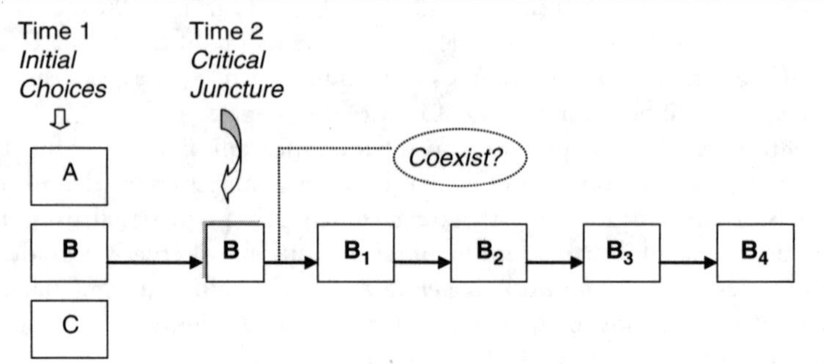

- During Time 1, the initial conditions, the Protectorate administration had completed constructing the Uganda railway. The administration had a keen interest in recouping the costs of construction and in making the railway pay for its maintenance and more generally making the East Africa Protectorate self-sustaining.

- Though the administration could pursue several ways to meet this objective, it chose to encourage European immigrants, who through agriculture and other commercial activities would generate revenue through the taxation of their imports and exports. This is option B, which gets selected out of all other feasible options during the critical juncture period at Time 2. At this time also, the administration encouraged a policy of segregation in which the settlers would be separated from native communities.

- B_1 represents the appropriation of land from Maasai, Kikuyu, and other native communities for the settlement of European immigrants. The settlers demanded individualized property rights in order to gain security for their investments. The Crown Lands Act enabled this appropriation of land and set in motion the individualization of rights in areas taken up for European settlement. The Maasai and other ethnic communities were bundled up in reservations where rights to land were predicated upon membership in their respective communities.

- B_2 represents the different commissions and plans that were set up to first investigate land rights and later to create individualized rights. These included the Kenya Land Commission (KLC), the East African Royal Commission (EARC), and the Swynnerton Plan. The KLC defended the property rights of the settlers and crystalized the notion of exclusive communal rights in the reservations. The EARC reversed the notion of exclusive communal rights and instead encouraged the development of individualized rights as the most appropriate model to enhance economic development. The Swynnerton Plan was the apogee of the drive to individual, private land rights. It was created to defuse political tensions in the African reservations, where demands for individualization and formal registration was high as this was regarded as the most viable way of securing African lands against further appropriations. The Plan recommended the undertaking of vigorous land adjudication and registration in the communal African areas.

- B_3 is specific to the Maasai. It represents the creation of group ranches, a property rights structure that is exclusive to a group of individuals within subsections of the Maasai. It was a reaction to the large-scale individualization of Maasailand, which saw Maasai land being distributed to an influential clique of individuals and to non-Maasai. It was also intended to restrain state appropriation.

- B_4 box represents the current subdivision of Maasailand (see chapters six and seven).

Figure 4.1 Path Diagram Showing Institutional Continuity across Time

alternative property regimes within the colony. The predominance of private, individual rights to land gains clarity in later years particularly in the 1950s just about one decade before Kenyan Africans gained self-governing status and independence from Britain. During this period, private property was perceived as a solution to growing tenure insecurity (and political tensions) within the African reserves. After all, it had served well to secure immigrant land rights. Africans thus supported the implementation of the Swynnerton Plan.

Events in Maasailand were embedded within a similar logic. Maasai rights, institutions, interests, and demands were not only subordinated to that of European settlers who appropriated the most productive of their land assets but also in later times to that of the land needs of the neighboring agricultural communities such as the Kikuyu. The Kenya Land Commission strongly supported the influx of Kikuyu into the better parts of Maasailand such as Ngong and Loitokitok as they were expected to help in developing and sedentarizing the shiftless pastoralists. In addition, several parts of the remaining Maasai reserve were annexed by government for the conservation of wildlife resources.

By the time the land adjudication and registration program was introduced by the state, the Maasai tentatively accepted it. Though ordinary Maasai rejected large-scale individualization of their lands, some elite demanded it and were obliged. The majority of the Maasai however supported the administration's decision to codify collective land rights through the enactment of the Land (Group Representatives) Act of 1968. They anticipated that this codification of their rights in law would guard against further appropriations by the state and influential individuals. On the contrary the security that group ranches were anticipated to afford would be systematically eroded in later years due to opportunism and lack of accountability by committees that were elected to oversee the management of group ranches. Committee collusion with influential politicians, with officials in the Ministry of Lands and Settlement, and with other elites within the Maasai community resulted in significant portions of group land being distributed among these individuals. Consequently, the early to mid-1980s saw Maasai once again clamoring for individualized land rights, on their own accord, against this new threat from within. It must be noted that this final reaction comes in the wake of a gradual narrowing of alternatives due to the nature of restrictions imposed by government policy in earlier times. Nonetheless, an element of choice does persist, however constricted; not all 52 group ranches in Kajiado district adopted the path of individualization, a small number opted to remain as group ranches.

Evidently, institutional choice for the Maasai has been severely narrowed over time. Private, individual rights have seemed the most appropriate for securing land rights. Individuals' and groups' attempts at securing their rights and privileges have resulted in reinforcing the dominance of private rights. The reversal of such rights and a resort to earlier forms of institutions are likely to come up against intense opposition from the beneficiaries of such a property structure, many of who have had (or still have) the state's backing.

CHAPTER FIVE
THE PUZZLE OF "PERVERSE" PROPERTY RIGHTS

Introduction

When viewed against the context of Maasai pastoral livelihoods that have evolved and adapted to conditions of climatic variability and resource heterogeneity, the decision to subdivide is puzzling. Subdivision and fragmentation impedes mobility, which is crucial for survival under such variable conditions if livestock is to remain the core economic activity. This chapter addresses the puzzle of why individual group ranch members supported the subdivision of their collective holdings into individual, titled parcels.

What prompted this decision? How was it arrived at? Who participated? Unlike the earlier donor-sponsored, government-driven initiatives that carved out group and individual ranches from the open, undivided Maasai range, the recent clamor for subdivision and individualization during these past two decades has emerged from within the community itself.

This chapter presents individual and group calculations underlying the decision to subdivide and the context in which these decisions were made. The incentives of a diversity of actors, differentiated according to age, gender, and wealth, and their interactions is analyzed. I also attempt to account for the "wave" of subdivision in which separate, seemingly autonomous group ranch units resolved to subdivide at roughly the same time—between 1987 and 1989.

Certain conditions within the socioeconomic sphere were identified in chapter one as motivating individuals and groups to seek to privatize/individualize property rights in land. These conditions may create a situation in which individuals and groups perceive the benefits anticipated in the new, individualized structure as outweighing the costs of transforming the old one and of maintaining the new structure. Changes in relative factor and product prices is one such condition (Demsetz, 1967; North and Thomas, 1973; North, 1990). An increase in product prices may, for example, increase land values. Individuals will then demand and invest in changing property rights toward greater exclusivity as they anticipate capturing the attendant gains. To them, the resulting gains outweigh the costs of initiating, transforming, and enforcing the new property rights structure. In areas closer to markets, these processes of transformation will be particularly pronounced as the higher rents to be gained precipitate intense competition (Alston et al., 1995).

Demographic pressures, perceptions of scarcity, and common-pool resource losses may also motivate individuals to seek alternative property rights structures. As populations increase on a relatively unchanging land resource base, perceptions of scarcity may set in motion demands for exclusive property rights as individuals attempt to eliminate uncertainty with regard to future shares in the collective holdings (Ostrom, 2001a; Platteau, 2000, 1996, 1995; Boserup, 1965). Perceptions of scarcity are rendered acute if accompanied by deterioration in the physical condition of the resource (Libecap, 1989). Actors in this situation may thus seek to transform property rights in order to mitigate losses that occur within the shared domain in order to realize the gains of individual management.

The demand for exclusive property rights does not occur within an economic vacuum. Often actors in government will supply services such as surveys, registration, titling, and enforcement crucial for the integrity of formal, individualized property rights. The incentives of individual government agents are important, as they will often seek to supply property rights when the transformation promises gains to themselves and/or their associates (North, 1990; Feeny, 1993). Active state involvement in land transformation is often justified under the guise of promoting economic "development," or safeguarding the management and conservation of natural resources or enhancing equity in resource distribution.

I use the above framework to explore the puzzle of why group ranch members supported the individualization of their collective holdings.

Presidential Exhortations and the
Call to Subdivide

The turning point in the race to subdivide group ranches in the Maasai districts of Narok and Kajiado came when President Moi on several occasions between 1983 and 1989 voiced his support for the process. In 1983,

President Moi, speaking at a fund drive in neighboring Narok district, urged members of group ranches to subdivide (*Daily Nation*, July 19, 1983; *Kenya Times*, July 19, 1983). He stressed the need for individuals to develop their own pieces of land. Noting the unviability of group ranch operations, he expressed the fear that group ranches may in future spark "trouble" because registered members were inviting their friends to reside in the group ranches. Two years later, in 1985, President Moi reiterated his call for subdivision in Trans Mara district. Here he advised Maasai leaders to begin land adjudication to enable each family to develop its own farm (*Kenya Times*, March 9, 1985). In 1986, the Narok District Commissioner announced that all group ranches in his district were dissolved according to the wishes of all members and that private, individual ownership would now make it possible for individuals to farm the land (*Daily Nation*, August 7, 1986). The District Commissioner urged the local land adjudication office to speed up demarcation and registration process.

Kajiado district joined the bandwagon in 1987, when political and civic leaders resolved that all group ranches in Kajiado district be subdivided *equally* among their respective members on the basis of the "family" unit (*Daily Nation*, January 23, 1987). The controversial nature of group ranch subdivision began to emerge at this meeting. Calling for local government administration's involvement in the process, the Kajiado leaders accused group ranch committee members of frustrating the subdivision exercise by victimizing some members. The leaders warned group committees against collecting funds from members and urged them to stop withdrawing group ranch funds from banks. The leaders also resolved that in order to guard against shoddy work, only those private surveyors that had been certified by government should be involved in subdivision. Speaking at another fund-raising event in Kajiado town, President Moi directed that all loans given to dairy farmers in Kajiado district by the Agricultural Finance Corporation be written off because cattle died in the 1984 drought and farmers consequently had no means through which to repay their loans (*Daily Nation*, April 15, 1989). The President also directed that the process of group ranch subdivision be speeded up so that owners of parcels could get title deeds to their land. He instructed the head of the Civil Service to send a team of surveyors to Kajiado district. He once again noted that "the issue of having group ranches will create problems in the future."

The President's encouragement for subdivision, likely originating from pressures within Maasai community itself,[1] had two effects. First, it fostered an acceptance of subdivision from a reluctant bureaucracy that had been advocating greater caution in the subdivision of group ranches. Second, it served to cap local debates on the issue. Group ranch members in Kajiado district began to vote for the dissolution and subsequent subdivision of their group ranches into individual parcels. The four group ranches studied in this research resolved to subdivide in 1987, 1988, and two in 1989. This was consistent with the general trend in the district.

A second issue that President Moi touched on was the "rescheduling" and eventual writing off of loans borrowed from the Agricultural Finance Corporation. Though this was intended to benefit the elite individual ranchers, who had experienced extensive livestock losses in the 1984 drought, it appears to have been broadly interpreted to apply to group ranches as well. As a result, those group ranches that, owing to loan encumbrances, had been denied consent to subdivide by the Registrar of group ranches, were now free to start subdividing their land. These group ranches had earlier taken loans for the implementation of group ranch projects and were prevented from subdividing because they had not completed paying off their loans. By tipping public opinion in the favor of subdividing, by supporting the "rescheduling" of loans taken by ranchers, and by overriding a reluctant bureaucracy, the President's policy endorsement may have accounted for the apparent "wave" among group ranches to subdivide.

Prior to the President's announcements, government officials from the departments of Lands Adjudication and Range Planners from the Ministry of Livestock Development urged caution on subdivision. According to the minutes of the annual general meeting at Enkaroni group ranch of February 26, 1985,[2] for example, the Registrar of group ranches emphasized "the grave consequences of ranch subdivision without basic infrastructure." At the same meeting, the Range Officer noted that "it was unfortunate that members' wish to subdivide the group ranch would result in unviable units which would be expensive to develop because of their small sizes." He further pointed out that if the land were partitioned equally, each member would be entitled to 79 acres (34 hectares) in which one would be able to keep no more than seven head of cattle. Present also was the District Land Adjudication Officer who strongly reiterated the inordinate expenses of individual parcel management and requested members to reconsider their decision. The President's pronouncement thus served to silence the bureaucracy, forcing it into action where previously it was cautious. Government surveyors were assigned to the process, while range officers from the Ministry of Livestock Development and Planning were enlisted to ensure that subdivided parcels were viable.

Official sanction for subdivision came at a time when most group ranch members had seen the necessity to subdivide. Records for the group ranches studied indicate that there had been considerable debates on the merits and demerits of subdivision prior to the President's 1989 encouragement. Minutes of Enkaroni group ranch meetings in February and May 1985 had as their sole agendas discussions on the merits and demerits of subdivision.[3] Not all meetings and debates were recorded. Those that did not occur under the auspices of a formal annual general meeting of members, such as those organized through the local chief's administrative umbrella (the local *baraza*), were not recorded in writing. Such *barazas* were numerous in each of the group ranches in the run-up to subdivision.

If the President's remarks merely quickened the pace of decision making, and if the bureaucracy was not actively encouraging group ranches to subdivide, then what is it that motivated group ranch members to subdivide? In the next section I show the complement of factors that drove individuals' preferences for subdivision. These included increasing population within the group ranches and the normative imperative to keep recruiting new members from the pool of maturing youths; the notion of "development" and progress associated with individual land ownership; the problem of differential access to and exploitation of group resources owing to variations in livestock ownership among group members; the problem of outsiders, primarily the neighboring individual ranchers, who grazed their livestock within group-held land without fulfilling reciprocal obligations; and the fear that group-held land may easily be interpreted as "vacant" land that could be issued for the settlement of population overflowing from the densely populated highland regions of the country.

I categorize these motivations as economic, demographic, and defensive strategies. As we shall see, though many of these motivations are important in each of the group ranches studied, the salience of each of the motivations varies due to the unique features and experiences of each group ranch area. Table 5.1 illustrates individual preferences for subdivision according to age set and status for each group ranch. Table 5.2 goes further to list the various reasons that individuals gave for wanting their group ranches subdivided. These reasons are provided for each group ranch and also aggregated across all group ranches. The figures in the following tables, together with more extended explanations offered by each individual in their interview session, form the basis for analysis and discussion in the following sections. All figures in tables 5.1 and 5.2 relate to *registered* members of the group ranch whose membership status conferred upon each of them rights to decision making. They each received individual parcels upon group ranch subdivision. All were interviewed during the first phase of fieldwork in 2001.

Table 5.1 Breakdown of Group Ranch Members' Preferences for Subdivision

Age Set/Status	Enkaroni		Meto		Nentanai		Torosei	
	Favor	*Disfavor*	*Favor*	*Disfavor*	*Favor*	*Disfavor*	*Favor*	*Disfavor*
Ilterito	—	—	1	0	—	—	—	—
Ilnyankusi	2	2	4	2	6	1	0	0
Iseuri	11	1	14	1	8	0	8	7
Ilkiseyia	17	1	16	7	3	2	9	3
IrangIrang/Ng'orisho	10	0	10	3	3	0	9	3
Ilking'onde/Ilkishili	3	0	5	0	—	—	13	10
Widows	2	2	12	3	2	2	2	2
Total	45	6	62	16	22	5	41	25
	(88.24%)[a]	(11.76%)	(79.49%)	(20.51%)	(75.86%)	(10.34%)	(63.08%)	(38.46%)
Grand total	170	52						
	(76.58%)	(23.42%)						

Note: [a] Proportion of registered members who were interviewed in 2001.

Source: Own field work.

Table 5.2 Factors that Motivated Group Ranch Members to Prefer Subdivision

Factors	Enkaroni		Meto		Nentanai		Torosei		Total
	Elders	Widows	Elders	Widows	Elders	Widows	Elders	Widows	
Acquire title	15	0	50	15	19	3	42	4	148
Increasing population	20	0	43	11	12	0	47	3	136
Non-Maasai may take	15	0	41	12	6	2	53	2	131
Individual ranchers	12	0	15	2	9	2	2	0	42
Herd inequality	8	1	—	—	1	0	1	0	11
Problem with group decisions	7	0	5	1	3	0	5	0	21
Government required	1	0	4	0	1	0	3	0	9
Politicians influenced	1	0	6	0	2	0	2	0	11

Source: Own field work.

Subdividing the Group Ranch: Members' Motivations

"Land Does Not Give Birth": Population Increase and a Static Resource Base

Group ranch members in Enkaroni, Meto, Nentanai, and Torosei were concerned with increasing human numbers in the context of a fixed land resource base. Land, unlike people, does not give birth. The periodic registration of new members as age sets matured had direct implications for the size of parcel that each would receive in the event that land was subdivided. As young men matured, they were recruited into group membership. This recruitment involved collective registration of an entire age set. Consequently, members' shares to group ranch land were gradually diminishing with the expansion of membership. The anticipated outcome was that parcels would be small and unviable upon the eventual subdivision of the group ranch, at some unknown though certain time in the future. This concern also reflects a general sense that land subdivision was unavoidable, a sense that is tied to events in Kajiado district and elsewhere in Kenya. The historical origins of this perception of inevitability have been analyzed in chapter four.

Tables 5.3 and 5.4 present population figures for each group ranch for the past 20 years and incorporate three population census data. Table 5.5 gives an indication of new registrations across time in some of the group ranches.

Table 5.3 Number of Members in Each Group Ranch in Three Time Periods

Ranch	1982	1984	2002[a]
Enkaroni	190	336	356
Meto	408	425	(645)?
Nentanai	51	51	56
Torosei	165	165	300

Note: [a] For the subdivided group ranches, the year 2002 refers to number of members who were eventually registered and to whom land was allocated.

Source: District Land Adjudication Office, Kajiado district.

Table 5.4 Total Population in the Study Areas

Name of Locationa[a]	1979		1989		1999		2002 Projection at 4.5% Growth Rate	
	Male	Female	Male	Female	Male	Female	Male	Female
Enkaroni	[b]	[b]	731	757	1209	1340	1384	1534
Meto	1629	1766	2401	2551	2529	2511	2895	2875
Nentanai village	[b]	[b]	[b]	[b]	192	234	210	268
Bissil	[b]	[b]	1922	1878	4567	4851	5229	5554
Torosei	1696	1607	987	897	1209	1340	1384	1534

Notes: [a] Each of the locations coincides with a group ranch, except Nentanai, which falls under Ilbissil location.
[b] Data not available.

Source: Central Bureau of Statistics, Ministry of Finance and Planning (Kenya, Republic of, 2001b, 1994, 1981).

Table 5.5 Number of Individuals Registered

Group Ranch	Registrations[a]
Enkaroni	1984: 89 registered
Meto	1980: 23
	1985: 134
	1989: ?
	1992: 38
Nentanai	

Note: [a] Registrations refer to the number of times new members were added to the group ranch register and thereby became official group ranch members and shareholders. For Nentanai, there was no record of new registrations after the group ranch had been formed.

Source: Own field work.

By the time the Enkaroni group members were debating whether or not to subdivide in 1985, many group ranches in Kajiado were engaged in the same discussion while others such as those in Kaputiei and in Ngong divisions had already subdivided about a decade earlier or were at advanced stages. Arguably, subdivision in Kajiado district began in the late 1960s with the initial enclosure of the larger, Maasai range into the group ranches as we currently know them. This large-scale enclosure was punctuated by the demarcation of a few, very large, individual ranches that were issued to Maasai that were willing to pursue lives independent of the collective, the so-called individual ranchers. The late 1970s and early 1980s saw key areas of northern and eastern Kajiado district individualizing formerly group-held land. This general tendency toward individualization can be seen in other parts of Kenya such as amongst the Kikuyu, Kamba, Kisii, and Kipsigis communities who neighbor the Maasai and whose land is now largely held under individual title.

The links between increasing numbers of registered group ranch members and accompanying perceptions of land scarcity is reflected in the increasingly stringent rules for recruiting individuals into group membership. In all the group ranches studied, registration began with the combined registration of the Ilterito, the Ilnyankusi, the Iseuri, and the Ilkiseiya age sets at the time when group ranches were formed (see table 2.4 of chapter two for age-set chronology in the study areas). In Meto and Enkaroni group ranch areas, recruitment of new members ended with the registration of the Irang Irang age set in 1984 and the register was "closed" to any future member recruitment. This coincided with the time when members of both group ranches were beginning to debate subdivision. More junior age sets such as the Ilkingonde, who were initiated around the time when these group ranches were ready to subdivide, found the register closed and were shut out of a process by which they too would have formalized their entitlement to group land. The same applied to even more junior age sets such as the Ilmajeshi and the Ilkilaku/Ilpaang'u that were formed several years after the Ilkingonde. All were excluded because their inclusion would have reduced the share of group land available to each registered member. In Nentanai group ranch, which is Kajiado's smallest, even the Irang Irang age set was not registered!

When the group ranches were first carved out of vast open Maasai territory that used to be controlled by specific sections of the Maasai, the intent was to register those families living in territory that was controlled by the section of Maasai that held claim to that particular territory. This first registration required that community elders and government chiefs verify the residential status of each individual prior to his registration. Anyone certified as a genuine resident and whose identity was endorsed by a select group of elders was registered. Male household heads and some of their young male sons were registered. Included in this first registration were non-Maasai from Kikuyu, Kamba, Somali, and wa-Arusha (of Tanzania) ethnicities who at the time were variously employed as cultivators and traders. They were affiliated either through marriage or friendship with local Maasai and were incorporated into Maasai sociocultural structure through the age-set and clan institutions.

Each of the four group ranches studied of Enkaroni, Meto, Nentanai, and Torosei had a very small minority of non-Maasai as registered members. For Enkaroni group ranch, in particular, the first registration was conducted under a somewhat peculiar circumstance. Enkaroni is inhabited by the Purko, the smallest Maasai section in Kajiado district. The boundaries of most group ranches are contiguous with the government's administrative locations, which are the smallest administrative units in the country. Since the Kajiado Purko were very few, it was not administratively prudent to create a location specific for the Purko. Proposals at the time intended to annex the Purko to a neighboring section, the Ildamat. The Purko resisted this proposal by registering any male resident in the area, whether adult, child, non-Purko, and even non-Maasai as a way of preventing this artificial assimilation into the Ildamat section.

Apart from residency and gender, there were no other restrictions in the first few years following the establishment of group ranches. Later years saw greater stringency in the application of the rules of membership. While earlier registrations were open to all adult male residents, later registrations limited eligibility to a set of criteria that were simultaneously applied. An individual thus had to have been born and raised within the group ranch, had to have been initiated into adulthood according to Maasai custom, had to be endorsed by the entire membership during annual general meetings, had to possess a national identity card, and had to pay a registration fee. These rules were ultimately negated with the closing of the register of members when each group ranch resolved to subdivide.

Closing the register of members locked out eligible males such as the Irang Irang in Nentanai, the Ilking'onde in Enkaroni, and Meto and the Ilkishili in Torosei. Women, who were excluded from rights from the inception of the group ranches, were eventually, as widows, registered at the insistence of government officials. They were also registered as a matter of expediency. Registering a single widow on behalf of her eligible sons as opposed to registering the adult sons of the deceased husband reduces the ultimate number of individuals registered. This plays into the numbers and scarcity situation.

More strictly enforced rules of eligibility to membership are just part of a wider exclusion mechanism. Questions of identity and belonging also emerged when group ranch members resolved to subdivide. In Meto group ranch, for example, the wa-Arusha, migrant laborers from Tanzania, who were resident on the group ranch and who came to assist in cultivation, were struck off the register because they were of Tanzanian origins. Similarly, individuals whose names were double registered in Meto as well as in the registers of adjacent group ranches were requested to select which group ranch they wished to remain in. Their names were consequently deleted from the register of their choice. Within the group ranch itself, some individuals were registered several times under different names. This was also corrected. Exclusion was thus a prime theme in group ranch subdivision. Earlier forms of exclusion were based on gender. In later years age became the basis of exclusion. Yet later still identity, that is, whether one was Kenyan or not and/or whether one belonged to one group ranch or the other became the basis of exclusion. These efforts at exclusion fed off notions of land scarcity that were in turn fueled by expanding human population in the group ranches.

The Individual Ranchers: Land Titles, Land Grabbing, and Competitive Grazing

In addition to an increasing membership, the impact of the early individual ranchers in motivating group ranch members to subdivide cannot be overemphasized. As indicated in chapter four, individual ranches were established in the early 1960s to early 1970s. Very few were established in the 1950s. Because individual ranches were expected to serve as models for proper livestock and pasture management, the government provided them with necessary infrastructure and support to ensure their success. Using their land titles as collateral individual ranchers had access to development loans from the Agricultural Finance Corporation. They also had access to extension services from relevant government departments such as the Ministry of Livestock and Water Development. With this kind of support many individual ranchers appeared successful. Many constructed permanent stone houses, put up temporary and permanent watering facilities, increased the quantity, and improved the quality of their herds. With time group ranch members, who were faced with increasing challenges to collective decision making, began to find the group concept unworkable and to see in individual ranching a reasonable and viable alternative. Group members were eager to access these loan facilities and achieve similar success.

The individual title was viewed as the gateway to development. Privatizing land was perhaps the "magic bullet" that would unleash development in Maasailand. A title to land represented complete and secure ownership, but more. It could be used as collateral to acquire loans for farm and livestock improvement; it could be used as security against which unforeseen circumstances such as illness could be confronted. For the poor in particular, individual ownership represented not only their extrication from a grazing interaction in which they were exploited but also an opportunity to manage their livestock in harmony with pasture availability; an ability to earn alternative incomes either by leasing out excess pastures, cultivating, selling charcoal, and, in extreme cases, selling off part of their land. With individuation, the poor would become property owners and have access to alternative productive resources that would enable them improve their status within the community.

This association of "development" with individually owned assets is particularly strong in Meto, where large individual ranches virtually surround the entire group ranch save for the hills on its border with Tanzania. Group members witnessed individual ranchers using land titles as collateral to take loans; they used these loans to increase the number and quality of livestock and to improve on-farm infrastructure. The livestock enterprise seemed to succeed and indeed to thrive under individual ownership.

Meto is perhaps one group ranch where the role of alternative subsistence strategies was given serious consideration during the decision to subdivide. Being periodically ravaged by East Cost Fever, livestock populations were increasingly threatened and cultivation assuming increased importance in the livelihoods of group ranch members. Under an individualized system each individual would determine how much land to put under cultivation relative to grazing. Also the returns to investments of labor and seed would be realized by the same individual. Land use restrictions under group ranching made cultivation difficult, this in addition to the risk of crops being destroyed by free ranging livestock. The increasing incidence of cultivation was noted with concern by the group ranch chairman during Meto members' general meeting of September 27, 1989. Cultivation in Meto was greatly facilitated by the hired labor of the wa-Arusha of Tanzania or through kinship ties with the Kikuyu. Though crops may fail in bad years' grain, surpluses in good years would be sold to members of the neighboring Torosei group ranch. Others, however, prefer to transport their surplus to Bissel market 56 kilometers away. Competitive pricing of maize in Tanzania hampers sales in Torosei, while Bissel sales are rendered less profitable by the high costs of transportation.

The success of the individual ranchers and group members' envy of it must be qualified. To some group ranchers, the very creation of individual ranches in the late 1960s and early 1970s was the equivalent of a land grab in which huge chunks of the community's land were hived off and transferred to exclusive individual use without the community's consent. Some individuals also harbored a fear that this land grabbing might renew itself and the remaining parts of the group ranch might be taken in very much the same way as had happened during the creation of the individual ranches. These fears were especially acute among the members of Nentanai group ranch, who have seen the mushrooming of individual ranches around them and who have also witnessed the grabbing of livestock holding grounds in nearby Bissel town by influential individuals.

The members of Enkaroni group ranch viewed individual ranchers as a menace. Though some may have admired and even envied the "development" exemplified by individual ranchers, most group members had more reason to resent than to admire the individual ranchers' successes in the livestock enterprise because it occurred at their expense. Individual ranchers would release their livestock to graze in group ranch pastures during the wet season and retreat into their fenced and exclusive ranches in the dry, while denying group members the use of their ranches during this time. The individual ranchers were in effect using the group ranch as a wet season grazing area and setting aside their own land as dry season grazing areas (*olopololis*). These *olopololis* were exclusive, accessible only to the individual ranch owners themselves.

Why did Meto and Nentanai group ranches tolerate the herds of individual ranchers, while Enkaroni did not? Enkaroni, which in Ol-Maa means the "place with no river," is inadequately supplied with water. Its location places it in a somewhat distant position to any alternative source of pasture and water. Meto, on the border with Tanzania, seems to have unrestricted access to dry season pastures and water in nearby Tanzania. Nentanai's closeness to the Maparasha Hills accords it the same advantages as Meto. Nentanai is often referred to by individuals in Enkaroni as one of the last pasture refuges during the dry season. Both Nentanai and Meto were also severely ravaged by East Coast Fever, and the declining herds may have reduced competitive tensions with the individual ranchers.

Thus the individual ranchers' "successes," in some sense, achieved one of the goals that had driven the establishment of individual ranches in Kajiado district: to act as a model that could be replicated by the wider Maasai community. But this demonstration effect was counterbalanced by their exploitative grazing on surrounding group lands. It was also offset by perceptions among some group members that the individual ranchers represented a land grab. These latter situations generated resentment rather than envy. All three reasons—demonstration effects, exploitative grazing, and land grab—appeared to motivate interest in the subdivision of collective holdings.

Livestock Holdings and Grazing Interactions
inside the Group Ranch

Herds within the group ranch were a collection of livestock belonging to both livestock-poor and livestock-rich individuals. Livestock ownership was not factored into pasture availability, and the livestock of all group members grazed on the same pastures. Livestock-poor individuals were discontented with this arrangement, as it did not differentiate between the pasture demands of different members with varying livestock holdings. They felt that they were subsidizing the livestock enterprise of the rich, with no apparent gain to themselves. This was particularly evident in the drought periods when all livestock belonging to both rich and poor would be forced to migrate out of the group ranch after exhausting available pasture. These migrations would result in substantial herd losses. Losses were particularly acute for the poor who, having set off with only a few cattle, would often return with none. Livestock-poor individuals were thus bearing the costs of collective herding, yet the benefits were concentrated among the wealthy few. These grazing differentials among group ranch members themselves dovetailed with the exploitative tendencies of the individual ranchers and pushed group members into viewing subdivision as a desirable alternative. With subdivision, each individual would acquire his own parcel and be forced to manage his pastures according to the number of cattle that he owned.

Challenges with Collective Decision Making
in the Group Ranch

The group ranch committee members were particularly sensitive to difficulties in collective decision making. This group of 10 individuals, elected from the wider group ranch membership and mandated with tasks of running and overseeing all development efforts on the ranch were frustrated by several issues. Enforcing livestock quotas and getting individuals to limit or reduce stock quantities as part of ranch management planning was impossible. Livestock under indigenous Maasai herd management is owned and managed by individuals. Herd size is individually determined. The economic and symbolic value of cattle occasioned a focus on accumulation among rational herd owners. Milk is a crucial component of basic subsistence. Cattle are important for cementing social relationships either through bride wealth or stock exchanges among friends and relatives, as well as an insurance against droughts. The committee was unable to mediate against this strong set of incentives and to convince herd owners to reduce their herds. Without an agreement on a limit to herd size, the group ranch did face a tragedy of the commons.

In addition to the uncontrolled accumulation of livestock by some group ranch members, the committee faced considerable defiance of their attempts to define and enforce grazing and settlement patterns within the group. Individuals would, for example, graze livestock in areas deferred for dry season grazing, or even construct homesteads in the same. Similarly, group members would invite kin and friends to graze on group land without consulting the committee.[4] Others would set wild fires to decimate tick infestations and to improve pastures. Yet still others were guilty of nonpayment of their contributions for the financing of group projects such as water and schools.

While most of these challenges were resolvable and some were actually resolved, for example, by forcibly evicting unauthorized settlers or chasing away nonmembers, these solutions were untenable in the long run. The committee thus encouraged and even campaigned for subdivision as a way of divesting themselves of these responsibilities. Recalling some of the trials the group scheme underwent, the Enkaroni group ranch chairman during an interview observed that "it is only the government that can manage large pieces of land like group ranches."[5]

Consequently, the group ranch committee members invested much effort in encouraging subdivision. They not only campaigned for subdivision by presenting it as a government requirement, emphasizing President Moi's previous advice to the community, but they also stirred deep-seated fears by suggesting that future, post-Moi governments may settle non-Maasai in the group ranches if left undivided. This may have played a pivotal role in hardening members' resolve to subdivide. This fear of immigrants and especially the Kikuyu must be contextualized. Though the wa-Kamba were rewarded for their role in the World War by being given land in parts of northern and western Kajiado, the Kikuyu were perceived as a bigger threat in spite of historical symbiotic Maasai-Kikuyu relations. Not only were the Kikuyu more numerous and economically stronger, but recent experiences of unfair land transactions in other parts of Maasailand have left Maasai suspicious of Kikuyus. The validity of such arguments can easily be called into question because group ranches are legally titled and have this far represented a most effective form of protection of Maasai land, at least from government appropriation. Indeed, all evidence suggests that recent losses to Kikuyu were through direct sales, the result of subdivision itself. Nonetheless, land remains a deeply emotive issue for the Maasai in their memory of the state's historical capacity to seize their land regardless of local community interests and in the wake of unequal land transactions with "market-savvy" outsiders.

Clearly a multiplicity of factors underlies group ranch members' decisions to subdivide their collective holdings. The demand for exclusive, individual property rights in land follows quite closely economic predictions.

An increasing human population heightens perceptions of scarcity while titles acquired after subdivision are envisioned to open up previously inaccessible opportunities. Both these reasons seem to have created an incentive among individuals and groups to want to subdivide. But also difficulties in enforcing rules for resource appropriation within the group ranch and in excluding outsiders raise concerns over distribution. Members viewed subdivision and individualization as a solution to distributional asymmetries. Similarly, claims to external threats of dispossession create a powerful incentive for subdivision. Such claims are validated by a historical examination of Maasai land relations (chapter four).

Though the preceding account has laid out factors that motivated demand for exclusive, individualized property rights, it is incomplete. It homogenizes a host of differentiated preferences among actors, and it obscures the concrete struggles, bargains and controversies that defined the decision-making process. As illustrated below, this was a process that closely followed the age and gender differentiation of Maasai society and one that was characterized by conflicting agendas and disparate abilities by individuals to influence the nature and direction of change. An analysis of the preferences of individuals and groups of actors, and the ways in which they pressed their claims in the run-up to subdivision greatly enhances the understanding of this dynamic process. It places in perspective the problem of why subdivision happened in the first place.

The following section presents the heterogeneity of actors and interests in subdivision. It illustrates how these interests were articulated, mediated, and tempered within the framework of a mix of formal-legal and customary institutions, to achieve the outcome of subdivision.

Differential Preferences for Subdivision among Group Ranch Members

Maasai in the four group ranches of Enkaroni, Meto, Nentanai, and Torosei belong to the Purko, Matapato, and Loodokilani sections. The section is a territorially defined unit. Yet the sociopolitical organization of the Maasai across sections is almost identical, with cross-cutting linkages afforded by age sets and clan affiliations. Minor differences in dialect, terminology, and dress may occur between sections. In general Maasai society can be categorized into the elders, the *ilmurran*, the youth, the women, and the children. Elders can further be disaggregated into three groups—junior, senior, and retired elders. These categories of elders personify a power and authority structure that is entrenched in ritual, is defined by age and experience, and is given expression by decision-making responsibility and privilege within the community.

Among the communities of Enkaroni, Meto, Nentanai, and Torosei group ranches, the senior most grouping of elders that featured prominently in the conversations on subdivision belonged to the Ilterito and Ilnyankusi age sets. The Ilterito, if alive today, would be roughly between 85 and 100 years old, while the Ilnyankusi may be between 70 and 80 years old. The Iseuri may be about 60–70 years; the Ilkitoip (Ilkiseiya and Irang Irang) early forties to late fifties; the Ilkingonde, mid-twenties to late twenties; and so on. The *ilmurran* are usually young men in their mid-teens to mid-twenties and comprise the "warrior" group in the community. Women, like children, are dependents. They have little to no decision-making authority outside of the household.

The Elders

In Enkaroni and Torosei group ranches, the age differential correlated closely with preference for subdivision, while in Meto and Nentanai it did not. In Enkaroni, for example, the most senior elders during the time when subdivision decisions were being debated were the Ilterito and the Ilnyankusi. Majority of individuals in these age groups, though few in number, were strongly opposed to subdivision. To them land subdivision symbolized the end of Maasai pastoralism, the beginning of poverty, of a disintegration of community, and, in the extreme, of land sales. In their reasoning subdivision would reduce the amount of land available for livestock, leading to a reduction in the number of livestock that each could potentially own ultimately resulting in poverty. Such poverty would then motivate individuals to sell parts of their land in their bid to survive. Such sales, if to outsiders, would result in the loss of Maasai land to non-Maasai. This restricted movement and "caging in" of individuals in their parcels would undermine community cohesion. The senior most elders of Enkaroni and Torosei preferred not to subdivide. By contrast the senior Ilnyankusi of Meto and Nentanai group ranches strongly supported the subdivision. The reason for this preference is discussed later in this section.

Despite the senior elders' interjections, Enkaroni group ranch was still subdivided. Torosei group ranch resolved to subdivide and is still organizing for a formal survey and demarcation. In Enkaroni, the elders' voices of dissent did not go unheeded, judging by the widespread acknowledgment that elders' were the main stumbling block to subdivision. The Ilterito and Ilnyankusi here were ineffective in pressing for their interest. They were few and kept dying as the debates progressed. The Ilterito in particular were too old and weak to leave their compounds and attend meetings, while many Ilnyankusi disgusted with the whole idea simply refused to attend meetings convened to discuss subdivision. When the matter was taken to a vote[6] among group members, the senior elders were outnumbered by the more numerous Iseuri and Ilkitoip who were not only younger and stronger but who comprised the larger part of the 10- member group ranch committee. The composition of group ranch committees is discussed in greater detail in the next chapter.

Remarkably, the elders did not evoke their powers to curse those that went against their wishes because their "sons" continuously appealed to them about the gains of subdivison. Their official sons are the Ilkiseiya, the right-hand or older grouping within the Ilkitoip age set. Father-son relationships across age sets serve to solidify interage-set relationships. While proximate age sets struggle against each other for power, leadership, and community recognition, alternate age sets usually separated by a minimum of 14 years are characterized by a supportive, though paternalistic, relationship characterized by deference for the older age set. Within an age set, on the other hand, individuals enjoy bonds that are cordial and mutually reinforcing; solidarity is a fundamental organizing principle. Thus the Ilkiseiya, the recognized "sons" of the Ilnyankusi, many of whom were in favor of subdivision, appealed for their "fathers" blessings at many *barazas* that were convened by the group committee to discuss subdivision. These meetings seemed to have been an exercise in public relations designed to contain the disapproval of the seniors because their will was virtually ignored. The Iseuri and the Ilkiseiya, the younger, more numerous, and most powerful elders on the group ranch, got the subdivision that they preferred.

The preference for subdivision by the Ilnyankusi elders in Meto and Nentanai departs radically from the "conservatism" expressed by the Ilnyankusi of Enkaroni.

The Ilnyankusi of Meto and Nentanai favored subdivision. Their preference for subdivision in these two cases was conditioned on the fact that members of their age set own the numerous individual ranches surrounding Meto and Nentanai group ranches. In the whole of Maasai in general, the Ilnyankusi were the first to be issued individual ranches, and have used their large parcels as collateral to develop their ranches and even to acquire more land.[7] The Ilnyankusi in Meto and Nentanai group ranches at the time of subdivision were in favor of subdivision because they felt that their peers who had obtained individual ranches had cheated them out of their land. Most regretted their earlier choices of not taking individual ranches when they were up for grabs. Here, the Ilnyankusi that disfavored subdivision were few and did not matter. Some disfavor until now, though at the time of subdivision they recognized that it would still happen and chose not to resist.

The remaining groups of elders, the Iseuri and Ilkiseyia, were much in favor of subdividing. Both these age sets had good representation within the group's management committee, as will be discussed in detail in the next chapter. For the Iseuri and the Ilkiseyia a key motivator was the need to "develop" following the example of the individual ranchers. Each of the individuals envisioned a greater security with subdivision and the ability to make independent decisions with regard to cultivation, to livestock management, and to the development of infrastructure and housing.

Rich and Poor Livestock Herders

The rich and the poor, who belong to different age sets, can also be grouped into preference categories. The rich, who own large numbers of livestock, and cattle in particular, were initially not in favor of subdivision. Their large herds would not be sustained under restricted, smaller-sized parcels. Free grazing of their herds within the group ranch made them the disproportionate beneficiaries of the group ranching system. They did not favor change.

The poor on the other hand favored subdividing, though some expressed a "fear" of the rich whom they anticipated would influence decisions and acquire larger parcels during the process of subdivision. The livestock-poor individuals were interested in the transition primarily because they did not have large herds; restricted grazing within the confines of their individual parcels was expected to enable them to better manage their small herds. Subdivision would also open up new income generating opportunities for the poor. They could lease excess pastures to the rich and could benefit from milking the herds of the rich as they grazed in the leased pastures. They could also cultivate. They could sell charcoal or even a part of their land. Subdivision would thus create avenues for livestock-poor individuals to generate much needed income from alternative activities and uplift their status within the community. Thus in spite of the shadow of a possible land grab by the rich herd owners during subdivision, the poor had considerable incentives to support the drive for subdivision.

The Women

Since women were not registered as group ranch members, they were not allowed into group ranch meetings. The nonregistration of women may have followed Maasai cultural interpretations in which land and land use decisions are the responsibility of male elders. Women acquired rights through their relationships with males either as wives, daughters, or sisters. Women in the studied group ranches thus did not participate in the decision of whether or not to subdivide. They "followed their husbands decisions" or "took their husbands stand." Those that attempted to confront their husbands over the issue were met with indifference and sometimes hostility. On matters to do with land, women were decision takers. Though widows, as the executors of their deceased husbands' shares in the group ranch, were sometimes permitted to attend group ranch members' meetings, they could not address men publicly. Several widows did not attend the meetings because their in-laws represented them. However their votes counted when time came to vote on whether or not to subdivide. Similarly, the registration of widows as replacement for their deceased husbands helped contain the numbers problem. Instead of registering the adult sons, it was more convenient to register widows, who in turn would distribute to their sons.

Women thus had no forum within the structures of the group ranch to pursue and articulate their interests and claims. They did not attempt to challenge the basis of their exclusion. The same elders who had crafted the rule to exclude them could not be relied upon to change the rules in their favor. Though women were denied participation, it did not deprive them of a preference and an opinion regarding subdivision.

Many married women favored subdivision on several grounds: inheritance for children, land ownership, and freedom to conduct independent decisions. The few who were wary of subdivision cited restricted access to grazing and a breakdown of shared life patterns as fundamental constraints. Their lack of involvement in the process may also have colored their opinion against subdivision. Today, these same women who disfavored subdivision are even more resentful of subdivision; not only have the conflicts over trespass increased but inconveniences to their daily lives have also increased. Subdivision has made their daily provisioning activities even more difficult. While before they had the entire group ranch to draw on for fuel wood, a woman is now forced to get fuel wood from a finite source within the confines of her parcel. Parcel owners have also sealed off the usual, shorter access routes to water. Married women with young sons were particularly opposed as they knew their children had no chances of being included in the exercise.

The widows favored subdivision because it would allow them to become landowners through the inheritance of their deceased husbands' shares in the group ranch. This would ultimately give them some independence and control within the group ranch and their sons' futures would be assured. Land ownership by women seems unprecedented in Maasai culture. It is a turning point in gender relations and likely the beginning of subtle shifts in the status of Maasai women.

The Youth: Struggles for Inclusion

In this study, youth are defined as those male individuals who had not yet been initiated into elderhood but had been initiated into adulthood through circumcision by the time the process of subdivision begun in the group ranches of Enkaroni, Meto, Nentanai, and Torosei.[8] When subdivision issues were being discussed in mid-1980s, and by the time members resolved to subdivide into individual parcels, several groups of youths in these ranches were eligible for registration as members. These were the Ilkingonde of Enkaroni, the Ilkingonde of Meto, some Ilkishili (same age as Ilkingonde) of Torosei, and the Irang Irang of Nentanai. In all sections of the Maasai, the Irang Irang (referred to as Ng'orisho among the Matapato) are the immediate seniors of the Ilkingonde.

These sets of youths favored the idea of subdivision for very much the same promise of individual progress and development suggested by individual land ownership. Perhaps even more significant was the measure of independence from their fathers that the individual ownership of land promised. Maasai youths are typically reliant on their fathers for the initial acquisition of cattle and other stock to start them off in the livestock enterprise. This dominance by older folk is evident in other spheres of an individual's lifetime, such as in the rites of passage. The younger folk are often at a less powerful end of a power continuum. Land, a basic resource in the livestock, enterprise is highly valued. The youth saw in land ownership the ability to strip themselves, at least in an economic sense, of part of the hold their fathers, and ultimately elders, had over them. The urge to break away was all the more pressing due to the polygynous structure of most Maasai households. Not all wives in a polygamous household were treated equally, and the probability of disfavor trickling down to children could not be discounted. It was not unlikely that such disfavor would manifest itself in the distribution of assets from father to sons. Even though the youths favored subdivision, they were excluded from membership and subsequently an avenue through which they, by right, would have acquired a critical asset.

Though the excluded age sets varied somewhat, the basis of their exclusion was remarkably consistent across all group ranches: increasing the number of members would reduce the size of parcels that each would ultimately receive. The perception of the severity of the problem also varied depending on the group ranch. That the Irang Irang age set, relatively more advanced age wise, were excluded in Nentanai is an indication of a more acute version of the problem. The small size of this group ranch made the range of whom to include even more restrictive. The inclusion of Ilkingonde/Ilkishili in Torosei group ranch on the other hand may be attributed to the relatively large size of the group ranch and also to the timing of the decision to subdivide. Yet their exclusion in Enkaroni and Meto is difficult to explain but may be a consequence of the times at which different ranches began serious discussions on subdivision. Group ranch records indicate that Enkaroni and Meto began discussion as early as 1982 and 1985. It is unclear for Torosei as records do not have any indication. Nentanai, the smallest group ranch, began somewhat earlier than the rest and even resolved to subdivide two years earlier, in 1987, than the other three.[9]

In Torosei group ranch, majority of the Ilkishili, who are also known as Ilkingonde in other group ranches, were registered in 1985 around the time of their circumcision and four years prior to their members' resolution to subdivide. About 18 individuals were not registered because they were not circumcised by the time. Thus it is these individuals who initially sought registration. The issue of youth registration in Torosei becomes complicated due to the delay in formal survey and demarcation. Although group ranch members here resolved to subdivide in 1989 only an informal demarcation has been conducted by the committee. There consequently seems to be a general feeling that there is room for adjustments. As a result youths initiated much later than the Ilkishili, that is, the Ilmajeshi age set, have also begun to agitate for their registration.

In Enkaroni, which resolved to subdivide in 1988 but had begun negotiations over subdivision earlier in 1985 but could not proceed due to outstanding loans to the Agricultural Finance Corporation, the Ilkingonde were not registered. Though they had been initiated into adulthood by the time members resolved to subdivide, they were still excluded because the decisions to subdivide had been made, at least in principle, by 1985 when the Ilkingonde were still undergoing initiation. By 1988, the Ilkingonde though now *Ilmurran* or warriors, were still excluded on the grounds that their registration would result in smaller parcels for other members after subdivision. They were advised by the committee to seek land from their individual fathers upon completion of subdivision. The situation in Meto group ranch was very similar to Enkaroni in this regard.

Nentanai, Kajiado district's smallest group ranch, was unique in that a more senior age set to the Ilkingonde were denied registration. Once again the primary reason for excluding the Irang Irang here was the anticipated decline in parcel sizes for the rest of the members if the Irang Irang were registered. They were also advised by their committee to wait for their fathers to distribute land to them. Nevertheless, about seven Irang Irang were secretly registered by the committee in 1987 when the group ranch members opted to subdivide.[10] This was justified on the basis that these Irang Irang were members of large families that had many eligible sons.

The exclusion of youths in these group ranches did not go unchallenged. Youths argued that land in traditional customary practice belonged to all, access being conferred to adult males via the community rather than by inheritance from their fathers. As such, they were well within their rights to demand for registration. They subsequently organized to challenge their exclusion and did this using various avenues both internal and external to the community. They sought the intervention of the elders, from the local administration, from government officials, and even from Maasai politicians of national stature. They did not succeed.

The excluded Irang Irang of Nentanai were the least organized, and their unsuccessful confrontations did not go beyond the committee level. In Torosei, the 18 excluded Ilkingonde actively sought registration from the committee in 1989. The group ranch committee did not accede to their demands. Three years later, this group, supported by their registered age-set members together with their *Il-Piron* that is their "fire-stick" fathers of the Iseuri age set, sought to convince the rest of the group members to support their bid for registration. This attempt was unsuccessful, as the Ilkiseyia and Irang Irang denied support. The Ilkiseyia and Irang Irang argued that they would only support Ilkingonde registration if their underage sons would be registered too. This denial is not surprising because it closely mimics the historical rivalry between members of adjacent age sets that is characteristic of the Maasai sociopolitical structure.

In 1996, when the Ilmajeshi, the age set immediately junior to the Ilkingonde, came of age they sought registration as well. The committee referred the Ilmajeshi to seek support from the Ilkingonde and from the Iseuri. This was a natural decision because the Ilmajeshi at a future time will be united with the Ilkingonde to form a single age set, with the Iseuri as their sponsors and fire-stick fathers. Though the Iseuri offered support for Ilmajeshi registration, the Ilkingonde insisted that their own unregistered 18 must first be registered before they even considered supporting the registration of the160–200 Ilmajeshi.

The Ilkiseyia and the Irang Irang age sets, at the Torosei annual general meeting in 1998, categorically refused to support this second attempt at registering Ilkingonde and Ilmajeshi. Once again they reiterated that any new registrations must include their underage sons. Although the determination of such a meeting should have been conclusive, the question of the registration of these age sets is still pending. The committee itself is undecided on the issue. Out of the 10 committee members, five, including the chair are Iseuri and desire the registration of their "sons"—the Ilkingonde and Ilmajeshi. The other five, being of the Ilkiseyia age set, do not want this. In addition, the unregistered youth have threatened to disrupt the activities of the surveyor when and if he comes to formalize the committee's earlier demarcation.[11]

Currently, the unregistered Torosei youths are anticipating being joined by the Ilpaang'u, the most junior age set in the hierarchy. These are the official "sons" of the Ilkiseyia and will likely gain support from the Ilkiseyia. This tug of war among rival age sets is one of the factors contributing to the continued delay of Torosei group ranch's subdivision process.

The process by which Ilkingonde in Enkaroni and Meto advanced their claims took very much the same form as in Torosei. It was defined by similar alliances across age sets that were built around long-standing competition and rivalries among adjacent age sets and cordial, paternalistic relations between age sets twice removed. The Ilkingonde youth used their leader the *Ilaiguenani* or age-set spokesman to approach the elders. The age-set spokesman or *Ilaiguenani* is a respected individual who represents a crucial component of traditional Maasai leadership structures. The selection of spokesman is widely vetted by the elders (in particular the fathers of the individual's age set) and is based not only on personal integrity and charisma but also on family reputation and untainted family history. The *Ilaiguenani* for each age set is inaugurated during the *Eunoto* or shaving ceremony that admits the *ilmurran* into elderhood, a ceremony where the *ilmurrans'* dreadlocks are shaved and in which they exchange their characteristic spears for the sticks typically held by elders. All spokesmen whether of younger or older age sets have the power to discipline and even to curse individuals within their age sets. In addition, they are treated in much the same way as elders—they have direct access to the elders and sit together in exclusive elders' meetings.

In negotiating for their registration as members, the Ilkingonde of Enkaroni, by way of their *Ilaiguenani*, organized for a meeting with the group committee and influential group ranch elders in the period following group ranch members' resolution to subdivide and close the register. The elders were approached in the traditional fashion with blankets and local brew. Some elders, especially those with sons of the Ilkingonde age set, agreed to support them. The elders of the Ilnyankusi who disfavored subdivision were also in support of the Ilkingonde registration. The issue of Ilkingonde registration was however not resolved during this meeting; they all reached a consensus that it be put to vote at a more formal general meeting of all group ranch members.

Meanwhile, the Enkaroni committee members were running a parallel campaign against the registration of the Ilkingonde. They would, for example, cite the problem that each individual's share would reduce by an amount proportional to the number of new additions to the register. This agitated most peoples' immediate concern that they would get small parcels. Part of the decision to subdivide the group ranch hinged upon this concern.

As part of their campaign against the Ilkingonde registration, the committee also made specific assurances to those in support of the Ilkingonde (in particular their fathers) that they would increase their parcel sizes to enable them accommodate their sons. In other instances, the committee would threaten to reduce the amount of land allocated to specific individuals supporting Ilkingonde registration. In addition, the committee pressured the Ilkingonde *Ilaiguenani* to control and quieten his group, failing which they would engineer his removal from leadership. Each *Ilaiguenani* has the power to curse as a way of enforcing compliance. The committee also silenced the most vocal Ilkingonde leaders by promising them registration or promising them that they would see to it that their fathers were given large enough parcels to cater for their sons. These strategies were effective in dividing the Ilkingonde. It saw some individuals dropping out of the group; it saw their spokesman backing down and appealing to his Ilkingonde compatriots to drop their agitation.

The Ilkiseiya and Irang Irang age sets (collectively known as the Ilkitoip) had their own argument against the registration of the Ilkingonde, not too different from the Ilkiseyia and Irang Irang of Torosei. They said that if the Ilkingonde were to be registered, then even their sons, then some of the Ilmajeshi age set that falls directly behind the Ilkingonde and others even younger, should be registered as well, since they too have rights to land in Enkaroni. By the time this matter was taken to vote during a general meeting, majority of the members voted against the registration of the Ilkingonde. A resolution was passed that no Ilkingonde (save for orphaned ones) be registered and that all Ilkingonde be allocated land by their fathers.

Dissatisfied with this resolution, the Ilkingonde sought alternative means to have it reversed. They first appealed to the locational chief. He was indifferent. The Enkaroni chief, a group ranch member belonging to the Ilkiseiya age set, was reluctant to address the youth's problem. Next they took their complaints to the district officer in Kajiado town, who was also indifferent to their plight. The youths finally resorted to the District Commissioner, the highest government authority within Kajiado district. Events at the District Commissioner's office in early 1989 demonstrate the group committee members' determination to lock the Ilkingonde out of membership. It also demonstrated the extent of their influence as well. The District Commissioner initially declined to see the Ilkingonde. The Ilkingonde on their part refused to move from his office, claiming that they would camp at the District Commissioner's office until he responded to their request for a meeting or showed them where to go and settle. The District Commissioner agreed then to meet with the Ilkingonde but only in the presence of their locational chief.

When the chief came to the meeting, he pointed out to the District Commissioner's that these were a bunch of unruly youths intent on subverting the subdivision of Enkaroni group ranch. The chief further noted that he could not recognize the youths as hailing from his location. He dismissed them as imposters and suggested that they be disciplined for creating disturbances within his location. He recommended that they be jailed. Several of the youths were indeed jailed for a few days. This served to deter the youths. They were defeated and did not seek an alternative. Going to court was not a viable option as some were still in school and many were dependent on their fathers. Financing a court case would have been impossible. The youths returned home and reapproached the committee, which would not give them a hearing.

It is instructive that the Ilkingonde did not seek intervention from the Lands Office in Kajiado. The land adjudication officer in Kajiado was also the assistant Registrar of the group ranches. This office in Kajiado, as it relates to group ranch matters, closely follows the Group Ranch Act of 1968. This Act only recognizes group ranch-registered members and accords complete control of new member registration to existing group members by way of a 60 percent majority voting rule. The role of government is advisory and supportive. Any government involvement in matters of group ranch registration would be in excess of their mandate and in contravention of the law. Recourse to the district administration provided a leeway, albeit a very narrow one, to getting their concerns addressed. The District Commissioner heads the Kajiado Land Arbitration Committee. Although this committee settles disputes, it settles disputes of a specific kind: those having to do with land that is individualized and. belongs to private, individual entities. The District Commissioner would have been unable to use his office to solve the registration of the Ilkingonde. At best he would have used his stature as the top administrative agent in Kajiado to appeal to group ranch officials and members to register the youth.

The attempts of unregistered youths in Meto took the same form and followed the same pattern as in Enkaroni. About 216 youths, mainly Ilkingonde, variously sought support from the elders, the committee, and the local and district administrations in their bid to have their names added onto the register of members. As with Enkaroni, they organized under the leadership of their age-set spokesman and sought support from the Iseuri, their fire-stick fathers. As with Enkaroni, they were denied support by the Ilkiseyia and Irang Irang and for the same reasons. The youths in Meto also wrote a letter to the District Land Adjudication Officer dated June 10, 1991, who referred them back to the committee. They were not registered.

Unlike the Enkaroni and Torosei youths, the Meto youths took their complaints further afield. They took their case to the Registrar of group representatives, a high-ranking government official in the Ministry of Lands and Settlement in whose portfolio group ranch administration falls. They also sought audience with the Vice President, who at the time was a leading politician in Kajiado and nationally and who had on several occasions intervened in group ranch matters in his home constituency.

The Registrar promised to convene a special general meeting to deal with this problem. This information leaked to the committee who went to see him before he took action and successfully blocked him from convening the meeting. The youths had placed their hopes in the Registrar and his failure to decisively address the issue dealt a huge blow to their efforts. In seeking assistance from the Registrar, the youth were in effect calling upon his open support for their registration several years earlier. During an annual general meeting on February 26, 1987, the Registrar speaking on member registration reminded the registered members that there were those who were minors during incorporation of their group ranch and who have now attained the age of majority and required registration. He informed the registered members that the nonregistered were their sons who had a right to seek registration from a court of law and whatever the judge rules will be final. He however cautioned the nonregistered youths to refrain from using violence.

The Vice President on the other hand arranged appointments with the youths but never showed up. The youths eventually gave up. They felt that the committee had used delaying tactics in solving their registration problem and that subdivision was too far gone to reverse. They had struggled with the question of registration over a period of four to six months. These struggles faced other setbacks such as the disappearance of the Meto group ranch file from the Land Adjudication Department's registry in Kajiado, as well as the periodic absence of those who were still in school and who also had taken a leadership role. About 100 youths were involved, though only 15 representatives were selected to forward their complaints beyond the group ranch.

The committee intimidated the youths with threats that if they continued pursuing the issue of registration, then their fathers would be given small parcels and/or issued parcels in unfavorable locations. One Ilkingonde had the following to say: "[T]he committee threatened me that if I don't remove from my age group my mother will be given land in a terrible area; so I removed from my age-group because I knew the committee had the power to do it." In addition to threats and intimidation, the committee took up their complainants' leaders and registered them as a way of weakening the group.

Conclusion

The events outlined in this chapter demonstrate that individuals and groups will seek to alter property rights in their anticipation of net gains from a new structure. To the group ranch members, the benefits expected in the new, individualized property rights structure outweigh the costs of transforming the old as well as the additional costs of maintaining the new structure. This new property rights structure also promises to eliminate disadvantages that were present in the status quo property rights.

The costs and benefits as well as risks of institutional change were however distributed unevenly because of the differentiated structure of group ranch communities. For the excluded youths and women, the costs of institutional change outweighed the benefits as it created new uncertainties with regard to future access to productive resources. As a result, the youth contested their exclusion and used diverse forums to articulate and press their claims. Women on the other hand, lacking a forum to articulate their preferences, disengaged from the process. Rules created to exclude women had a cultural basis that they were neither ready nor equipped to challenge.

In the case of the livestock-poor individuals, the costs of organizing to transform property rights and subsequently to defend the new rights were outweighed by the promise of specific benefits within the altered property rights structure. These included new income opportunities such as leasing pastures and cultivating, accessing capital markets by using titles as collateral, and the management of individual herds in tune with pasture resources thus eliminating or reducing the need to migrate during dry spells.

The incentive structure of the wealthy herd owners is unclear. Though they disfavored subdivision because restricted access to pastures would threaten the viability of their large herds, they did not organize to alter the direction of decision making. That individuals who would logically be most disadvantaged by change, and who had the resources and influence to delay or deter change, made no effort to do so is curious. The outcome of change, evidenced by the distribution of land parcels, greatly favored these individuals as will be shown in the next chapter. The prior negotiation of such an outcome may have accounted for the wealthy cattle keepers' acceptance of change.

The conditions that influenced individual benefit-cost calculations are consistent with predictions made by property rights theorists, and these conditions were outlined in the introduction to this chapter. Land titles issued by the state upon completing subdivision would be used by individuals to access capital markets that were previously inaccessible to them. By freeing capital and creating opportunities for investment, titles are ultimately expected to increase the value of land. In this regard, titles can also be viewed as lowering the cost of obtaining development credit. In addition, the title as a symbol of ownership security acts as a signal to potential buyers who do not have local knowledge (Alston et al., 1995). It thus broadens the land market to remote purchasers beyond local buyers.

Population growth, typified by the progressive increase of group ranch members and an almost automatic recruitment of groups of maturing youth, was an important motivator for subdivision. For many members, it became obvious with time that a land shortage was pending. By increasing resource scarcity population pressure enhanced the value of the resource.

Individuals then found it beneficial to invest resources in meeting the costs of privatization.

The group ranch, like all collective goods, was subject to various kinds of incentive problems that created high governance costs for collective organization. Because in the traditional indigenous Maasai system livestock are individually owned and managed, the "symbolic" function of cattle as well as a need to maximize family welfare in a relatively risky environment created an incentive for rational herders to accumulate livestock. The group ranch committee, mandated with the management and administration of the group ranch, was unable to enforce livestock quotas and impose limits on grazing capacities. This would have gone against traditional values. More importantly, the committee, being wealthy herd owners themselves, would likely not have acted against their own self-interest. Consequently, the size of herds went unregulated, with wealthy herd owners reaping disproportionate benefits from the collective and the livestock-poor shouldering the uncompensated costs of collective grazing.

These grazing externalities imposed on the poor by the wealthy, most pronounced during drought, undermined the provisioning abilities of poor herders, undermined the reproduction of pastoral livelihoods, and negatively affected herders' incomes. The grazing of individual ranchers' herds in the group domain only served to exacerbate the problem. Sanctioning the politically influential individual ranchers may not have been in the best interests of the committee. Thus both wealthy herd owners' and individual ranchers' activities became an externality that poor herders could no longer ignore. Since with private property the potential yields and profit expectations can be attributed exclusively to the individual, a strong incentive was created for the livestock-poor individual to support group ranch subdivision. This would eliminate the costs of collective herding. For the committee as well, private property eliminates governance costs such as those incurred to reach collective agreement and to organize a community of users. The opportunistic tendencies of members to circumvent rules, for example, when they cultivated or constructed settlements in prohibited areas, or when they invited their friends to graze in the group ranch, further increased the costs of governance.

Thus the theoretically unexpected transformation of property rights from group ranches to individual holdings can be attributed to both efficiency and distributional considerations as predicted by theorists. Beyond affirming the predictions of property theories, this chapter also begins to draw attention to the conflictual nature of the process of transformation. The struggles of the youth for inclusion, and their search for help across multiple forums ranging from local cultural institutions to government administration and national politicians is an indication of the multiple forums they were able to draw upon as they articulated their claims. Their multiple identities as sons, as adults in indigenous Maasai custom, as citizens of the republic, and as constituents provided their access to these forums. The advantages of claiming multiple identities in order to access multiple forums for resolution were not realized in this instance. Such manipulation of identities is not unique and is consistent over much of Africa and elsewhere where access and control over land and resources is contested and negotiable, where successful competition for access requires investment in social relationships, and where shifting identities are used in contestation (Meinzen-Dick and Pradhan, 2002; Berry, 1993, 1989).

The changing structure of land ownership transcends the transformation of economic and political relations, into transforming entire cultural structures and practices (Kanyinga, 2000; Bates, 1989; Okoth-Ogendo, 1991, 1976). The youth can no longer gain access to land by virtue of being adult members in their communities as was the case in earlier times. They are now dependent on their fathers for land. Inheritance has taken on new meaning; and youth are now not only dependent on their fathers for livestock but for land as well. Women, widows in particular, now exercise formal rights over their deceased husbands' land.

Though institutional change, and specifically the transformation of property rights in land, may be triggered by changes in relative prices and other factors within the economic sphere, it is a political process involving negotiation and bargaining among diverse agents that is embedded within local sociocultural structures and involves the state in crucial ways. These struggles over claims to land are further explicated in the next chapter in which the actual process of dividing the collective holding and the subsequent distribution of resulting parcels among group ranch members is discussed.

Chapter Six
Subdividing the Group Ranch: Allocating Land and Distributing Wealth

Introduction

In the preceding chapter group ranch members' motivations to reassign property rights were assumed to be driven by individuals' responses to changing relative factor scarcities as well as by their desire to reduce losses inherent in the status quo as they anticipated gains in the new arrangement. Distributional concerns were at the core of individuals' investing resources in transforming property rights.

This chapter builds on the previous one by discussing and analyzing decisions and procedures following group ranch members' resolution to subdivide the collective holdings and to distribute resulting parcels among individual members. These decisions related, first, to the organization of on-ground demarcation and survey, and second, to principles guiding land allocation and distribution following demarcation and survey. The chapter also discusses the outcome of the process of subdivision, the challenges to the outcome, and how resulting conflicts were addressed.

In characterizing the process of subdivision, several puzzles emerge. Why did rational individuals, that is, the group ranch members, expect the management committee to conduct subdivision and land distribution according to the agreed principles of equal allocation? Why did the management committee end up distributing land in an overtly unequal manner? Why did those who were least likely to be advantaged by equal land distribution, notably the wealthy herders, not oppose the proposed allocation formula? This chapter addresses these puzzles as it discusses land allocation and distribution during the process of group ranch subdivision.

The structure and content of decision making in all the four group ranches studied of Enkaroni, Meto, Nentanai, and Torosei were remarkably similar. So were the procedures for land allocation and the outcome of parcel allocation. All group ranches are treated together except where individual peculiarities call for special explanation. I use the theoretical tool kit provided by property rights scholars to characterize and account for the processes and interactions leading to observed outcomes.

Different property rights arrangements distribute costs and benefits in society in different ways. Thus distributional issues with regard to the allocation of benefits, such as wealth and power, will likely be a fundamental concern in the transformation of property rights, and the process a highly politicized and controversial one (Libecap, 1989; Knight, 1992; Firmin-Sellers, 1995). Actors in the political milieu will compete to define and redefine the distribution of wealth and power under the new arrangement. Potential losers and winners will attempt to protect their benefits under the status quo or seek new advantages promised by the new structure. Societal actors with varying capacities to influence outcomes will engage in bargaining and negotiation to assert their claims and to influence outcomes. Thus a careful analysis of this distributional conflict and how it is resolved will provide a better understanding of the evolution of property institutions (Libecap, 1989; Knight, 1992; Firmin-Sellers, 1996).

Negotiation and bargaining over property rights occurs in diverse arenas (Lund, 2002). It may occur in courts, village hearings, local councils, village chiefs, development projects, civil servants, or any societal institution that is approached to lend authority to certain property arrangements. Consequently, there is also a need to extend beyond the narrow scope of formal-legal political institutions, such as politicians and courts, and to include diverse political institutions, such as customary institutions, that actors use to pursue their goals.

The nature and intensity of distributional conflict is influenced by whether benefits in the new arrangement will be concentrated and on how diverse are the interests of the bargaining parties (Libecap, 1989). Both these aspects are heavily dependent on the formula used to allocate and distribute benefits. For example, rents can be divided among customary users in proportion to their respective rates of use in the status quo arrangement or they can be divided equally among previous rights holders (Platteau, 2000). Proportional division, having higher information requirements, disadvantages low intensity users whose membership in the group entitles them to equal use of collective resources. Though equal division has low information requirements, it is likely to generate intense opposition from individuals who are benefiting disproportionately from high intensity usage of community resources. Scholars seem to suggest that proportional division is a more politically desirable alternative (Libecap, 1989; Roemer, 1989). Others would argue that this is an empirical determination that is very much dependent on social norms of equity and fairness (Ensminger, 1992).

The outcomes of political bargaining will thus depend both on the power and influence of actors as well as on how the proposed distribution of wealth and power will blend in with prevailing institutional norms. Institutional change may be slowed and indeed blocked if the proposed distribution in the new arrangement is very concentrated.

How is conflict resolved so that the new property rights structure is implemented? Some actors may invoke the authority of the state to terminate severe conflicts over distribution (Firmin-Sellers, 1996). In other cases, powerful actors with a relative bargaining advantage are able to constrain others to comply with new institutional rules (Knight, 1992). How do they do this? Knight argues that the relative bargaining power of actors, itself a function of the resources available to actors, affects the credibility of commitments during bargaining. Weaker parties with less resources, who face higher costs in case of extended or a breakdown in bargaining, are less likely to challenge a stronger parties' commitment. In addition, threats of retaliatory action from a stronger person, though less desirable, may serve to increase pressure on the weaker party to adopt a less-preferred alternative. Thus outside of direct state intervention power asymmetries can resolve conflicts in social interactions. Nonetheless, Knight recognizes the possibility of weaker parties having marginal influence, in which case conflict is not resolved and instead recurs.

The above framework creates several expectations. These include the following:

1. Distributional conflict, determined by the mode of allocation chosen, is greatest where the new arrangement concentrates benefits in the hands of a few interests, particularly where social norms of fairness dictate a more equitable if not equal solution;
2. Actors utilize a variety of political institutions, formal and customary, to assert their claims to achieve the assignment of their preferred property rights;
3. Conflict is resolved either through coercion using the instruments of the state or through a more decentralized bargaining process among societal actors, but a process characterized by power asymmetries among actors. The more powerful actors constrain the choices of weaker ones forcing compliance to the new property assignment.

The following sections analyze the fit between these theoretical predictions and empirical reality in the subdivision of group ranches.

Subdividing the Group Ranch: Decisions and Procedures

The four group ranches at separate annual general members' meetings resolved to subdivide their collective holdings into individual parcels for distribution among each of their members. Nentanai group ranch was the first to make this decision on March 1987, Enkaroni followed in May 1988, while Meto and Torosei were the last to make this resolution in September 1989. Although these dissolution and related meetings occurred separately across the group ranches, the decision rules adopted for the conduct of subdivision were remarkably similar.

First, members resolved that subdivision be conducted in a manner as to ensure that all parcels are equal in size. But this equal allocation formula was qualified on two counts to cater for variability in resource attributes and to cater for differences in family size and therefore resource demands. Enkaroni and Meto group ranches, for instance, explicitly agreed that those individuals whose parcels would end up on hills or near streams/rivers during subdivision would be provided with larger parcels.[1] The same would apply to those families with a large number of adult, unregistered, though married, sons. This equal allocation draws its inspiration from two sources. The Group (Land Representatives) Act specifies that group ranch land is the property of the registered collectivity, held by each member in *equal, undivided* shares. More significantly, it draws from shared customary understandings where all recognized users have equal access to land, an indivisible territory. As a result if this previously indivisible territory is to be divided among its legitimate users, then it must be done so in recognition of this basic principle. It must be divided equally.

Second, though the officially elected committee would oversee the process of subdividing the group ranches and allocating parcels to individual members, each group ranch selected an additional group of about 10 individuals to assist the committee in the task of demarcating the group ranch. This new committee was referred to as the *"kamati ya panga"* (machete committee) or, more appropriately, the demarcation committee. Its responsibility was to help the official committee with the physical task of marking parcel boundaries. Its life lasted only for as long as it took to physically demarcate parcel boundaries.

Third, the group ranch members were to send in applications to the official committee for the areas in which they preferred to have their parcels located. Individuals were required to make their applications either verbally or in writing to the committee members, usually the vice chairman. However, no detailed arrangements were made on how this distribution would take place and how conflicting choices would be resolved.

Fourth, each committee advised that all members remain at their current locations until completion of subdivision to prevent opportunistic movement to choice areas prior to subdivision. Also no member was to fence off any part of the land, not even for their private *olopololis*, an exclusive zone of land close to each homestead for the grazing of young and/or sick livestock. They finally instructed individuals that there would be no land sales prior to the acquisition of titles. The committees assured members that all registered members would get land.

In accordance with the Land (Group Representatives) Act, each annual general meeting and in particular general meetings where group members' sole agenda was the dissolution of their group ranch were presided over by the Registrar of group ranches or by his appointed representative. At each of these meetings, following majority of group members' resolution to subdivide, the Registrar would outline the government's official procedure for dissolution and subdivision.[2] First, the official committee would apply for dissolution on special application forms. To this application form they would attach a 100KShs (about $1.2) processing fee and the minutes of the annual general meeting at which the majority of the members voted to dissolve their group ranch and subdivide among the members.

Second, after verifying that a group ranch had no outstanding loans and that the group ranch title is not charged or borrowed against, the Registrar would consent to its subdivision. And the group ranch can then engage a surveyor to embark on demarcation. Third and following the Registrar's consent, the group ranch seeking to subdivide would apply to the district's Land Control Board for its consent to subdivide. The Land Control Board is charged with monitoring and vetting land transactions within the district. It is a panel of experts, administrators, women, and elders drawn from local communities. It is chaired by the District Commissioner, who is the head of government administration in the district. Other members of the board are representatives of different government offices in the district. The secretary of the board is the district representative of the Commissioner of Lands. Other technical individuals include the District Land Adjudication Officer and a representative from the local authority, the Kajiado County Council. In addition, landowners in the district have representation on the board as well and are required to comprise three-quarters of the board. The Land Control Board, not to exceed 12 individuals and to comprise less than eight individuals, is appointed by the provincial commissioner and is gazetted by the Minister of Lands. At this stage of the subdivision process the land board has several responsibilities. It verifies and confirms whether or not the group ranch title deed is encumbered by loans; it seeks to establish the size of the land and the reasons for its proposed subdivision; it seeks to know the number of parcels that will result from subdivision of the land and whether/which public utilities will be set aside from the land. If satisfied with the results the board awards its consent for the group ranch to undertake subdivision.

Fourth, after the group ranch has completed demarcation, survey, and mapping it must seek further consent from the Land Control Board so that the collective group ranch title can be discontinued and instead converted to individual titles by the district land Registrar. At this point the Land Control Board's duty is to confirm that all registered group members have been allocated parcels and that parcels are relatively equal because group ranch land is held by its members in equal, undivided shares. It does this by examining the area list, a list that indicates the registered members, their parcel numbers, and the size of parcel that each will receive. The board must also determine that there is no dispute over the resulting subdivision and consults landowner representatives on the board and is open to disputing parties. The Land Control Board must confirm that public utility areas such as schools, trading centers, water points, health centers, access roads, and so on have been set aside. In all these decisions the Land Control Board depends heavily on technical experts such as the district surveyor and the District Land Adjudication Officer. If satisfied, the board consents to the transfer of title from the collective to individuals.

The district land Registrar then begins to process the titles. Group representatives, which includes the committee, usually chair, vice chair, and, secretary will sign the title transfers to individuals once they pay the required processing fees. The land Registrar will be a witness to this transfer process. Once all titles have been transferred, and every member has obtained title, a meeting will be convened and the Registrar of group ranches will officially dissolve the incorporated group and its representatives. This has not happened yet for any group ranch in Kajiado district as not all titles have been claimed even in the Kaputiei group ranches that were the first to subdivide in the late 1970s to early 1980s.

The group ranches also had a procedure for on-ground demarcation. After receiving the consent to subdivide, the group ranch would then engage a certified surveyor, either government or private, to conduct the on-ground demarcation. Prior to this the official committee and the temporary demarcation committee would traverse the entire group ranch, marking out boundaries of individual parcels using distinct natural features such as trees, rivers, rocks, and hills as markers. Following this, a team of certified private or government surveyors would be engaged to formalize and/or rectify the committee-determined boundaries. The surveyors would place beacons to mark parcel boundaries under the committees' instructions. This was an arduous, time-consuming process. The surveyors would charge fees for the work done and individuals were expected to pay these fees as a precondition to being shown their parcels. The fees varied from 1,500KShs (i.e., about $19) in Enkaroni, which was surveyed by a government surveyor, to 4,500KShs in Meto and 5,000KShs in Nentanai, both of which were surveyed by private surveyors.[3] Survey fees were decided by the committee, and the surveyor then communicated to group members. After the official survey and mapping, the committee would then show those individuals that had paid survey fees the location of their parcels. Individuals would then on their own seek their titles, at cost, from the land Registrar in Kajiado.

Before discussing the outcomes of the subdivision, it is worthwhile to reflect on why group ranch members expected the official committee to manage the process as agreed upon by the majority and to safeguard the majority's interests. This is puzzling because members endorsed the process before obtaining clear information on the attributes of land they would receive. Neither did they attempt to constrain the bounds of committee action nor deliberate on mechanisms for bringing the committee to account in case their expectations were not met. This is a significant omission if viewed from the perspective that individuals' livelihoods and the viability of the livestock enterprise, both dependent on access to adequate land resources, were at stake. Insights can be found in the factors that members considered when electing their official committee and in their selection of the demarcation committee.

Selecting the Committee: Traditional Norms of Trust and Reputation

The election of a management committee to run the affairs of the group ranch is mandated by the Land (Group Representatives) Act. This election is (or is supposed to be) an annual event, during which time group ranch members would place in office representatives of their choice, or remove those they dislike, or maintain those they preferred. In their election of the management committee, group members prioritized certain qualities such as honesty, integrity, sense of justice/fairness, industry, good behavior, and oratory skills. Some members elected to the committee were age-set leaders (*ilaiguenani*) or deputies to age-set leaders (*inkopirr*). This was a rather common occurrence in Enkaroni, Meto, and Torosei. Those who were not age-set leaders were often chosen because they were educated and their skills needed for record keeping and in the group ranches' external relations with government and with financiers. This was usually the case for the positions of secretary and treasurer. Thus group ranch management committees were a unique combination of traditional authority, by virtue of the qualities and criteria that group members used to select them, and of state or formal-legal authority as they were given force by the Land (Group Representatives) Act that provides for the administration of group ranches.

Prior to the actual on the ground subdivision, each group ranch selected another group of between seven and twelve individuals, the demarcation committee, to assist the official management committee in the physical task of subdivision. The demarcation committee, which lasted only for as long as it took to physically demarcate boundary parcels, was again selected along similar criteria as that of the official committee. Personal integrity, fairness, and industry were valued attributes. But to these attributes were added other pragmatic considerations. In some group ranches, achieving clan, and age-set balance across both committees was deemed important, as was the need to ensure that all the settlement regions within each group ranch were represented within the demarcation committee.

In Torosei group ranch, for instance, apart from the three educated individuals who were the chairman, secretary, and treasurer, all other committee members were deputies to their age-set leaders with the exception of one who was an age-set leader. But Torosei's committee structure is unique in the sense that the question of age-set and clan membership were taken into account so as to ensure equal representation among the age sets. The committee here was drawn from equal proportions of the age sets currently in power. Since the Iseuri and Ilkiseyia are currently in power, the Torosei committee comprises five of each. Similarly, the two major clans of the Maasai, the Odoomong'i and Orokiteng', must be represented in equal portions in the 10-member management committee.

The selection of the demarcation committee in Torosei followed the same logic as that of the official committee. First, the 10 were to represent the two major clans of the Maasai: five Odoomong'i and five Orokiteng'. In addition, they attempted to balance out those subclans that were inadequately represented within the main committee. In this case, subclans poorly represented on the main committee such as Ilaiser, Ilataiyiok, and Inkidong'i were included within the demarcation committee. Also, like the official committee, the equal balance between the "ruling" age sets, five Iseuri and five Ilkiseyia, was maintained. Finally, the area/locality that each of the demarcation committee members resided in was factored into their selection decision in order to ensure that all settlement/residential areas or localities were represented. Thus the work of the demarcation committee in Torosei, beyond providing much needed muscle power for a tedious task, was also to serve as the "eyes of the members."[4]

In Enkaroni, the 10 elected official committee members were again elected on the basis of personal integrity, but some were drawn from the traditional leadership structure as well. The chairman was the age-set leader of the Iseuri age set, while one of the members was age-set leader of the

Ilkiseyia age set. The secretary was educated, with secondary school education. While there was no special effort to equalize age-set distribution among the committee here, there seemed to be an equitable distribution of age set, with two Ilnyankusi, four Iseuri, and four Ilkiseyia. The first is the oldest age set, while the latter two are younger age sets that were coming into power at the time of their election. There was no effort to achieve clan representation. The demarcation committee here also comprised 10 members whose criteria of selection was typically the same as that of the official committee: personal integrity and fairness in dealings. However, the demarcation committee was also selected to represent the different areas or localities of the group ranch.

The constitution of the committee in Meto group ranch also was based on criteria similar to that in Enkaroni and Torosei. Personal integrity, maturity, and spokesmanship were important personality attributes. A large proportion of the individuals in the committee were also drawn from the traditional leadership structure. The chairman and his secretary were age-set leaders, while two other committee members were deputy age-set leaders. Education was also factored very highly in the decision to select committee members as group ranch members felt that educated individuals would be much more conversant with land issues and would provide good representation with government. Consequently, the core of the group ranch officials — the chairman, vice chairman, secretary, and treasurer—comprised individuals who were educated to various levels. Meto group ranch made no effort to balance out age sets or clans; indeed majority of the official committee members belonged to one age set, the Ilkiseyia. It was argued that this was their moment of leadership, which had been officially handed over to them from their immediate seniors, the Iseuri. More likely though, the Ilkiseyia, having a dominant vote among the group ranch members, may have used the election of committee members as an opportune moment to nudge the Iseuri out of leadership. The demarcation committee in Meto comprised 12 individuals chosen mainly according to the main settlement/residence areas. They were chosen in this way because "they are the ones who knew how people lived in their respective areas."[5] Their ability to work was also considered here.

In Nentanai, the official committee was also elected on the basis of leadership qualities and personal integrity. Here, there was no attempt to draw upon the traditional authority structure, perhaps because of the unique creation of Nentanai, which drew individuals from different, though close and strictly Matapato areas. Here the main effort was to balance age-set representation, with four Ilkiseyia, five Iseuri and the chair as Ilnyankusi, and clan representation. However, to the secretary's and vice chair's positions were elected individuals with substantial educational backgrounds. The demarcation committee was chosen to balance out clan representation, but it also reflected the dominance of the Ilkiseyia age set, a situation similar to Meto's. Both Meto and Nentanai belong to the Matapato section of the Maasai. As we have seen in earlier chapters, though age-set and traditional structures are almost identical among all groups of the Maasai, the details of structural dynamics may vary. It seems like in the case of Meto and Nentanai the Iseuri had ceded power to the Ilkiseyia much earlier than in Enkaroni or Torosei. Nentanai's being a small group ranch, indeed the smallest in Kajiado district, questions of settlement representation did not arise.

Clearly, group ranch members put considerable effort into the selection of their leaders. Though the management committee had been elected earlier, they had personal attributes that instill confidence in their leadership and in their ability to conduct subdivision as per agreed procedures. In any case, the management committees (with the exception of Nentanai) had organized and spearheaded the initiation, supervision, and maintenance of infrastructure projects within their respective group ranches. Seasonal water pans (also referred to as dams), boreholes, and cattle dips were installed during their tenure of office. In the demarcation committee, which was constituted for the sole purpose of subdivision, there was a special attempt to ensure that the outcome of subdividing the group ranch tallied with their expectations. By ensuring diverse and crucial forms of representation, between age sets, between clans, and with a strong regard for settlement patterns, group members made an attempt to bridge the gap between expectations of the process and the outcomes of the process. The considerations by which individuals were chosen to the two committees amount to a vetting procedure, and if added onto the bureaucratic procedures and vetting by the district's Land Control Board, they theoretically provide for a sound way of reducing uncertainty and assuring confidence that outcomes would indeed meet individuals' expectations. Thus rational individuals, to the extent possible, established a system that was based on traditional norms, and on past experience, which was anticipated to induce a measure of accountability among those to whom they had entrusted with the responsibility of subdividing their land.

Outcomes: "Fingers on the Hand Are Not Equal"

The result of subdividing the land was met with widespread dissatisfaction; not only had the committee dishonored the agreement to equalize land parcels, but many members were not allocated parcels in the areas of their choice. Some group ranch members organized to challenge committee allocations using various institutional mechanisms. Other group ranch members though dissatisfied did not launch an organized challenge against the committee's unequal subdivision.

Location of Parcels

Although individuals applied for their desired locations, not many were allocated parcels where they had requested. Some individuals were even relocated from prime sites close to water, transportation, schools, or with favorable pastures to remote and unfavorable sites not of their choice. Many such individuals either had personal conflicts with some member or other of the committee or had come in direct confrontation with the committee during the process of subdivision. Individuals who were friendly to the committee, or who comprised family to committee members, were allegedly issued the areas of their choice. The committee members awarded themselves prime land. Some individuals in Meto claimed that the opportunity to choose was not afforded to all but rather to the wealthy and to the friends and family of committee members.

Though the Enkaroni committee did not communicate its criteria for allocating member's particular sites, apart from individual applications, there seemed to be an underlying pattern to their decisions. Length of residence in a locality is one example. An individual who had lived in one locality for a long period of time without relocating would be allocated the spot that he wished. But this decision rule was complicated by the fact that settlement in the group ranch was collective. Maasai homesteads constituted a pool of households comprising an extended family and some close friends. It was thus not uncommon for several individuals to apply to be located in the same site or specific locality. Besides, it is only expected that individuals would apply for those localities that represent specific advantages to them such as closeness to schools, to water, health and trading centers; such advantages are commonly recognized and desired.

To reach a decision in such a situation where several applicants applied for the same locality, the committee supplemented the extended residency rule with a first-come-first-served rule. If all applicants, however, insisted on being located at the site, the committee complied but would ensure that their parcels were smaller since, as they argued, many would be squeezed into one area. The committee on the other hand promised those who agreed to move to alternative locations a larger share wherever they were moved to. While the thought of getting a smaller parcel may have worked to intimidate a sizable number of members into accepting areas they did not like for fear of receiving small, unviable parcels, some individuals were adamant and refused to move.

Where more than one person applied for the same site, which was the case in Meto because group members had already settled in their preferred sites long before subdivision, the committee based its decisions on several criteria.[6] First, the age factor was taken into consideration and older individuals given first preference. Second, the length of time in which a resident had lived at a site and whether the individual had invested in some "development" such as wells, dams, or other watering facility would be considered. Third, widows had to be "taken care of" and could not be moved away from their "guardians." Beyond these criteria, some individuals who had the foresight to realize that not all could be accommodated in their areas of choice because of overlapping interests, selected alternative sites, which they were given. Those who insisted on being located at the site they requested, even when the demand was high, were moved elsewhere while those who were not in the group ranch during subdivision were relegated to the hills and other less desirable locations.

In Meto, the requirement that individuals pay clearance fees before being shown their parcels served to disadvantage those unable to raise the fee at the time, because those who paid clearance fees earlier were allegedly given good areas often displacing those who were originally resident in those areas prior to subdivision.[7] As at the time of fieldwork in Meto, the committee was also sanctioning the transfer of land parcels belonging to those who had not yet obtained official titles to those able to raise title fees. The chairman was allegedly issuing out "vacant" parcels to those who were able to pay.[8] This means that though an individual may have paid his clearance/survey fees and may have been shown the location of his parcel, the committee could still overturn this earlier decision and reissue the land to someone else who was able to raise land title fees.

Parcel Sizes

Majority of the members were unhappy with their parcel sizes. Many argued that their parcels were small, while the committee had issued itself, its friends and family large parcels. They complained that the principle of equal parcels they had negotiated in meetings was not followed. Table 6.1 provides a synopsis of the parcel sizes and their distribution among group ranch members following subdivision.

The results indicate that the process of subdivision was not equal, as expected, and far from equitable.[9] In all three group ranches where subdivision was completed and formalized via surveying, mapping, and the issue of land titles, in Enkaroni, Meto, and Nentanai, two-thirds or more of the registered members have parcel sizes that fall below the averages. In addition, more than 25 percent of former group ranch land is owned by only 9 percent of its registered members. Finally, the committee members, who spearheaded the subdivision exercise and who were expected to conduct the subdivision fairly, ended up owning between 25 and 35 percent of the land that they were entrusted to subdivide. The average size for the committee

Table 6.1 Summary of Parcel Sizes in Enkaroni, Meto, and Nentanai

	Enkaroni	*Meto*	*Nentanai*
Area (hectares)	11,802.5	27,358.02	4,038.48
Number of members	332	548	56
Average parcel size after subdivision	35.56	49.92	72.12
Largest parcel (hectares)	200.5	152.79	214
Smallest parcel (hectares)	3.6	4.27	14.21
Standard deviation	27.23	21.87	51.06
Other information	Sixty-four percent of members have less than average parcel size.	Sixty percent of members have less than average parcel size.	Sixty-three percent of members have less than average parcel size.
	Twenty-five percent of former group ranch land is now owned by 9% of the former members.	Thirty-five percent of former group ranch land is now owned by 9% of the former members.	Twenty-six percent of former group ranch land is now owned by 9% of the former members.
	Thirteen individuals with single digit parcels.	One individual with single digit parcel.	
	Committee members (i.e., 10 individuals) own 9 percent of former group ranch land.	Committee members (i.e., 10 individuals) own 4% of former group ranch land.	Committee members (i.e., 10 individuals) own 30% of former group ranch land.
	Committee average = 100 hectares.	Committee average = 113hectares.	Committee average = 133hectares.

Source: Own field work.

members parcels following subdivision was 100 hectares for Enkaroni (as compared to the Enkaroni average of 36 hectares), 113 hectares for Meto (as compared to the Meto average of 50 hectares), and 133 hectares for Nentanai (as compared to the 72 hectares average for Nentanai). Committee parcels were thus more than twice the average size of ordinary members' parcels.

In Enkaroni, where the entire group membership had reached an understanding that group land would be divided equally among the members, each member's entitlement was about 75 hectares. This did not happen. Instead, the committee began by allocating themselves large parcels. Then individuals with close ties and affinities to committee members were rewarded with large-sized parcels. Wealthy individuals with large herds were also allocated large parcels. They were able to adequately entertain the committee by slaughtering cows and giving them gifts of livestock.[10] They successfully negotiated their preferred parcel sizes. Those that could not "entertain" the committee, notably the poor, did not succeed in negotiating a preferred parcel size and ended with considerably smaller-sized parcels. Widows too received small parcels as they were unable to defend their claims.[11] Yet those with disagreements, personal or political, with the committee had no space to negotiate—they were punished with smaller-sized parcels.

It is also observed that the committee kept those with large parcels well informed about the process, such that when subdivision was technically over, and land titles released by the Registrar of lands in Kajiado district, they hurriedly obtained their title deeds, long before the committee announced to the general membership that parcel titles were ready to be collected.[12] This is a significant move. Precolonial policy enacted during the emergency period at the time of the Mau Mau uprising privileged the holders of first titles, usually indigenous Africans who were in collusion with the colonial government. This was their reward. This policy was aimed at preventing other claimants, usually returning freedom fighters who had been actively involved in the uprising. Current land policy still upholds this antiquated and discriminatory clause, articulating that first titles issued can only be reversed if proven that they were fraudulently acquired. Proving fraud is a protracted, expensive affair as seen in the case of Ilpartimaru and other group ranches.

In Meto, the same pattern as in Enkaroni can be noted: majority of the members were unhappy with their parcel sizes; many argued that their parcels were small while the committee had issued itself, its friends and family large parcels. They complained that the concept of equalization contrary to general agreement was not followed. According to the Meto secretary, the committee members felt they had to be compensated for the tedious and unpaid work of subdividing the group ranch. This they did with issuing themselves "some extra land."[13] He also contended that those whose whereabouts were unknown, though their names appeared on the register, were given small parcels.

In both Enkaroni and Meto, when the demarcation committee at first marked out boundaries by visual assessment, they underestimated and some registered members ended up without parcels. The surveyor rectified this mistake when he came to plant beacons on the ground. Since land was not enough for all members, the parcels of some individuals, committee members included, were reduced to create land for those without.

It is appropriate that group ranch members' demands for equal allocation and concerns over the unequal outcomes of land distribution be properly understood because it raises important questions of equity that must be interpreted both within the material realities of the past and present, and in the context of Maasai culture. Obviously the outcome of subdivision has favored the wealthy cattle owners and the committee; many in the committee were wealthy herd owners too. A simple Pearson's product moment correlation between land allocated after subdivision and livestock holdings suggests that both size of parcel and livestock[14] holdings vary positively together in Enkaroni, Meto, and Nentanai (table 6.2). For cows, in particular, the association is always significant and relatively strong. Goats and sheep are significant only in Nentanai.

While it may be difficult to evaluate just how much of the committee's proportional allocation (which disregarded members' demands for equal subdivision) was driven by their own interpretations of equity or just due to a plain lack of transparency (which is what members suggest), it might be relevant to remember that the group ranch members' demands for equal allocation and distribution of land occurs against the backdrop of severe inequalities between families/households' livestock wealth in both current and historical times. Why then the demand for equality, why then the surprise and discontent with the unequal distribution?

These inequalities in livestock holdings, discussed at length in chapter two, suggest imbalances in the appropriation of joint resources across time.

Table 6.2 Correlations between Land and Livestock

	Cows	*Goats*	*Sheep*
Enkaroni			
Pearson correlation	.354[a]	.074	.200
Sig. (2-tailed)	.023	.645	.216
N	41	41	40
Meto			
Pearson correlation	.568[b]	.170	.194
Sig. (2-tailed)	.000	.175	.122
N	65	65	65
Nentanai			
Pearson correlation	.583[b]	.578[b]	.515[a]
Sig. (2-tailed)	.003	.004	.012
N	23	23	23

Notes: [a] Correlation is significant at the 0.05 level (2-tailed).
[b] Correlation is significant at the 0.01 level (2-tailed).

Source: Own field work.

But today's circumstance is radically different from that which prevailed in the colonial times, and possibly even during the phase of group ranching. In prior times, though livestock holdings were unequal, and though there may have been some competition for prime grazing land and water among individuals, land was available and accessible to *all* Maasai as a birthright.

Though each individual's herds varied according to stochastic events such as drought, epidemics, and raiding, and according to livestock management skills, there seemed to be an *equality of opportunity*. Land resources were available to all, and the extent of mobility determined access. Each individual would manage his herds within the constraints imposed by stochastic events and labor, subject to luck, misfortune, skills, and so on. Chapter three illustrated how significant portions of Maasailand were appropriated at different times by different actors for different reasons throughout its history. Thus with time land became a scarce resource, assuming an ever-more critical role in the Maasai livestock economy.

As the range closes in on the Maasai and as portions of it get allocated to a wealthy few, which has been the case in previous times and during subdivision, the production opportunities shift in favor of these wealthy herd owners. With significantly less land available to them and an increasing restriction on mobility, poor individuals are likely to get locked into the situation of poverty. Where previously an individual may have had a good chance of rapidly accumulating or losing herds, currently an individual's ability to accumulate is more strongly influenced by the availability of land. Those with small herds and small parcels but without alternative modes of livelihoods outside pastoral subsistence are disadvantaged. It is therefore not surprising that individuals would raise objections against a skewed distribution of land following subdivision. Not only does it strip them of their birthright, but it also undermines the very basis of their livelihoods in a marginal environment where alternatives are severely limited. Indeed, contrary to early times when livestock wealth was fluid, subdivision threatens to lock in wealth distribution.

Outcomes: Disaggregating the Bundle of Rights in Individual Property

An emerging trend after subdivision is that individuals and groups seem to be renegotiating rights to the access and appropriation of pasture and water; resources that have now been individualized and secured under a single, titled owner. Individuals are pursuing several strategies, separately or concurrently. One strategy is reaggregating their individualized parcels and pursing joint pasturing and management of their herds. This reaggregation of parcels seems to be occurring among neighbors, or within families and

Table 6.3 Post-Subdivision Arrangements

Arrangement	Enkaroni (N = 46)	Meto (N = 76)	Nentanai (N = 25)
Reaggregating parcels between friends, neighbors, family, in-laws.	6 (13%)	42 (55%)	11 (44%)
Do not have sharing arrangements.	40 (87%)	32 (42%)	9 (33%) (an additional 4 do not live on their parcels and neighbors graze freely)
Pasture leases.	8 (17%)	4 (5%)	0 (0%)
Redistributed herds with friends, family, in-laws.	20 (43%)	29 (38%) (2 not indicated)	9 (36%) (1 not indicated)

Note: Most interviewees allowed others into their pastures during times of drought and stress; N = total number of observations.

Source: Own field work.

in-laws, or in relatively few instances among friends whose parcels are not necessarily adjacent to each other. In addition, some individuals with few livestock and having pastures that exceed their herd requirements are now leasing out (at a cost) parts of their parcels to those whose parcels are insufficient to meet their herd requirements. Interestingly, parcel owners have continued with the Maasai practice of splitting their herds among friends and kin. Table 6.3 provides a summary of these arrangements and their frequencies in the individualized areas of Enkaroni, Meto, and Nentanai. This information was obtained from the "livestock ownership and grazing management" section of the interview schedule that sought to establish post-subdivision livestock and pasture management. Not all respondents interviewed agreed to answer all questions, while others, primarily from Nentanai, do not live on their parcels as they have opted to pursue alternate livelihoods in nearing urban centers.

In Enkaroni, only 13 percent managed pastures jointly with others, while up to 87 percent did not and actively enforced their boundaries. The latter category claimed that livestock and land were unequal and that pursuing joint strategies would leave them vulnerable to exploitation by those with larger herds. Those pursuing collective strategies did so as a matter of economic expediency. Not all allocated parcels have the complement of ecological niches necessary for the sustenance of livestock. By reaggregating and collectively rotating livestock between different parts of the joint pasture at different times individuals are attempting to re-create albeit at a smaller scale the complement of pasture and water they find necessary for livestock management. Whether this effort improves livelihoods and sustainability outcomes for the Maasai is yet to be empirically determined; however it seems like best they can do for their production system and their livelihoods under a radically altered property structure. These individuals have also, out of their shared holding, carved out an area (the *olopololi*) for the exclusive pasturing of young animals as well those that are sick and/or old.

About 14 percent admitted to leasing out pastures to those requiring more and who were ready to pay, while about 43 percent of those interviewed in Enkaroni had part of their herd not resident on their parcel, but away having been gifted or loaned out to friends or extended family. Some, who owned parcels in other parts of Kajiado district, had trekked to leave them there.

Meto and Nentanai had fair proportions of individuals engaging in shared arrangements, 55 percent and 44 percent, respectively. Leasing of pastures is not a popular arrangement for individuals in these two areas, while a fair proportion of them have also split their herds between different locations. Just about a third of interviewed individuals in Meto and Nentanai did not have shared arrangements for herding and pasture management. The reasons provided for engagement in these arrangements are very much similar with those given in Enkaroni: collective management as an effort at assuring the viability of the pastoral enterprise; redistribution of herds aimed not only at spreading/minimizing risk but also meeting social obligations; and those unwilling to share ultimately concerned with compensation for unequal land and livestock. It seems that herd redistribution and leasing of pastures might compensate for low levels of joint pasture/herd management such as in Enkaroni, an area with no streams. On the other hand, where individuals are able to reach understandings on joint pasture/herd management and also have access to mechanisms of redistributing herds, leasing arrangements do not seem to be very important, such as in Meto and Nentanai.

Though the content of the leasing and sharing arrangements beg for greater elaboration, these initial findings are distinctive. First, they reinforce arguments provided in chapter four that strongly suggest that individuals' primary motivations for subdividing their collective holdings were defensive. Subdivision was a strategy to secure their land claims against unsanctioned appropriation by non-Maasai and by the Maasai elite.

Second, having secured their land against these threats, individuals are now seeking ways to enhance the viability of their production system. In their attempts to do so in a marginal environment, they are beginning to renegotiate and trade their rights of access, of resource withdrawal and resource management among themselves. Each individual title holder retains the right to dispose/alienate his resource. The rights that had been collapsed and consolidated within a land title is now being split into its component rights, presumably adding some value and some certainty to a precarious system rendered even more precarious by the subdivision of collective holdings.

This is an unfolding phenomenon, the nature of the arrangements, the mechanisms for enforcing them, and the impacts on mobility and livelihoods can be further investigated. Nonetheless, it is instructive to many proponents of privatization whose primary inspiration has been the economic benefits of alienability. Indeed, it begins to question whether the transition from common to private property does represent a more efficient form of rights. It also forcefully suggests that locally evolved property institutions are often designed to meet specific social and environmental objectives.

The next section discusses the mechanisms by which dissatisfied individuals and groups contested (or not) the committees' highly unequal distribution of the former collective holdings among its members.

"Malalamiko ya Beacon": Contesting Outcomes

In Enkaroni, individuals who were outraged with the outcome of subdivision, largely those unhappy with their parcel sizes, organized to challenge the committee's allocations. Included in this group were widows who had not been allocated their deceased husbands' parcels, as well as individuals who, though registered members, found themselves without land. This grouping of about 50 individuals was referred to as the *kikundi cha malalamiko ya beacon* or the beacon complaints group. When this group approached the committee to renegotiate parcel sizes; they were told that "the fingers on one hand are not equal," so how did they expect everyone to get equal sized parcels? The committee was not ready to discuss the complaints of unequal-sized parcels; they, however, allotted those who were legitimate members but had missed parcels altogether.[15]

Faced with the committee's reluctance the complainants' group approached the elders and asked them to appeal to the committee over the unequal allocations. The elders' *barazas* or public meetings were unfruitful, not surprisingly as the elders too had vested interests in the outcome of such deliberations. In any case, they would not have had sufficient powers to overwrite committee decisions. The group of complainants did not seek audience with the local chief and the local politicians, as they too were beneficiaries of the process.

They then took the case forward to government officials in the Department of Land Adjudication and Settlement. The Department of Land Adjudication had adopted an attitude of noninterference in matters of group ranch subdivision. The then District Land Adjudication Officer had on two prior occasions cited that the determination of parcel sizes depended entirely on the group ranch as a whole and that complaints be directed to the committee and not to his office as "all facts related to cases are present in Enkaroni."[16] This position was reiterated by the district officer, Central Division, during a closed meeting on March 23, 1992 between the district officer, group ranch secretary, chairman, treasurer, land adjudication officer, the chief of Matapato (in the neighboring Lorngosua group ranch), and five complainants. At this meeting all other complaints, for example, those to do with boundary disputes and irregular routing of cattle tracks, were solved save for the complaints on "small land parcels," which the district officer referred to the group ranch committee.[17]

Range planners in the then Ministry of Livestock and Water Development, unlike land adjudication officers, were less distanced from members' concerns. Faced with complaints on parcel sizes, they would make evaluations of site viability and, where necessary, urge committee members to reconsider their allocations.

It was the feeling among most individuals that their appeals to government officials went unheeded because of bribery. Though this study is not positioned to evaluate such claims, their validity cannot be discounted. One letter of February 19, 1990 from a widow to the District Commissioner is instructive. Not only does she complain of exceedingly small parcel size (her 15 hectares as compared to committee members' average of 300 acres) but charges that "government officers are corrupt and take bribes."[18] She also accused the committee of corruption and misuse of powers; she personally witnessed a day when the group ranches chairman "commanded an old man to kneel down and worship him, buy some beer for him and slaughter a fat he-goat so that he would give him a reasonable *shamba* [parcel]." Another letter dated March 16, 1990 was addressed to the district officer, land adjudication officer, District Range Officer, and district surveyor, from an individual complainant regarding a "further subdivision of his land" following his complaints to the location chief.[19]

The most compelling evidence of the members' dissatisfaction was a letter dated February 9, 1990 written jointly by an unidentified number of members addressed to the District Range Officer with copies to the District Commissioner, district officer, central division, Member of Parliament Kajiado Central, the location councilor, District Land Adjudication Officer, and the chief of Enkaroni location. In this letter the members cited their complaints, directly quoted, as follows:[20]

1. People in leadership i.e. committee and chiefs have allocated themselves huge chunks of land;

2. committee have failed to subdivide the ranch in an equitable manner;
3. close friends, relatives and in-laws of the committee are given bigger portions of land;
4. committee never ready to listen to members' complaints (heavy-handedness);
5. Chiefs are blocking people from going for further measures (i.e., seeking redress at alternative fora);
6. the chairman is demanding that those with personal differences with him must kneel down and beg for mercy;
7. there is bribing;
8. some members are allowed to participate in committees' private meetings; others are not;
9. some unregistered people have been given ranches by the committee without members' knowledge.

It seems that there may have been a general meeting to discuss the allegations raised above because two years later the District Land Adjudication and Settlement Officer (DLASO) reminded the group ranch chairman that group ranch members had agreed to the "adjustment of land parcels" for a group of eight named individuals in a resolution that was reached at an annual general meeting on August 27, 1990.[21] The records did not hold a reply to this communication, and subsequent events suggest that the resolution was not implemented. The minutes of the August 27, 1990 did not at any point mention the adjustment of parcel sizes. It is, however, clear that that meeting resolved mentioned cases and at the conclusion of the meeting the group members requested the DLASO to send a team of surveyors to the group for the purpose of final subdivision and to erect beacons "now that the complaints were over." The DLASO agreed. It is curious that these minutes failed to capture the consensus on adjusting parcel sizes.

The group of dissatisfied complainants appealed to the court of law as a final recourse to justice. Indications of this groups anxiety that their problem may not be meaningfully addressed within the framework of the group ranch came as early as May 21, 1990 in a letter from an advocate/lawyer who, writing on their behalf to the group ranch chairman, cited that his clients had been allocated small pieces of land while some other group members had been allocated large chunks of land. The lawyer said that his clients would apply to the High Court for an injunction to terminate subdivision unless the chairman confirmed that their clients' complaints would be investigated within 14 days from their receipt of his letter. In a rejoinder, dated May 24, 1990, the group ranch chairman acknowledged that complaints of unequal subdivision had been brought to his attention and to that of administrative authorities but that he and his committee were "unaware of your clients discontent."

The chairman suggested that

1. clients bring specific grievances/complaints to the committee
2. failing 1 above to notify DC through area chiefs and local DO
3. revert to you and to communicate to us on your views

"In the case of a complete collapse of arbitration, the option of the court remains."

From the previous accounts, it is clear that the complainants had followed the channel suggested by the committee and had failed. Six members from this group eventually to the case to the High Court against the group ranch committee as the legal representatives of Enkaroni group ranch.[22] The plaintiffs' demands were as follows:

1. Land be allocated equally among all its members
2. Land subdivision carried out on group ranch be declared null and void
3. Subdivision should be halted until suit is heard
4. that The group committee is subdividing land in a discriminatory manner
5. Plaintiffs had been allocated small land parcels while other members had been allocated large parcels of land.

A ruling by Justice Akilano Akiwumi of the High Court dismissed with cost the plaintiffs' application for an injunction.[23] The justice ruled that

1. The plaintiffs should show, *prima facie*, why it is wrong that they have been allocated smaller land parcels than others. The burden is on the plaintiffs to show that the discriminatory subdivision is for some cogent reason for instance, wrong, unlawful, or contrary to the objections of the defendant. This has not been shown.
2. The annexure to the affidavit of the plaintiff seem to show that it is rather the DLASO, the survey officer and the local chief who might be accused, if anything of unfair distribution of land, if it is so.
3. The plaintiff must show beyond mere allegation that they have been given smaller portions of land than those given to others. What are the actual sizes of the portions of land involved? There is no evidence on this.
4. The plaintiffs have not made out a *prima facie* case with a probability of success. They have shown no reason to support their allegation of discriminatory subdivision and why they should not have been allocated what they were given.
5. Plaintiffs' application for injunction dismissed with cost.

The burden of proof was shifted to the plaintiffs. As ordinary group ranch members, though they were theoretically by law entitled to access their group ranch records at will, they were denied such access. Group ranch records are tightly held by the group ranch committee secretary. The area list in particular is a document that is strictly guarded by the committee up till now, almost 10 years after the completion of subdivision. The area list indicates members' names, their group registration numbers; their parcel sizes, and plot numbers. It is a document endorsed by the DLASO as an authentic representation of an equitable subdivision of group land. The area list is an authoritative document that formally endorses the completion of subdivision; it acknowledges that every group ranch member has been allocated a parcel, that no deserving member was omitted and that there is no disputation. The area list authorizes the Registrar of lands in Kajiado district to begin the issue of formal land titles to individual group ranch members. Following this defeat in the court of law, their final recourse to justice, the group of complainants conceded defeat. They did not reorganize to appeal the High Court ruling. They realized no help was forthcoming. Their advocate advised them to give up the case because "everybody was against them including the Registrar of the High Court who is a member of Enkaroni and whose *shamba* is among the big ones."[24]

During this contestation the committee resorted to its strategy of creating divisions within groupings that challenge the fairness of their decisions. It began by threatening to withdraw already allocated land or to reduce its size. It also quietly increased the parcel sizes of certain selected individuals, presumably the most vocal ones. Where did the committee get the land to achieve this? It is alleged that there were some unclaimed parcels allocated to individuals who had registered, but had not been seen for a long while. Some of the complainants may have benefited from these "floating farms." These selective allocations not only eroded group cohesion but saw a systematic decline in group size from about 50 individuals to about six individuals, which eventually lodged an appeal in the High Court.

In Meto, individuals dissatisfied with their parcel sizes did not team up to confront the committee but rather complained individually. The committee was unresponsive and argued that because many people were complaining about their parcel sizes, nothing could be done about it. Some individuals chose not to register their dissatisfaction because they found others with even smaller parcels and felt they were better off as they were. Those who had the courage to confront the committee were threatened that their parcels would be taken and given to other more interested parties, or their parcels would be further reduced. One individual was told that he would be taken to jail in Nakuru, a town more than 300 kilometers away.

Others were asked to identify whose land would be reduced in order to cater for the increase in their parcels. Still others were told that parcel sizes could not be equal as the attributes of land vary from one place to another. When asked why he did not pursue his complaint about having been allocated a small parcel on a hilly area where he can barely cultivate, one Ilkiseyia man said that he was not financially well-off to pursue the matter and just accepted what was allocated to him. Some individuals were absent from the group ranch, and many were scattered over the group ranch, while others had been told to wait for the surveyor who would come with a "light" to equalize the parcels! Meto group ranch is located adjacent to Ilpartimaru and Lorng'osua group ranches. Both these group ranches began their subdivision long before Meto; however, long-standing conflicts have prevented the subdivision from proceeding to more advanced levels. The Meto group ranch committee reminded group ranch members that their raising issues may derail subdivision to the extent it has in their neighboring group ranches. Thus organizing to contest committee decisions was a big challenge in Meto.

In Nentanai, individuals did not contest their committees' unequal allocation. Nentanai is also a neighbor to Ilpartimaru group ranch, and individuals here claimed that they learnt from their neighbors how expensive and destructive it was to derail the process of subdivision. Nentanai is an interesting case because during the course of my fieldwork I found that many residents of Ilpartimaru were residing with relatives and friends in Nentanai as a way of escaping the escalating conflict in their own group ranch. In any case, even if discontented individuals wanted to organize, it would have been challenging. Many of those affected were very poor and did not even reside in the group ranch itself but in nearby urban areas, as well as Nairobi, where they were pursuing alternative livelihoods.

Conclusion

Subdividing a total of about 90,000 hectares of variously endowed group ranch land between about 1,400 registered members by about 40–80 committee members of the respective group ranches of Enkaroni, Meto, Nentanai, and Torosei is difficult. The committee faced serious challenges such as the terrain, members' unwillingness to move when relocated, boundary disputes, uprooting of beacons, and difficulties in the payment of surveyor's fees.

The committee backtracked on a general members' resolution that all land parcels be equalized among members except for those families with many unregistered young men, or in areas where resource attributes compromised productivity. When the exercise was completed, parcels were found to be unequal, with more than 60 percent of registered members having holdings substantially smaller than the average. Much of this land was concentrated in the hands of committee members, their friends, relatives, and the wealthy herders. Individuals also did not get the locations of their choice; many were relocated to remote areas. In addition to the unequal parcel sizes and locations, there were complaints over poor planning of roads and public routes. In Meto, for example, there were complaints that shorter routes to water points were blocked and instead allocated to the committee, thus making these routes longer.

The committee also exchanged the parcels of those who had paid clearance fees and who had been shown their parcels, but due to financial constraints had not yet claimed their land titles, with those who were/are able to pay the title fees. All individuals were required to pay a uniform title fee regardless of parcel size and land attributes, yet the land registry at Kajiado ordinarily assesses differential title fees depending on parcel size and land potential. Nothing has been done to solve these cases; they are pending.

That subdivision resulted in parcels of unequal size, the distribution of which was based on kinship and friendship ties as well as wealth and status, is hardly surprising. Similar processes in different parts of the world point to similar outcomes. Group members dissatisfied with this outcome contested the decision both via local means of arbitration, such as through the council of elders, via government administration, and via the adversarial courts of law. They did not win. Others, fearing victimization by a vengeful committee, did not contest the outcomes. Still others due to a lack of resources or due to being widely dispersed in different areas simply could not organize an effective challenge.

The state through both its administrative arm under the office of the District Commissioner and its development-related departments were important players in this process. While the administration was called in as an arbiter to resolve parcel imbalances, the lands and livestock departments were mandated with advising group ranches in the method and conduct of subdivision. The potential role that both could have played in the subdivision was subdued by the Group (Land Representatives) Act, whose ambiguity and silence over the conduct of subdivision resulted in tremendous power reverting to the committee. Though this Act contains a clause that allows for the dissolution of group ranches, it does not articulate obligations and procedures required for the dissolution of the group ranches. It however reiterates the group ranch committees' powers by requiring that the committee continue to act in their capacity up until the time when *all* titles have been collected by their respective owners, at which they and the group ranch would be formally dissolved.

Thus the "how" part of subdivision was absent, leaving extensive discretion to the committee. To reiterate, the committee took advantage of this fundamental flaw and filled the gaps in the law with rules that benefited themselves, their families, and the wealthy. They unilaterally determined the sizes of land parcels, where to locate individuals after subdivision, and most importantly, ensured their role as signatories to the emerging land titles. The failure of the Land Control Board to enforce accountability assisted the committee achieve its end, and it in turn raises questions of its own transparency and accountability. The same applies to the judiciary. Thus the committee had legal recognition and state sponsorship. Not only did the committee have direct access to the bureaucracy, but they also had a privileged knowledge and understanding of the process, a process that is unprecedented in Maasai history. Added to this, and as we saw earlier, the committee's influence and authority also derived legitimacy from traditional customary institutions.

What can we make of this process of subdivision in the group ranches that were studied? To be sure, theoretical expectations were lived out by empirical experiences. Concern over distribution provided the impetus for institutional change. This concern saw members agreeing on an equal share allocation mechanism. Uncharacteristically, those likely to be most disadvantaged by the proposed assignment, the wealthy herd owners, were silent and did block or reverse it. Indeed, they appeared to endorse the equal allocation formula. This is significant and seemingly inconsistent with theoretical expectation. However, the outcome of subdivision favored these wealthy herders as they received larger parcels than most others. They used their influence to negotiate in a potentially disadvantageous situation. The committee subverted the agreed-upon formula and instead implemented one that preserved status quo relations. Side payments did occur.

However, this did not end the conflict over distribution as a new set of individuals dissatisfied with the wealth distribution emerged. The committee, using their authority and power, both state and traditional, intimidated some individuals into submitting and accepting the undesirable allocation under the new property rights allocation. Their threats of withdrawing parcels from complainers and redistributing to other interested parties were indeed credible, and some individuals from Meto and Nentanai did not organize to further challenge the committees' allocation. Some were frightened, others just grateful that they received parcels in the light of possibility of missing out, yet others were too scattered or too poor as in Nentanai to offer a forceful challenge. All these individuals accepted the outcome. But in Enkaroni, some dissatisfied individuals contested the committee's decisions. But they lost at the level of the courts and eventually gave up. The committee thus was able to use the state to induce compliance with the new institution.

Power asymmetries between the group ranch members and the committee resulted in the suppression and/or in the quashing of conflict. The committee effectively resolved conflict over property rights assignments either by credibly committing to pursue their threats by constraining group members from contesting their solution or by invoking the coercive power of the state, which forced individuals to comply with the new property assignment. Thus transformation is both about bargaining and negotiating among societal actors as well as the use of the state's coercive power to terminate conflict. The state is an active participant in these negotiations. It is analytically incomplete to leave out the state.

Power asymmetries among societal actors can serve to resolve conflict only so far as the so-called weaker parties are unable to or choose not to organize a challenge. Where societal actors are able to systematically organize and sustain contestation, power asymmetries among bargaining parties do not seem able to resolve conflicts, and consequently the state and its instruments are called into play.

The question of why mechanisms that would have achieved some control over equity in the distribution of resources at an earlier juncture did not have their intended impact merits further discussion. It seems to extend beyond the notion of committee power and control to touch on issues of accountability that have been alluded to earlier in this section. Many group ranch members who were not "well connected," drawing upon the prior reputation of the committee, presumed that the committee would be fair in the allocations. They were wrong. Traditional constraints did not work. Instead, the committee avoided an equal distribution and secretly gave more resources to the wealthy who were satisfied with the results and did not organize to block institutional change. Because the whole process was embedded in a corrupt administrative regime, as we have seen in this and previous chapters, the committee was sure of getting away with such an allocation. After all this was an unprecedented, onetime decision. Cultural constraints were severely undermined by the combination of corruption, of top-down external decision making, of secrecy, and of one-off decision making. Quite clearly, simply moving decisions from the center to the periphery in a system that has lost accountability and the capabilities of earlier institutions does not necessarily improve equity or efficiency.

Scholars over the past decade or so have expressed concern over the concentration of land in Africa. Much debate continues to focus on whether or not concentration is happening (Berry, 2002, 1988) or on advocating research on class formation as an inevitable end point to land concentration (Peters, 2002). This study demonstrates one out of the many diverse ways in which land concentration may occur in African pastoral communities. It cautions that decentralized land reforms, which seem to be on the rise in certain parts of Africa, may not necessarily achieve their intentions of improving efficiency and equity.

Chapter Seven

The Subdivided Group Ranch: Exploring Ecological Implications

Introduction

This chapter explores the ecological implications of transforming property rights regimes from collective holdings to private, individually held parcels as has happened in the four group ranches in this study. The specific question that it addresses is whether these different land use and management regimes (i.e., reaggregation versus non-reaggregated) significantly affect vegetation cover within the study areas, after the influence of dominant environmental factors has been accounted for. The reasons why herders adopt the diverse land use and management arrangements/strategies that they do have been provided in the previous chapter.

Privatizing land resources in highly variable semiarid or arid areas may threaten the integrity of ecological systems. Empirical studies in different parts of the world indicate that a decline in the structure of vegetation resources, such as species composition, abundance, and diversity, occurs when communal resources in semiarid grassland areas are increasingly privatized (Dahlberg, 2000; Sneath, 1998; Harry et al., 1996; Li et al., 1993; Sheehy, 1993; Tserendash and Erdenbataar, 1993; de Carvalho, 1974; Odell, 1981). Thus the characteristics of the resources being privatized do seem to matter.

Though understanding of long-term ecological processes in highly variable arid and semiarid areas is at best incomplete, extensive pastoralism practiced for centuries by communities residing in such areas are instructive to our quest for defining appropriate tenure regimes under such environmental conditions. Pastoralism and the mobility of pastoral herds often prove to be a rational and sustainable system for exploiting rangeland plant resources (Coughenour, 1991).

The initial intent of this part of the study was to investigate ecological differences between group ranches that had been subdivided and individualized and those that had not. But as discussed in chapter three, these categories hardly exist because most group ranches in Kajiado district are at different points of the transition toward complete individualization. In these individualized areas, some individuals are reaggregating their parcels on the basis of kinship and friendship to create larger management units, while others are actively enforcing their individual ownership. The sizes of these individual parcels and the densities of livestock vary. These different management strategies formed the basis for stratifying vegetation and soil sampling within this study.

Table 3.5 in chapter three presented how vegetation and soil samples were obtained from five different management regimes that included (1) reaggregated parcels; (2) large parcels supporting large livestock herds; (3) large parcels supporting few herds; (4) small parcels supporting large herds; and (5) small parcels supporting small livestock herds.

The determinants of savannah ecology have been widely documented (see chapter one). The availability of water and soil nutrients is a primary determinant of vegetation composition and structure, while grazing and fire are important modifiers of these base effects. In this scheme of determinants, however, the role of previous history is crucial. Past land use may obfuscate the effects of the biophysical environment as well as current use. Nonetheless, obtaining samples from sites that are in close proximity and that have similar land use histories should minimize the role of history. The four group ranches from which samples were drawn share similar environmental conditions as well as similar histories of pastoral land use. Vegetation species and abundance, rainfall amounts, soil nutrient levels, soil depth, and slope steepness were recorded from a series of plots located in each of the five management categories.

This chapter explores the influence of different management regimes on vegetation cover and distribution in the subdivided group ranches using Canonical Correspondence Analysis (CCA) while taking into account the primary biophysical factors of precipitation, soil nutrients, and slope steepness. CCA is an important tool used by community ecologists for the analysis of principal relationships between plant species and environmental variables. Using multiple linear regression it constructs linear combinations of environmental variables along which the distribution of species is maximally separated (ter Braak, 1995, 1994, 1986; Hill, 1991; Palmer, 1993). Like multiple regression, it can accommodate nominal environmental variables by defining dummy variables. Unlike multiple regression, it performs well with skewed species distributions, is not sensitive to high noise levels in the data, and to high correlations among explanatory variables. All data were standardized by transforming original values to their logarithms in order to become scale-independent and to make the different units of measurement comparable (Legendre and Legendre, 1998; Jongman et al., 1995).

The following hypotheses were investigated:

1. Management arrangements that involve the reaggregation of parcels after subdivision will have higher plant cover (trees, shrubs, and grasses) than strictly individualized arrangements because grazing pressure will be less concentrated/diffused over wider areas. Species composition here will tend toward more favorable/desired plants such as valued perennial grasses or less weedy shrubs.
2. For individualized arrangements, both large and small parcels, plant cover will be generally higher (and composition more favorable) where livestock numbers are less.
3. Smaller parcels that have larger livestock numbers will have the lowest plant cover and have the least favored species composition.

Results of Soil Chemical and Physical Analysis

Tables 7.1 and 7.2 provide a summary of the soil nutrient concentrations, pH, texture, and slope steepness across the five management regimes. Soil samples were taken at two depths, 0–10 centimeters and 10–20 centimeters, each of which was analyzed separately. In the Canonical Correspondence Analysis, readings from the 0–10 centimeters level were used for herbaceous and grassy species, while the 10–20 centimeters level was used for the shrubby and tree species.

Tables 7.1 and 7.2 show that the modal values for each soil factor, including slope steepness, is not very variable across the different management types. There is also not much variation between the two soil depths. Although there is some measure of local variation at some sites, given the differences between maximum and minimum values, the soils in the study area can generally be characterized as similar.

Management Arrangements–Vegetation-Environment Relationships

Herbaceous and Grass Component

Table 7.3 presents the CCAs multiple regression results, which represent a regression of plots in species space against the environmental variables. The canonical coefficients, which represent the unique contribution of individual

Table 7.1 Soil Characteristics for the Five Management Types, 0–10 Centimeters Depth

0–10 Centimeters Depth	Soil pH	Nitrogen (%)	Organic Carbon (%)	Phosphorus ppm (M)	Potassium me(%)	Calcium me(%)	Magnesium me(%)	Manganese me(%)	Sodium me(%)	Slope (%)	Texture
Communal											
Maximum	7.5	0.31	2.63	320	3.56	28.4	7.25	0.78	2	42	
Minimum	5.3	0.16	1.39	100	1.28	6.6	0.35	0.35	0.58	4	
Mode	5.5	0.16	1.39	100	1.28	7	0.35	0.58	0.74	4	Sandy clay loam
Large-many											
Maximum	6.9	0.3	1.98	308	1.94	11.6	5.25	1.04	1.04	45	
Minimum	4.5	0.07	0.52	22	0.41	0.6	1.1	0.28	0.2	4	
Mode	6.2	0.1	1.09	60	0.64	6	3.1	0.38	0.44	9	Loamy sand
Large-few											
Minimum	4.8	0.08	0.1	10	0.32	2.6	0.85	0.28	0.25	1	
Maximum	7.4	0.35	2.35	272	2.64	30.4	6.65	0.81	1.72	4	
Mode	5.6	0.18	1.5	58	1.42	6.8	3.4	0.45	0.62	4	Sandy clay loam
Small-many											
Maximum	7.7	0.34	2.34	272	1.88	30	5.15	0.76	1.16	8	
Minimum	4.9	0.1	0.88	17	0.44	1.5	1.35	0.17	0.28	1	
Mode	6.1	0.13	1.61	44	1.08	10.8	3.45	0.56	0.38	6	Sandy clay loam
Small-few											
Maximum	8.1	0.36	2.39	308	2.44	19.6	6.35	0.89	1.34	12	
Minimum	5	0.07	0.02	0	0.1	4	0.5	0.03	0.46	1	
Mode	5.8	0.24	1.08	44	1.17	7	4.45	0.45	0.88	1	Sandy clay loam
						1					

Note: Ppm = parts per million; me = milli electron volts.

Source: Own field work.

Table 7.2 Soil Characteristics for the Five Management Types, 10–20 Centimeters Depth

0–20 Centimeter Depth	Soil pH	Nitrogen (%)	Organic Carbon (%)	Phosphorus ppm (M)	Potassium me(%)	Calcium me(%)	Magnesium me(%)	Manganese me(%)	Sodium me(%)	Slope (%)	Texture
Communal											
Maximum	7.4	0.38	1.92	330	3.76	30	6.85	0.74	1.62	42	
Minimum	4.7	0.08	0.69	10	0.28	0.4	0.15	0.12	0.18	1	
Mode	6.1	0.13	1.18	273	2.02	11	0.4	0.43	0.99	4	Sandy clay Loam
Large-many											
Maximum	6.7	0.16	1.34	286	1.34	10.2	4.45	0.63	0.88	45	
Minimum	4.7	0.05	0.29	25	0.25	0.4	1.25	0.25	0.14	4	
Mode	6.2	0.09	0.72	179	0.54	0.65	2.35	0.38	0.46	9	Sandy loam
Large-few											
Minimum	7.2	0.3	2.92	238	2.52	37.6	7	0.85	1.9	4	
Maximum	5.1	0.07	0.6	5	0.14	3	0.84	0.12	0.22	1	
Mode	7.2	0.3	2.92	238	2.52	37.6	7	0.85	1.9	4	Sandy loam
Small-many											
Maximum	7.7	0.27	1.69	282	1.46	34.8	5.85	0.71	1.08	8	
Minimum	4.4	0.07	0.63	10	0.24	3	1.65	0.15	0.2	1	
Mode	6.2	0.1	1.53	35	0.55	9.6	3.9	0.25	0.3	6	Sandy clay Loam
Small-few											
Maximum	8	0.32	2.4	320	2.56	17.2	6.85	0.87	1.64	12	
Minimum	4.9	0.05	0.44	0	0.16	4	0.67	0.03	0.04	1	
Mode	6	0.15	1.73	17	0.88	11.2	3.4	0.43	0.98	1	Sandy clay Loam

Source: Own field work.

Table 7.3 Regression of Plots in Species Space on Environment for Herbaceous and Grass Species

Variable	Standardized Canonical Coefficients		
	Axis 1	*Axis 2*	*Axis 3*
pH	0.086	0.379	0.345
Nitrogen	0.023	0.063	0.019
Carbon	−0.008	−0.020	−0.105
Phosphorus	−0.007	−0.054	−0.050
Potassium	0.011	0.025	0.141
Calcium	−0.044	−0.141	0.018
Magnesium	−0.078	−0.299	−0.097
Manganese	0.013	0.030	−0.045
Sodium	−0.028	−0.146	**−0.533**
Slope	−0.031	−0.151	−0.298
SL-SCL (T)	−0.009	−0.054	0.168
Sa-Loam (T)	−0.018	−0.111	−0.141
Sa-Clay (T)	−0.003	−0.028	−0.054
Sand (T)	0.016	0.061	0.030
Loamy-Sa (T)	−0.020	−0.144	−0.345
Loam (T)	**0.951**	0.300	−0.090
Cla-Loam (T)	−0.018	−0.094	−0.042
CCL (T)	0.003	−0.009	−0.086
Clay (T)	−0.009	−0.055	0.063
Small-few (M)	−0.015	−0.035	−0.221
Small-many (M)	−0.011	−0.082	−0.506
Large-few (M)	0.002	−0.016	−0.489
Large-many (M)	0.022	0.108	−0.130
Rain	−0.142	**−0.417**	1.129
Eigen values	.629	.589	.363
Significance	.0110	.0010	.0030

Note: Figures in bold denote highest canonical coefficients in each axis. M = Management Type; T = Soil texture; SL-SCL = Silt Loam-Silty Clay Loam; Sa-Loam = Sandy Loam; Sa-Clay = Sandy Clay; Loamy-Sa = Loamy Sand; Cla-Loam = Clay Loam.

Source: Own field work.

environmental variables to the regression solution, indicate the following:

1. Axis 1, with the highest canonical coefficient of 0.951, is the dominant factor. It represents a soil texture gradient in which loam texture is an important determinant of herbaceous/grass species cover.
2. Axis 2, with a coefficient of −0.417, is predominantly a rainfall gradient, with declining plant cover as rainfall increases;
3. Axis 3 is a soil nutrient gradient (coefficient of −0.533), in which increasing sodium concentration constrains the cover of herbaceous plants. This axis also seems to demonstrate a small effect of management regime on herb/grass species cover, with the *small-many* and *large-few*

management categories demonstrating the most negative effect on plant cover and the *large-many*, the least negative effect. All coefficients are relative to reaggregated/communal, which is the base category.

Shrubby Species

Results of the CCA multiple regression (table 7.4) reveal that the first axis defines a rainfall effect in which shrub cover values decline with increasing rainfall. The second axis defines a management effect that suggests a decline in shrubby species cover with respect to management type. In this solution, the *small-few* category has the most negative effect on shrub species cover,

Table 7.4 Regression of Plots in Species Space on Environment for Shrubby Species

Variable	Standardized Canonical Coefficients		
	Axis 1	Axis 2	Axis 3
pH	−0.066	0.371	0.054
Nitrogen	0.124	0.081	−0.147
Carbon	−0.054	−0.041	0.119
Phosphorus	−0.109	0.140	**0.798**
Potassium	−0.127	0.195	−0.251
Calcium	−0.029	−0.092	−0.392
Magnesium	−0.060	0.267	0.004
Manganese	−0.027	−0.104	−0.431
Sodium	0.152	−0.405	−0.238
Slope	−0.093	0.430	−0.185
SL-SCL (T)	−0.016	−0.003	−0.070
Sand (T)	0.010	0.004	0.088
Loamy-Sa (T)	0.099	−0.038	−0.280
Sa-Loam (T)	−0.056	0.209	−0.338
Cla-Loam (T)	0.002	0.035	−0.176
Sa-Clay (T)	−0.165	0.138	−0.197
Clay (T)	−0.102	0.181	0.171
Small-few (M)	0.450	**−0.678**	0.123
Small-many (M)	0.395	−0.541	0.040
Large-few (M)	0.549	−0.362	0.091
Large-many (M)	0.202	−0.443	0.151
Rain	**−0.845**	−0.435	0.136
Eigen values	.362	.172	.127
Significance	.0100	.0100	.0100

Note: Figures in bold denote highest canonical coefficients in each axis. M = Management Type; T = Soil texture; SL-SCL = Silt Loam-Silty Clay Loam; Loamy-Sa = Loamy Sand; Sa-Loam = Sandy Loam; Cla-Loam = Clay Loam; Sa-Clay = Sandy Clay.

Source: Own field work.

followed by the *small-many* category. *Large-few* category is found to have the least negative effect and suggests a higher percentage cover of shrubby species. The third axis defines a soil nutrient gradient that is characterized by an increasing shrub cover as soil phosphorous concentrations increase.

The Tree Species

Canonical coefficients show that rainfall and soil nutrients (i.e., sodium and potassium) are principal factors affecting tree species cover (see table 7.5). Axis 3 seems to demonstrate a small management effect, which is characterized by a negative effect on tree cover consistently across all management regimes. These coefficients are larger than those for shrub and herb/grass species. The third axis suggests some management effect that is characterized by a consistently high and negative effect on tree cover. *Large-few* and

Table 7.5 Regression of Plots in Tree Species Space on Environment

Variable	Standardized Canonical Coefficients		
	Axis 1	*Axis 2*	*Axis 3*
pH	0.053	0.200	0.049
Nitrogen	−0.228	0.345	−0.117
Carbon	0.076	−0.005	−0.010
Phosphorus	0.283	0.243	0.087
Potassium	0.199	**−0.649**	0.746
Calcium	−0.083	−0.081	−0.067
Magnesium	0.288	−0.584	0.454
Manganese	0.005	0.016	−0.050
Sodium	−0.285	0.477	**−0.766**
Slope	0.135	0.046	−0.194
SL-SCL (T)	−0.027	−0.012	−0.023
Sand (T)	−0.080	0.106	0.097
Loamy-sa (T)	−0.149	−0.200	−0.073
San-loam (T)	0.016	0.045	0.087
Cla-loam (T)	0.022	−0.040	0.171
San-clay (T)	0.057	0.447	0.046
Clay (T)	−0.092	0.258	0.028
Small-few (M)	−0.278	−0.292	−0.505
Small-many (M)	−0.384	0.101	−0.411
Large-few (M)	−0.446	−0.327	−0.588
Large-many (M)	−0.196	0.283	−0.573
Rain	**0.822**	−0.066	−0.373
Eigen values	.376	.211	.206
Significance	.0100	.0100	.0100

Note: Figures in bold denote highest canonical coefficients in each axis. M = Management Type; T = Soil texture; SL-SCL = Silt Loam-Silty Clay Loam; Loamy-Sa = Loamy Sand; San-Loam = Sandy Loam; Cla-Loam = Clay Loam; San-Clay = Sandy Clay.

Source: Own field work.

Table 7.6 Summary of CCA Results

	Most Negative Effect on Cover	*Least Negative Effect on Cover*
Herbaceous	Small-many (−.506) Large-few (−.489)	Large-many (−.130)
Shrubs	Small-few (−.678) Small-many (−.541)	Large-few (−.362)
Trees	Large-few (−.588) Large-many (−.573)	Small-many (−.411)

large-many categories have the greatest negative effects and *small-many* the least negative effect. This result reverses the trend observed for herbaceous and shrubby species.

The data presented above can be summarized in table 7.6.

The points to note are that these coefficients are relative to the reaggregated/communal category (the base category) and that none of the canonical coefficients for any of the management regimes is positive.

In order to better understand the relationship between vegetation cover and management regimes, a summary of the 10 highest scoring plant species and their cover values across each of the management regimes for the herbaceous/grassy layer, shrubby and tree layers was calculated. Tables 7.7, 7.8, and 7.9 show the total cover percentages for the highest-ranking 10 species in the herbaceous, shrubby, and tree layers, respectively. These values were derived by aggregating each species cover value across all the plots in which it appeared. These aggregated values were then divided by the total area covered by all the plots sampled for each category. The result was then multiplied by 100 to get a percentage. This then became the cover percentage for each species.

The tables show that the species mix across the herbaceous/grassy, shrubby, and tree layers is typical of semiarid vegetation and that cover percentages for each layer is in general relatively low. The dominant grasses (table 7.7), found consistently in all the five management types such as *Themeda triandra, Digitaria macroblephara, Pennisetum masaicum, Pennisetum mezianum,* and *Cynodon plectostachyus* are all perennial grasses that form valuable grazing. Some annual grasses such as *Aristida keniensis* and *Eragrostis aethiopica,* each with low grazing value, are also among the dominant grasses. These two annuals are commonly found on degraded, disturbed soils.

Themeda triandra, Digitaria macroblephara, and *Pennisetum masaicum,* all valuable perennials, show consistently higher cover values in the Communal management type and lowest values in the *small-many* management type. The *large-many* category also has high cover values for these perennial grass species.

Table 7.7 Herb and Grass Species Cover Percentages (The Herbaceous Layer)

Species Name	Communal, 58 Plots	Large-Many, 45 Plots	Large-Few, 46 Plots	Small-Many, 42 Plots	Small-Few, 44 Plots	Species Notes
Themeda triandra	16.81034	9.222222	4.56	1.41	4.8	Perennial grass, often dominant on open grassland/ bushland; valuable grazing.
Digitaria macroblephara	14.05172	8.289	3.845	2.03	2.23	Perennial found in open deciduous bushland, often with *Acacia* on black clayey soils.
Pennisetum masaicum	13.62069	—	5.3	2.67	3.48	Perennial, open or bushed grassland often on seasonally clogged clayey soil, reasonably good grazing.
Cynodon plectostachyus	13.10345	12.15556	—	2.2	61.44	Perennial, valuable grazing.
Eragrostis caespitosa	7.103448	14.11111	5.225	3.25	2	Perennial, found in overgrazed areas.
Pennisetum mezianum	5.896552	—	2.1	2.8	4.75	Perennial, palatable when young, very woody when mature.
Eragrostis aspera	3.534483	9.022222	—	—	—	Annual, disturbed places and old cultivated land, often on poor soils, average forage value.
Microchloa Kunthii	3.293103	—	—	—	—	Perennial, open or bushed grassland, shallow soils with underlying rock, of no grazing value.

Continued

Table 7.7 Continued

Species Name	Communal, 58 Plots	Large-Many, 45 Plots	Large-Few, 46 Plots	Small-Many, 42 Plots	Small-Few, 44 Plots	Species Notes
Solanum incanum	2.448276	—	—	—	1.18	Abundantly found in waste grounds.
Gutenbergia cordifolia	?	—	—	1.7	—	Annual herb found on rocky, eroded grassland often on shallow soils.
Barleria sp.	—	5.222222	2.25	2.82	—	Spiny herb.
Eragrostis aethiopica	—	4.111111	3.16	3.37	1.97	Annual grass common on disturbed ground, weed on poor soils, little grazing value.
Enkaroni Shrub1	—	3.377778	—	—	—	
Aristida keniensis	—	3.355556	1.66	1.42	2.9	Annual grass found on dry, eroded soils in bushland and waste places; grazed when young.
Ocimum gratissimum	—	3.355556	—	—	—	Shrub common in disturbed bushland.
Chloris virgata	—	—	3.63	—	—	Annual grass common in overgrazed grasslands and disturbed habitats; valuable grazing.
Nentanai grass 4	—	—	1.65	—	1.75	

Source: Own field work.

Cynodon plectostachyus, a valuable perennial, has highest cover values in the *small-few* management type and lowest values in the *small-many* category.

Table 7.8 showing cover values for the shrubby layer indicates that *Solanum incanum* is a local dominant across all the management regimes. Highest cover values for *Solanum incanum* are found in the *large-few* and *small-many* categories, while its lowest cover values occur in the communal and *large-many* categories. *Solanum incanum* is a weedy, undesirable shrub species in grasslands. *Aspilia mossambicensis* also reaches fairly high cover values in most of the categories.

In the tree layer (table 7.9) the communal management type has consistently higher tree cover values for most species, across the five management regimes.

Table 7.8 Shrub Species Percentage Cover Values (The Shrub Layer)

Species Name	Communal, 59 Plots	Large-Many, 45 Plots	Large-Few, 45 Plots	Small-Many, 42 Plots	Small-Few, 45 Plots	Species Notes
Solanum incanum	2.371216102	5.772791	18.35063	14.81897	4.170189	Shrubby species; weed in grassland; common in wasteland and secondary vegetation.
Acacia mellifera	1.209255932	—	6.588764	—	—	Found in dry bushlands or woodlands often as a dominant.
Enkaroni shrub 1	1.002744068	2.371352	—	—	—	
Ocimum bacillicum	1.001132203	3.452791	—	1.917724	1.75851	A branching annual, sometimes woody at base common in disturbed dry country.
Hibiscus aponeurus	0.820423729	2.00371	—	2.216774	1.154296	Short-lived perennial common in dry grasslands.

Species						Notes
Lantana trifolia	0.688500847	—	1.011468	2.407304	0.963999	Common in bushed grasslands.
Aspilia mosambicensis	0.647984322	2.661251	2.559593	2.733383	3.301458	
Hibiscus calyphyllus	0.515482203	—	—	2.934523	1.428836	Bushed grasslands.
Melhania ovata	0.475844492	—	—	—	—	Common in dry grasslands.
Barleria spinosa	0.417467797	—	1.183064	—	—	Spiny herb/shrub.
Acacia brevispica	—	3.851389	—	7.186354	—	Found often on rocky/stony soils.
Lantana camara	—	3.203423	2.464045	14.81897	3.955272	Serious weed in secondary vegetation.
Grewia similis	—	2.402373	—	2.056855	—	Found in bushed grassland.
Ocimum gratissimum	—	1.767956	1.004231	2.105787	—	Annual.
Cordia gharaf	—	—	1.615278	—	—	Found on moister sites.

Continued

Table 7.8 Continued

Species Name	Communal, 59 Plots	Large-Many, 45 Plots	Large-Few, 45 Plots	Small-Many, 42 Plots	Small-Few, 45 Plots	Species Notes
Grewia bicolor	—	—	0.824202	—	0.942746	Found in dry *Acacia* bushland/ grassland, often on rocky sites.
Hoslundia opposita	—	—	0.818527	—	—	Common in disturbed sites, though not in very dry localities.
Dyschoriste thunbergiiflora	—	—	—	—	4.599463	Woody herb or shrub uncommon in dry, rocky country.
Rinus ateriensis	—	—	—	—	1.735417	

Source: Own field work.

Table 7.9 Tree Species Percentage Cover Values (The Tree Layer)

Species Name	Communal, 53 Plots	Large-Many, 45 Plots	Large-Few, 36 Plots	Small-Many, 41 Plots	Small-Few, 39 Plots
Acacia tortilis	0.01804	0.015122	0.565932	0.00637	0.006803
Acacia drepanolobium	0.006233	0.007083	0.05211	0.001689	0.002114
Acacia mellifera	0.005437	0.003567	0.724021	0.006774	—
Balanites aegyptiaca	0.003647	0.001789	0.430096	0.009564	0.010369
Acacia nilotica	0.003517	0.004552	0.133625	0.000394	0.001079
Acacia xanhtophloea	0.002865	—	—	0.003249	0.00062
Commiphora Africana	0.002532	0.014425	0.768736	0.024418	0.006933
Acacia Senegal	0.001826	0.001181	0.685446	0.004169	0.000454
Baeg	0.001343	0.006442	—	0.000442	—
Ol	0.001006	—	—	—	—
Combretum sp.	—	0.000758	—	—	—
Azanza garckeana	—	0.000334	—	—	—
Zanthoxylum chalybeum	—	—	0.220143	—	0.00085
Albizia anthelmitica	—	—	0.05211	0.000251	—
Cordia gharaf	—	—	0.017357	—	—
Lannea Schweinfurthii	—	—	—	—	0.000905
Pappea capensis	—	—	—	—	0.000629

Source: Own field work.

Acacia tortilis is the most dominant species, with higher cover values across the different management types.

Discussion

Only a modest portion of variability in species cover can be explained by the selected environmental variables and by management regime: 8.6 percent of variance in herbaceous cover, 6.7 percent in shrubby cover, and 8.0 percent in tree cover. The rather low proportion of total variance explained is thought not to be a concern as the goal is not to explain 100 percent (Ter Braak, 1987). Ohman and Spies (1998) suggest that low proportions may be associated with large numbers of plots sampled and high numbers of species recorded. The large number of plots mean that more rare species are encountered, which have restricted spatial ranges, narrow habitat specificity, or small, nondominant population sizes. They act to increase the total variation in the species-by-plot data matrix.

This study set out to answer the following question: how do herders' post-subdivision strategies affect resource sustainability (proxied by plant cover and species)? The expectations were as follows: higher plant cover and more favored species in reaggregated/communal parcels as compared to other arrangements; higher plant cover and more favored species in large parcels with less grazing pressure; small parcels will have low plant cover and less-favored species.

This expectation was only partially fulfilled, and results were mixed as follows:

1. There is generally some negative effect of management regimes on plant species cover and composition. All four management arrangements, relative to reaggregated arrangements, are associated with lower plant cover, lower cover of favorable species, and higher incidence of unfavored species.
2. Management regime has in general a negative effect on tree cover.
3. In the case of herb/grass species, the *small-many* management category can be associated with the largest negative effect on cover, while the *small-few* with a low negative effect.
4. With regard to shrubby species, *small-few* and *small-many* categories have the most negative effect on cover.
5. For trees, the negative effect on cover is high and consistent across all arrangements. However, the effect is highest for large categories and lowest for the *small-many* category. This is a reversal of the trend observed for herbaceous and shrubby species.

In addition, valuable perennial grass species show consistently higher cover values in the reaggregated arrangement. Less desirable shrubby weeds such as *Solanum incanum* has lower cover in the reaggregated but highest cover in the *small-many*. *Lantana camara*, another shrubby weed, also has highest value in the *small-many* category. Reaggregated management regimes had consistently higher cover values for the perennial grasses. This observation tallies with our hypothesis that the reaggregation of parcels under this arrangement results in a less concentration of livestock within one place and thus decreases the grazing intensity. Consequently, cover values would be higher here than in the other regimes where livestock are more concentrated within smaller spaces.

These outcomes are generally within expectation. However, there are some complications: the *large-few* and *small-few* categories have, unexpectedly, the most negative effect on herbaceous and shrubby cover, respectively, while *large-many* has the least negative effect on the herbaceous. The study suggests that the expected relationship may be complicated further by herders' livestock distribution strategies, over and above parcel reaggregation. A closer examination of herding practices uncovers several crucial issues. First, many herders, particularly those with large livestock holdings, tend to not keep all their herds on their parcel of land. Not all of their livestock are resident on their land at all times. Instead, many tend to split up their herds, redistributing their holdings to other parcels that they own at other locations. This is a measure against the rapid depletion of pasture that would tend to occur if their entire livestock holdings were concentrated in one parcel. Or, in keeping with traditional Maasai norms of reciprocity, they tend to redistribute some of their holdings to their friends/stock associates or to relatives as a way of assisting those who have livestock herds that are inadequate to support their subsistence and to provide animals that recipients may use to rebuild their diminished herds. Of the six owners of parcels that had high stocking densities, and from whose parcels vegetation and soil samples were collected, five did not have their entire livestock holdings resident on their parcels. Some of their livestock were away in different places, having been loaned out to friends or relatives. Similarly, two out of the six owners whose parcels had low stocking densities had some of their livestock away. Table 6.3 in chapter six demonstrates the frequency of herd redistribution strategies commonly used to spread risk in a fragile and uncertain economic and ecological system.

Second, during times of scarcity and drought, almost all individuals cease to enforce and monitor their property boundaries. This practice also draws from traditional Maasai norms that constrains one who has pastures against excluding the stock of a needy herder, which might undermine his survival.

These mechanisms of livestock redistribution temper the potential effects of high stocking densities. These strategies tend to diffuse any distinct differences among livestock holdings that would otherwise be expected to result in variations in plant abundance across variably stocked parcels.

The effect of management regimes on trees merits further discussion. Even though trees are valued for shade and the pods used to feed small ruminants during lean times, there may also be a human harvesting concern with regard to tree cover, in addition to the general low cover imposed by environmental conditions. With group ranch subdivision, there has been an increase in charcoal burning as individuals seek to exploit a resource that was previously restricted. There is great need for studies on human use and tree cover.

Conclusion

This study's attempt at isolating the possible influences of different management strategies on sustainability aspects in the subdivided/individualized group ranches suggests that herders' post-subdivision strategies may matter. Parcel reaggregation is an early strategy that appears to offer promise for ecosystem sustainability as well as for economic sustainability. Reaggregation is an important strategy. It represents herders' attempts to manage or reduce climatic risk and vulnerability in the absence of formal insurance. Reaggregation and herd redistribution may permit herders to access resources that may otherwise have been cut off from them after obtaining individual title. Most importantly, reaggregation of parcels may offer some promise for sustainable land management and use, helping to deflect the seemingly inevitable ecological decline that is associated with the transition to more exclusive property regimes in arid and semiarid environments.

CHAPTER EIGHT
THE TRANSFORMATION OF PROPERTY RIGHTS TO LAND IN KENYA'S MAASAILAND

This book has focused on explaining why (and how) group ranch members in Kajiado district supported the subdivision of their collective landholdings. The puzzle of why property rights change is an ongoing concern for scholars of institutions in general and of economic development more specifically. Yet the quest to better understand and to explain institutional change has emphasized the triggers and outcomes of change at the expense of a more precise explication of the way in which change occurs or considerations of whether such change is reversible. Beyond highlighting the factors pressing toward change and the outcomes of a major change in property rights structure, this study of property rights transformation in Kajiado district illustrates the internal processes of change.

This concluding chapter recaps the study's main findings. It relates these findings to broader empirical settings and attempts to draw lessons for development policy. It also speculates on "the future of the Maasai."

Why Group Ranches Are Individualizing: Summary and Conclusion

The recent history of land relations in Maasailand from colonial times suggests that current processes are embedded within a longer-term process of change (chapter four). The appropriation of better watered areas of Maasailand for the settlement of European farmers/ranchers in the early twentieth century and the relegation of the Maasai to a smaller area of inferior quality were the first in a series of critical events that sowed the seeds of fear of land dispossession among the Maasai. Subsequent appropriations in the mid-twentieth century created national parks and game reserves for wildlife conservation. These protected areas removed more land from Maasai access and control increasing their tenure insecurity.

The creation of massive individualized ranches that were distributed to a few elite Maasai and the encouragement of cultivating groups to settle in Maasai territory to relieve congestion in neighboring areas was part of government policy in the run-up to independence between 1950 and 1963. This resulted in a further push of the Maasai into even more marginal lands and served to harden their resolve to protect their lands. Group ranches created by government in the late 1960s were accepted by ordinary Maasai because they anticipated that this property arrangement would protect them against losing land to non-Maasai and to local Maasai elites who wanted the entire Maasailand individualized in one broad sweep. Between the 1970s and 1980s, trust lands, land held in trust by the local county council on behalf of Maasai customary rights holders, were systematically grabbed, gifted out, or sold. Similarly, in some group ranches not only were management committees carving out large chunks and allocating them as individual ranches to their cronies or just outright selling, but administrators in the Ministry of Lands and Settlement, their spouses and friends, in collusion with the committee, were incorporated into adjudication registers and allocated parcels of land within Maasailand. None of them were Maasai.

Over time, the Maasai slowly but surely lost access and control over much of their land. The historical analysis in chapter four suggests that underlying the continued privatization of Maasailand, up to and including current processes of subdivision, is a defensive strategy. This strategy is designed to secure their political and economic position against other privileged groups, both from within and from outside the community. This argument is not intended to suggest that the Maasai are victims captured by a rigid, unchangeable history but rather to demonstrate the gradual narrowing of the institutional choice set across time.

Group ranch members' motivations for supporting subdivision were decidedly mixed (chapter five). By subdividing their group ranches individuals anticipated to capture the rents accruing from an increasing scarcity value of land, itself the result of a rising population. Individuals also anticipated that land titles acquired following subdivision could be used as collateral to access finances for on-farm development projects. Changes in relative prices are at the core of institutional change. The net gains of transforming property rights seemed to exceed the costs of change, and individuals were willing to invest in transforming property rights.

But the market is not the only force at work driving change. Politics is just as significant. Problems with enforcing internal governance arrangements such as controlling livestock numbers, settlement patterns, and other activities within the group ranch undermined the viability of the group ranch as a collective entity. Difficulties in excluding outsiders from grazing their herds in the group ranch, particularly wealthy individuals from neighboring individual ranches, were also important. These problems of internal governance and of exclusion of nonmembers have their origins in Maasai cultural norms. Decisions on herd management and livestock numbers are made by individuals to whom livestock belong. Strong incentives exist for herd accumulation, including those related to risk management and the fulfillment of social obligations. Similarly, cultural norms of reciprocity resulted in individuals inviting their nonmember friends and relatives to reside with them. The neighboring individual ranchers on their part were a great source of concern for group members. They grazed their extensive herds on group ranch land during the wet season and only retreated to their fenced enclaves during the dry season. They denied group members access to their exclusive pastures at this time. They exploited their friendships with committee members (and with their relatives) to ensure continued access to group ranch resources. By not honoring traditional reciprocal obligations they generated resentment from ordinary group ranch members who would also have wished to have access to individual ranchers' pastures during times of stress.

These problems over inequitable distribution in the appropriation of group ranch resources were particularly intensified by an increasing population and with the periodic occurrence of drought. High governance and exclusion costs under the collective framework made individualization desirable. To many individuals subdivision would help shed the burden of disproportionate and uncompensated costs of the collective enterprise.

The controversial nature of the dynamics of change is seen in the struggles by groups and individuals to either articulate their land claims (the youth—see chapter five) or to redress the skewed allocation of land parcels following subdivision (chapter six). The exclusion of the youth gives expression to the problem of impending land scarcity that also motivated change. Their customary right to land, itself a function of their membership in the community, was subordinated to existing group members' need to maximize the size of their landholdings in the face of subdivision. Community identity and membership ceased to be factors in land claims and were instead replaced by inheritance; the youth were expected to be allocated land by their fathers, absent of outright purchase. Attempts by youth to have this situation addressed at various forums, from elders' councils to the committee, to local and national politicians, and to government administration did not bear fruit. Group ranch members drew upon their discretionary powers provided for in the Land (Group Representatives) Act, to exclude and lock the youth out of the process.

Women were also excluded. Their fate having been sealed during the creation of group ranches in the late 1960s to early 1970s, during which (re)interpretations of customary rules by government administrators and local elders resulted in the registration of male household heads as the only members of the newly formed group ranches. The exclusion of women was formalized at this point. Women subsequently did not organize to challenge their exclusion during the subsequent division of group ranches because they were skeptical that the same elders/men who had designed their exclusion would reverse this decision. Widows were, however, registered upon the death of their husbands, but as we saw in chapters five and six they were not regarded as legitimate decision makers. Instead, their sons and brothers-in-law represented their interests.

Group members who were dissatisfied with the committee's secret reversal of the collectively sanctioned equal allocation formula challenged the distribution of parcels in the new individualized arrangement. They did not succeed. Other discontented individuals did not contest but rather succumbed to threats of dispossession by a powerful and credible committee. Those individuals who contested, like the youth, exploited a variety of institutions, from elders' councils to the court system. The courts, as state agents, thwarted any attempts at redress to force the implementation of the new, individualized property structure.

Control over the process of subdivision lay in the management committee, which is an artifact of government regulation. The committee is empowered by the Land (Group Representatives) Act to take a lead in the management of group ranch affairs but with due consideration of the wishes of the general group ranch membership. Committee leadership was legitimized by periodic elections. In electing these leaders group members drew from local cultural norms that define the attributes of good leadership. The committee was also elected to balance age-set and clan differentiation. It was also elected to ensure representation of the different settlement areas in the group ranch. This representation of diverse interests together with the leaders' good reputation instilled confidence among members that their expectations in subdivision would be met.

The committee on their part acted strategically to secure much of the resource for themselves, their relatives and friends and to the wealthy individuals who were able to influence them. Their ability to do this and to get away with it was a result of prevailing circumstances in the wider socioeconomic and political environment. There were many prior cases of unequal subdivision within the district. Land grabbing was also rife. It was tolerated by local and national politicians and by the district's government administration who often worked in collusion. The contrived "hands-off" approach by the district's Land Control Board and the Land Adjudication Department closed off avenues for the redress of member dissatisfaction. Ultimately, the subdivision exercise by the committee was a one-off exercise that was conducted in secret.

Despite the unequal and highly contested outcome of subdivision, individuals are adopting innovative arrangements to enhance economic viability within the individualized structure. Though some are actively enforcing their individual rights to exclude the rest, others are regrouping with their friends, neighbors, or kin to pursue collective herd/pasture management in their reaggregated parcels. Now confident in the security of their landholding, this latter group allows access to those with whom they have agreed to pursue shared strategies. Others still are leasing out excess pastures to those who have large herds and insufficient grazing. This is a significant post-transitional outcome that exemplifies the "bundled" nature of rights (even of private property rights) and the painstaking search for an arrangement that balances ecology and economy.

Attempts at evaluating the ecological outcomes of these varied arrangements (chapter seven) further reveal the complexity of Maasai adaptive strategies and the nontrivial interaction between ecological systems, property structures, and human use. As expected the biophysical factors of rainfall and soil nutrients are significant determinants of herbaceous, grassy, shrubby, and tree species cover and distribution. The vegetation is typical of that of semiarid, *Acacia* species-dominated bushed grassland. Only a modest proportion of the variation in vegetation cover can be attributed to the effects of management regime and environment. The reaggregated parcels seem to have higher plant cover, higher cover of favorable species, and lower incidence of unfavorable species than the other four management regimes. However, the interaction between management strategy and ecological system is complicated by redistribution of livestock herds, a hallmark of traditional Maasai livestock management systems. This redistribution was also achieved through the trading of rights following subdivision. Though these arrangements may serve to obscure expected outcomes, they are instructive because they reiterate the importance of factoring resource attributes (in particular ecology) into property rights decisions.

Study Findings: Theoretical and Empirical Perspectives

What this study finds is that property rights, like any institutional arrangement, do not stay static when the world around them changes dramatically. A major, though exogenous, change was imposed in the earlier system of property rights among the Maasai. This happened with the first wave of land appropriation in colonial times. The later creation of group ranches themselves *and* the allocation of individual ranches to Maasai elite were important. With these events and some government support for the further subdivision of group ranches, a situation was created where many reasons (which have been outlined) existed for members of the group ranch to support subdivision. Change seems remarkably path-dependent (North, 1990) and choices constrained across time, biased in favor of increased privatization.

The reasons that motivated members to support subdivision closely follow the predictions of property rights scholars such as North (1990); North and Thomas (1973, 1981); and Demsetz (1967) who argue that relative price changes motivate individuals and groups to want to capture benefits as new economic opportunities present themselves. But net gains by themselves are insufficient to explain change. The problem of how assets are distributed among rights holders in the ensuing property rights structure creates conflict among differentiated actors in society as they attempt to secure their claims (Libecap, 1989). This is evident in the conflicts between the excluded youth and the registered members and among group members that were allocated small parcels and the unyielding committee. This allocation was contrary to the equal allocation that had been endorsed by the entire group membership prior to subdivision.

As suggested by Knight (1992), conflict is resolved by credible threats from powerful community actors directed against weaker individuals. The committee was able to threaten those complaining over distribution with actually withdrawing their assets. But in some instances the committee was unable to sufficiently intimidate individuals and some parties organized to contest the inequitable distribution through the judiciary. In this case the court ruled against the plaintiffs and the power of the state was used to coerce the acceptance of those opposed and to see to the implementation of the new property structure. This conforms to Firmin-Sellers's (1996, 1995) arguments that state coercion is crucial in terminating conflict. Indeed, the new structure saw rational individuals, including the losers, "cutting their losses" (predicted as a post-transformational outcome by Firmin-Sellers) and choosing to recontract their bundles of rights to suit their production system. The process of transformation does not necessarily end with the acquisition of titles, especially since it was largely politically motivated.

Prior scholars (see chapter one) working in the higher potential areas of Kajiado district closer to Nairobi with greater ethnic heterogeneity find that the possibility of using land titles as collateral is an important motivator for individuals to support subdivision. In all these instances as well, increasing population provided more reason for individuals to want to subdivide *now*, rather than later. Galaty (1999a, 1999b, 1993) and Ole Simel (1999) demonstrate the insecurities that arise out of committees allocating group ranch land to their cronies. They also begin to demonstrate the controversies involved in subdivision. Thus although majority of prior studies were conducted in parts of Kajiado district having somewhat different conditions than in this study, the processes that triggered and motivated change are remarkably similar. The internal processes of change, though less elaborated, are also similar.

This research outlined in this book builds upon this prior body of knowledge in several important ways. First, by consciously systematizing analysis and by actively engaging a theoretical framework, it transports the significance of the events in Maasailand beyond the context of Kajiado and Kenya. The findings can be used to understand and inform development processes and decisions in broader settings. Second, this research has introduced an ecological perspective, beyond mere speculation, to the process of institutional change. This ecological perspective, though excessively complicated, serves to underscore Maasai commitment to their pastoral livelihoods. Third, by opening a new window into post-transitional behavior among the Maasai it considerably firms up arguments that subdivision is a conscious effort by economic actors to defend their claims to land. It places politics squarely at the basis of economic decision making.

The results presented here are not unique; many other studies in different parts of the world at different times seem to point to similar outcomes. In Mexico, Munoz-Pina et al. (2003) find that rising land scarcities and inequalities in livestock ownership among *ejiditarios* were important in motivating their support for subdivision. Unlike this study the *ejido* study finds that land allocation was based on a lottery system where land was of homogenous quality and allocation avoided altogether where resources were heterogeneous and unpredictable. Unlike this study, subdivision of the *ejidos* was conducted to incorporate the progeny of current *ejiditarios* and not to exclude them.

That the process of land allocation would be captured by the elite in society is not unexpected either. Bates (1989) shows that during land registration in colonial Kenya, educated and administrative elites were allocated larger land units. They understood the colonizer's language and his law. In Botswana, leaseholds were granted to large livestock owners (Thomas et al., 2000; Little, 1999; Peters, 1987); in Rajasthan in India, the land reforms of 1952 resulted in former common lands being transferred to wealthy families (Jodha, 1992, 1987); in Senegal, range privatization advantaged wealthy cattle owners (Thebaud et al., 1995), just as it did in Cameroon (Goheen, 1988).

This research has also demonstrated the unique advantage of investigating the dynamics of change in the real time, from which actors' lived experiences can be better accessed to inform our knowledge of such transformations. In this largely political process of transformation, actors draw upon cultural raw materials in their articulation of change. But this in turn transforms some cultural relations such as between the young and the older and between men and women. Many scholars have noted that a transformation of land tenure systems implies a wider transformation of cultural systems as well (Kanyinga, 2000; Okoth-Ogendo, 1991, 1976; Bates, 1989). But as we have seen in this study, this deeply political character of land institutions is continuously dogged by a very fundamental problem: that of separating land attributes and use from its system of holding. The emergence of new arrangements in the post-subdivision setting seems to point to the futility of this separation. This is a salient issue that will continue to pose significant challenges to public policy.

Implications for Policy

This study has illustrated the sociopolitical context in which property rights emerge. It has also paid close attention to the historical events that shaped current outcomes. The case for placing politics at the center of property rights transformations cannot be overemphasized. Struggles over the division of income and wealth in the new property assignment and the use of power to end conflict over assignments are hallmark features of the process. The exclusion of customary rights holders such as women and youths marks the beginning of property reassignment. What lessons do we draw for the conduct of policy and for the ability to reform policy?

A large number of state-led land tenure reforms are under way in Africa, Asia, and Eastern Europe, and this book suggests that change is strongly influenced by the governance regime in which individuals are embedded. Scholars studying processes of institutional creation and sustainability among local, self-governing communities have shown that the probability of adoption of effective rules is increased where governments provide backup mechanisms for local monitoring, sanctioning, and conflict resolution processes (Eggertsson, 1996; Schlager and Ostrom, 1996; Ostrom, 1990). The individualization of Maasailand strongly suggests that where systems in the wider social and political order are not accountable, it is unlikely that decentralized tenure reforms will be accountable but instead create opportunity for the capture of rents by elite groups in society. Large-scale privatization and formalization can represent an institutionalized excuse for land grabbing. Moreover, when a group is given substantial power to redistribute wealth, they may use that power in unfair or unjust ways. Enforcement of rules and procedures at multiple levels, including state actors, is necessary for equitable tenure reforms.

Private, individual property may not be suitable in all settings, especially where resource productivity is variable due to environmental variability as in most pastoral settings. The attributes of the resource being privatized matters. Because property in many parts of the developing world comprises a bundle of rights with different people holding different rights at different times, full ownership, all the time, over all the land, may not be necessary or even desirable (Meinzen-Dick and Pradhan, 2002; Ostrom, 2001b; Schlager and Ostrom, 1996). This Maasai case illustrates both points quite effectively. Collapsing rights in one individualized title disenfranchises those with customary rights to the same resources and creates conflict over access to heterogeneously distributed resources. Some resources are better managed under common property and some legal recognition of group rights (Runge, 1986).[1] Within groups, individuals' claims can be safeguarded by improving internal governance structures with some support from capable, nonpredatory external agents. These lessons are of direct relevance to Mongolia, where spontaneous enclosure of the range is practically underway, after a broader-scale shift from socialist to private enterprise (Fratkin and Mearns, 2003), and where there's increasing interest by diverse actors in the international development community.

Finally, the pessimism among commentators who have discussed "the future of the Maasai" is overwhelming. Earlier authors spoke of the "last of the Maasai" (Hinde, 1901). Others observed that the Maasai were a "doomed" race (Huxley, 1948; Commissioners of the Kenya Land Commission). Though the grimness of the situation cannot be trivialized, new opportunities are emerging out of current challenges (Zaal, 1999b; Kituyi, 1990; Holland, 1989). Education has rapidly gained currency, while Maasai are now using the age-set system as a foundation for collective action and responsibility in response to new economic and political opportunities. Recently Maasai from different parts of the district participated in and made specific demands to the Kenya Constitutional Review process. Maasai are increasingly active in local, regional, and international movements that press for the recognition and enforcement of their land rights. Time is yet to tell how these diverse futures will look.

Notes

One The Policy Problem: Group Ranch Subdivision in Semiarid Maasailand

1. Davis (1970) refers to a two-pronged structure for the group ranch management. A committee that is responsible for operational management as opposed to the group representatives, whose purpose was the safeguarding of traditional interests in the land and who were supposed to act to check committee excesses. While the terms committee and group representatives exist in the Group Ranch Act, there seems to be no difference in practice. Both terms are used interchangeably to refer to the group of individuals elected to manage group ranch affairs. My conversations with Dr. R. K. Davis reveal that it was the intent of the drafters of the group ranch legislation that decision-making power be divided between the committee and the group representatives and that veto powers be vested in the group representatives.
2. Kimana group ranch has made a conscious decision to restrict subdivision to those areas of the group ranch where such cultivation is possible.
3. The Institutional Analysis and Development framework acknowledges that frequently encountered situations comprise universal elements. In this framework, community actors can be disaggregated, their preferences and incentives outlined, and the influence of their resources of power and wealth on processes and outcomes evaluated. Actors' decisions and actions are embedded within prevailing biophysical, cultural, institutional, and material conditions. Theoretical approaches are then used to link actors, actions, and outcomes.

Two Background to Kajiado District, Kenya

1. Much of this information is obtained from the following documents: Kajiado District Development Plan, 2002–2008 (Kenya, Republic of, 2001a), Kajiado District Atlas (Kenya, Republic of, 1990), and Kajiado District poverty strategy report (SNV/SARDEP, 1999).

Three Research Design

1. During fieldwork, abandoned homesteads were found in the hills during the wet season. These were found occupied later during the dry season.

Four   The Footprints of History

1. The influx of settlers did not begin until 1903; many were of British nationality from Great Britain or South Africa.
2. The East African Syndicate comprised a group of British and South African entrepreneurs prospecting for minerals in East Africa.
3. This concession was in a extremely arid area around Lake Magadi, where the extraction of soda ash was the primary activity.
4. This unnamed and undated citation, titled "Section VII: The Masai Extra Provincial District," was retrieved from Box File A in the library of the Catholic Church in Kajiado town.
5. The notion of Maasai irrationality has since been forcefully refuted (Livingstone, 1986, 1977; Helland, 1980).
6. Letter dated November 11, 1944 from Veterinary Department to Officer-in-Charge of Masai District, based at Ngong, with subject reference as the Development Plan Masai District. The writer of the letter is unnamed. The letter was retrieved from Box File A in the library of the Catholic Church in Kajiado town.
7. See footnote 6.
8. Even though the amount of land occupied by Maasai at the time was substantial, its value was doubtful. Some commentators dismissed the Carter Commission's claim that the Maasai reserve had some of the best agricultural land in East Africa as a mere exaggeration (Tignor, 1976).
9. The changing title of the ALDEV reflects its transformation from an organization primarily concerned with resettlement to one that was more concerned with the technical issues of land management as it gained experience with local land issues. Between 1945 and 1946 it was the African Resettlement Board; 1946–1947 it became the African Settlement and Land Utilization Board; from 1947 to 1953 it was the African Land Utilization and Settlement Board; from 1953 to 1957 it was African Land Development Board; between 1957 and 1960 the Land Development Board (nonscheduled areas); and from 1960 onward, it became the Board of Agriculture (nonscheduled areas). Kenya, Government of, 1962.
10. See footnote 1, this chapter.
11. An individual ranch is a production enterprise in which an individual member of a "tribal" society may, with community consent and the authorization of the local country council, legally register communal land as private property.
12. Adjudication is the recording of individual or group rights over particular plots of land in a particular locality while registration is an exercise during which rights to clearly defined land units vested in clearly defined individual or group "owners" are documented and stored in public registries as authoritative documents, in most cases as title deeds.

Five   The Puzzle of "Perverse" Property Rights

1. One respondent mentioned that high-ranking officials in Moi's government mostly Kalenjin, including a member of Moi's family, were interested in land in both Narok and Kajiado districts. Subdividing the group ranches releases

control of land to the owner, who is then free to sell it. A huge chunk of land flanking the Nairobi-Namanga Road, between Kitengela and Kajiado town in the Kipetu-Kisaju plains, is now owned by several high-ranking individuals in former President Moi's administration.

2. Meetings File: Enkaroni group ranch, District Land Adjudication Office, Kajiado district.

3. Meetings File: Enkaroni Group Ranch, Department of Land Adjudication, Kajiado district.

4. This problem was particularly acute in Torosei group ranch, and subdivision here was also seen as a way of cutting off members from other neighboring group ranches particularly Shompole (which is much more arid than Torosei) who would bring their herds during the dry season. After exhausting Torosei pastures, they together with Torosei members would all be forced to move into Tanzania. In good times some Shompole people would refuse to return to their homes and would have to be chased away, but their friends would invite them again. Even if they left, they would leave a large proportion of their livestock behind. The poor in Torosei were the most notorious for inviting their friends as they would bene-fit from milking their friends' herds. Group members felt that subdivision would help them get rid of this problem, as anyone who would invite their friend would have to bear the burden of accommodating them on their individual parcel.

5. Interview: ENK/24/2001.

6. The Group Ranch Act of 1968 specified that all group ranch decisions must be made in the presence of a quorum comprising at least 60% of the total membership and that any individual decision must be put to a vote subject to a 60% majority rule. See chapter five.

7. The ownership of individual ranches within Kajiado and indeed Maasailand is dominated by the Ilnyankusi. This may be because Maasai political leadership at both national and local levels at the time when group ranches were being created and individual ranches demarcated in the 1960s comprised mainly of members from this age set. The Ilnyankusi have now been nudged out of lead-ership by their followers, the Iseuri, who are also facing increasing challenges from their followers, the Ilkiseyia age set.

8. Interviews across all group ranches studied indicated that circumcision was one of the requirements for registration. Galaty (2002) indicates that though this is a reasonable characterization for the current purpose, the notion of "becoming a man" is a process, defined by several sequential events, circumcision being just one out of these. Personal communication, October 26, 2002.

9. Meetings files for Enkaroni, Meto, and Nentanai group ranches. District Land Adjudication Office, Kajiado district.

10. Interview: NENT/26/2001.

11. Interviews with registered Ilkishili and the unregistered Ilkishili and Ilmajeshi of Torosei in October 2001 and July 2002.

Six Subdividing the Group Ranch: Allocating Land and Distributing Wealth

1. Lands on hills are highly erodible. Similarly the streams, which are seasonal, are susceptible to flooding during the rainy season. The force of the water creates

gullies in land surrounding such streams. Hills and streams are consequently not considered as desirable parcel locations.

2. Although the group ranch is technically dissolved, the committee stays in force, it is not disbanded. Dissolution is only to get the subdivision process going. Committee will only be disbanded after subdivision has been finalized and all registered members have received their land titles.

3. Torosei has not yet engaged a surveyor—persistent droughts and heavy cattle losses have made it difficult for members to raise survey fees. The committee in Torosei is now approaching one wealthy Kajiado businessman, who also owns land in Torosei to loan them an initial amount that would get the surveyor started on the ground. Nentanai members also had a problem raising survey and even title fees. The committee here received a loan from a neighboring cement manufacturer to get the survey process going. Those who could not afford to repay the loan were paid for by their friends and families in return for allowing the lender free grazing until the full amount is recovered. Some, however, opted to sell part or all of their land to those who paid the fees for them.

4. Interviews: TORO/2/2002; TORO/9/2002.

5. Interviews: MET/7/2002, MET/12/2002.

6. Interviews: MET/21/2001, MET/68/2001.

7. Interviews: MET/19/2001, MET/48/2001.

8. Interviews: MET/51/2001.

9. Torosei are not included in these results because they have not formally subdivided; thus parcel sizes are not confirmed.

10. Interviews: ENK/70/2001, ENK/8/2001.

11. Out of the 17 widows who were allocated land in Enkaroni, 12 have land below the group ranch average. Committees were hesitant to even issue land to widows because of the fear that in case the widow were to remarry their land would be lost to the family of the deceased. This fear was more acute in the event that the widow was remarried to an "outsider."

12. Interview: ENK/19/2001.

13. Interview: MET/21/2001.

14. The size and distribution of holdings was derived directly by asking the interviewee. These have not been verified by direct census and must be treated with caution as it is fairly uncommon for the Maasai to reveal their true wealth.

15. It is claimed that in order to settle the ones who had been unwittingly missed out, the committee members had to hive out parts of their huge chunks to accommodate those who had been overlooked during land allocation.

16. Minutes, Enkaroni Annual General Meeting, July 10, 1991. Meetings File, Enkaroni Group Ranch, Department of Land Adjudication, Kajiado district.

17. Minutes, Complainants Meeting, March 25, 1992. Disputes File, Enkaroni Group Ranch, Department of Land Adjudication, Kajiado district.

18. Letter written by Nenkitai ene Lolkinyei, February 19, 1990. Disputes File, Enkaroni Group Ranch, Department of Land Adjudication, Kajiado district.

19. Letter written by Pushati ole Leshinka, March 16, 1990. Disputes File, Enkaroni Group Ranch, Department of Land Adjudication, Kajiado district.

20. Unnamed author, February 9, 1990. Disputes File, Enkaroni Group Ranch, Department of Land Adjudication, Kajiado district.

21. Letter of April 15, 1992. Disputes File, Enkaroni Group Ranch, Department of Land Adjudication, Kajiado district.
22. Plaint, Civil Suit 3956 of 1992, July 22, 1992. High Court of Kenya.
23. Ruling, Civil Case 3956 of 1992, July 31, 1992. High Court of Kenya.
24. Interview: ENK/10/2002.

Eight   The Transformation of Property Rights to Land in Kenya's Maasailand

1. This opens up the possibility of pastoralists negotiating mutual accommodations with their cultivator neighbors and being allowed right of way and use rights over wider territory. Such arrangements have endured across time and space among pastoral communities and their neighbors (Arawal, 1999; Berge, 1998; Chakravarty-Kaul, 1996; Galaty and Johnson, 1990).

WORKS CITED

Agnew, A. D. Q., and S. Agnew. 1994. *Upland Kenya Wild Flowers: A Flora of the Ferns and Herbaceous Flowering Plants of Upland Kenya.* Nairobi: East African Natural History Society.

Agrawal, A. 1999. *Greener Pastures: Politics, Markets, and Community among a Migrant Pastoral People.* Durham, NC: Duke University Press.

Alchian, A., and H. Demsetz. 1972. The Property Rights Paradigm. *Journal of Economic History* 33: 16–27.

Alston, L. J., G. D. Libecap, and R. Schneider. 1995. Property Rights and the Preconditions for Markets: The Case of the Amazon Frontier. *Journal of Institutional and Theoretical Economics* 151(1): 89–107.

Anderson, D. M., and V. Broch-Due, eds. 1999. *The Poor Are Not Us: Poverty and Pastoralism in Eastern Africa.* Oxford: James Curry; Nairobi: East African Publishing House; Athens, OH: Ohio University Press.

Ault, D. E., and G. L. Rutman. 1993. Land Scarcity, Property Rights and Resource Allocation in Agriculture: Eastern and Southern Africa. *South African Journal of Economics* 61(1): 32–44.

Baland, J.-M., and J.-P. Platteau, eds. 1996. *Halting Degradation of Natural Resources: Is There a Role for Rural Communities?* New York: Food and Agriculture Organization of the United Nations.

———. 1998. Division of the Commons: A Partial Assessment of the New Institutional Economics of Land Rights. *American Journal of Agricultural Economics* 80: 644–650.

Banks, T. 2003. Property Rights Reform in Rangeland China: Dilemmas on the Road to the Household Ranch. *World Development* 31(12): 2129–2142.

Barfield, T. 1981. *The Central Asian Arabs of Afghanistan: Pastoral Nomadism in Transition.* Austin, TX: University of Texas Press.

Bates, R. 1989. *Beyond the Miracle of the Market: The Political Economy of Agrarian Development in Kenya.* New York: Cambridge University Press.

Baxter, P. T. W., and U. Almagor. 1978. *Age, Generation, and Time: Some Features of East African Age Organizations.* London: C. Hurst.

Beentje, H., J. Adamson, and D. Bhanderi. 1994. *Kenya Trees, Shrubs and Lianas.* Nairobi: National Museums of Kenya.

Behnke, R. H. 1985. Open-Range Management and Property Rights in Pastoral Africa: A Case of Spontaneous Range Enclosure in South Darfur, Sudan. Paper 20f. Pastoral Development Network, London: Agricultural Administrative Unit, Overseas Development Institute.

Behnke, R. H., and I. Scoones. 1993. Rethinking Range Ecology: Implications for Rangeland Management in Africa. In *Range Ecology at Disequilibrium: New Models of Natural Variability and Pastoral Adaptation in African savannahs*, ed. R. H. Behnke, I. Scoones, and M. Kerven. London: Overseas Development Institiute, International Institute for Environment and Development.

Bekure, S., P. N. de Leeuw, B. E. Grandin, and P. J. H. Neate, eds. 1991. *Maasai Herding: An Analysis of the Livestock Production System of Maasai Pastoralists in Eastern Kajiado District, Kenya*. ILCA Systems Study 4. Addis Ababa, Ethiopia: ILCA (International Livestock Center for Africa).

Bell, R. H. V. 1982. The Effect of Soil Nutrient Availability on Community Structure in African Ecosystems. In *Ecology of Tropical Savannas*, ed. B. J. Huntley and B. H. Walker. Ecological Studies, Volume 42. Berlin: Springer-Verlag.

Belsky, A. J. 1983. Small-Scale Pattern in Four Grassland Communities in the Serengeti National Park, Tanzania. *Vegetatio* 55: 141–151.

———. 1988. Regional Influences on Small-Scale Vegetational Heterogeneity within Grasslands in the Serengeti National Park, Tanzania. *Vegetatio* 74: 3–10.

Berge, E. 1998. The Legal Language of Common Property Rights. In *Land and the Governance of Renewable Resources: Studies from Northern Europe and Africa*, ed. E. Berge and N.C. Stenseth. Winnipeg, Manitoba: Hignell Book Printing.

Bernardi, I. M. C. 1952. The Age-System of the Nilo-Hamitic Peoples: A Critical Evaluation. *Africa* 22: 316–332.

Berntsen, J. L. 1979a. Maasai Age-Sets and Prophetic Leadership, 1850–1910. *Africa* 49(2): 134–146.

———. 1979b. Economic Variations among Maa-Speaking Peoples. *Hadith* 7: 108–127.

Berry, S. 1988. Concentration Without Privatization? Some Consequences of Changing Patterns of Rural Land Control in Africa. In *Land and Society in Contemporary Africa*, ed. R. E. Downs and S. P. Reyna. University of New Hampshire: University Press of New England.

———. 1989. Social Institutions and Access to Resources. *Africa* 59(1): 41–55.

———. 1993. *No Condition Is Permanent: The Social Dynamics of Agrarian Change in Sub-Saharan Africa*. Madison, WI: University of Wisconsin Press.

———. 2002. The Everday Politics of Rent-Seeking: Land Allocation on the Outskirts of Kumase, Ghana. In *Negotiating Property in Africa*, ed. K. Juul and C. Lund. Portsmouth, NH: Heineman.

Bill, J. C., and F. M. Anderson. 1980. Observations from Elangata Wuas Group Ranch in Kajiado District. Unpublished Report. International Livestock Center for Africa, Nairobi.

Blewett, R. A. 1995. Property Rights as a Cause of the Tragedy of the Commons: Institutional Change and the Pastoral Maasai of Kenya. *Eastern Economic Journal* 21(4).

Boserup, E. 1965. *The Conditions of Agricultural Growth: The Economics of Agriculture under Population Pressure*. Chicago, IL: Aldine.

Bourliere, F., ed. 1983. *Tropical Savannas*. Ecosystems of the World, Volume 13. Amsterdam: Elsevier.

Bradburn, D. 1982. Volatility of Animal Wealth among South-West Asian Pastoralists. *Human Ecology* 10: 85–106.

Breen, R. M. 1979. The Politics of Land: The Kenya Land Commission (1932–33) and Its Effects on Land Policy in Kenya. Unpublished PhD dissertation. Department of History, Michigan State University.

Bridges, R. C. 1991. Official Perceptions during the Colonial Period of Problems Facing Pastoral Societies in Kenya. In *Pastoral Economies in Africa and Long-Term Responses to Drought*, ed. Jeffrey C. Stone. Proceedings of a Colloquium at the University of Aberdeen, April 1990. African Studies Group. Aberdeen: Aberdeen University.

Bromley, D. W. 1989. Property Relations and Economic Development: The Other Land Reform. *World Development* 17(6): 867–877.

———. 1991. *Environment and Economy: Property Rights and Public Policy*. Cambridge: Basil Blackwell.

Bruce, J. B. 1988. A Perspective on Indigenous Land Tenure Systems and Land Concentration. In *Land and Society in Contemporary Africa*, ed. R. E. Downs and S. P. Reyna. University of New Hampshire: University Press of New England.

———. 1998. Country Profiles of Land Tenure: Africa, 1996. Research Paper No. 130. Land Tenure Center, University of Wisconsin, Madison, WI.

Bruce, J. W., and R. Mearns. 2002. Natural Resource Management and Land Policy in Developing Countries: Lessons Learned and New Challenges for the World Bank. Issue Paper No. 115. Drylands Program, International Institute for Environment and Development, London.

Bruce, J. W., and S. E. Migot-Adholla. 1994. *Searching for Land Tenure Security in Africa*. Washington, DC: World Bank.

Campbell, D. J. 1991. The Impact of Development upon Strategies for Coping with Drought among the Maasai of Kajiado District, Kenya. In *Pastoral Economies in Africa and Long Term Responses to Drought*, ed. Jeffrey C. Stone. Proceedings of a Colloquium at the University of Aberdeen, April 1990. African Studies Group. Aberdeen: Aberdeen University.

———. 1993. Land as Ours, Land as Mine: Economic, Political and Ecological Marginalization in Kajiado District. In *Being Maasai: Ethnicity and Identity in East Africa*, ed. Thomas Spear and Richard Waller. London: James Curry.

Chakravarty-Kaul, M. 1996. *Common Lands and Customary Law: Institutional Change in Northern India over the Past Two Centuries*. Oxford: Oxford University Press.

Ciriacy-Wantrup, S. V., and R. C. Bishop. 1975. "Common Property" as a Concept in Natural Resource Policy. *Natural Resources Journal* 15: 713–727.

Clayton, W. D. 1970. *Flora of Tropical East Africa: Gramineae (Part 1)*. London: Crown Agents for Overseas Governments and Administrations.

Clayton, W. D., and S. A. Renvoize. 1982. *Flora of Tropical East Africa (Part 3)*. Rotterdam: Balkema.

Clayton, W. D., S. M. Phillips, and S. A. Renvoize. 1974. *Flora of Tropical East Africa: Gramineae (Part 2)*. London: Crown Agents for Overseas Governments and Administrations.

Coldham, S. 1978. The Effect of Registration of Title upon Customary Land Rights in Kenya. *Journal of African Law* 22(2): 91–111.

Cole, M. M. 1982. The Influence of Soils, Geomorphology and Geology on the Distribution of Plant Communities in Savanna Ecosystems. In *Ecology of Tropical Savannas*, ed. B. J. Huntley and B. H. Walker. Ecological Studies, Volume 42. Berlin: Springer-Verlag.

Cole, M. M. 1986. *The Savannas: Biogeography and Geobotany*. New York: Academic Press.

Collet, D. 1987. Pastoralists and Wildife: Image and Reality in Kenya Maasailand. In *Conservation in Africa: People, Policies and Practice*, ed. David Anderson and Richard Grove. Cambridge: Cambridge University Press.

Cotula, L., C. Toulmin, and C. Hess. 2004. Land Tenure and Administration in Africa: Lessons of Experience and Emerging Issues. Report. International Institute for Environment and Development, London.

Coughenour, M. B. 1991. Spatial Components of Plant-Herbivore Interactions in Pastoral, Ranching and Native Ungulate Ecosystems. *Journal of Range Management* 44 (6): 510–542.

Cungu, A., and J. F. M. Swinnen. 2001. Case Study. The Dramatic Rise of Individual Farming in Albania: Causes and Effects. In *Access to Land, Rural Poverty, and Public Action*, ed. A. de Janvry, G. Gordillo, J. P. Platteau, and E. Sadoulet. A study prepared for the World Institute for Development Economics Research of the United Nations University (UNU/WIDER). Clarendon: Oxford University Press.

Curry, P. J., and R. B. Hacker. 1990. Can Pastoral Grazing Management Satisfy Endorsed Conservation Objectives in Arid Western Australia? *Journal of Environmental Management* 30: 295–320.

Dahlberg, A. C. 2000. Vegetation Diversity and Change in Relation to Land Use, Soil and Rainfall: A Case Study from North-East District, Botswana. *Journal of Arid Environments* 44: 19–40.

Dahlman, C. J. 1980. *The Open Field Systsem and Beyond: A Property Rights Analysis of an Economic Institution*. Cambridge: Cambridge University Press.

Daily Nation, July 19, 1983.

———. August 7, 1986.

———. January 23, 1987.

———. April 15, 1989.

Davis, R. K. 1970. Some Issues in the Evolution, Organization and Operation of Group Ranches in Kenya. Discussion Paper No. 93. Institute for Development Studies, University College, Nairobi.

———. 2000. The Kajiado Group Ranches: A Perspective. Unpublished Report. Institute of Behavioral Science, Boulder, CO.

De Carvalho, E. C. 1974. Traditional and Modern Patterns of Cattle Raising in Southwestern Angola: A Critical Evaluation of Change from Pastoralism to Ranching. *Journal of Developing Areas* 8(January): 199–226.

De Ridder, N., and K. T. Wagenaar. 1984. A Comparison between the Productivity of Traditional Livestock Systems and Ranching in Eastern Botswana. *ILCA Newsletter* 3(3): 5–7. Addis Ababa, Ethiopia.

De Soto, H. 2000. *The Mystery of Capital: Why Capitalism Triumphs in the West and Fails Everywhere Else*. New York: Basic Books.

Demsetz, H. 1967. Toward a Theory of Property Rights. *American Economic Review* 62: 347–359.

Doherty, D. A. 1987. Maasai Pastoral Potential: A Study of Ranching in Narok District, Kenya. Unpublished PhD dissertation. Department of Anthropology, McGill University.

Doornbos, M., and J. Markakis. 1991. The Crisis of Pastoralism and the Role of the State: Trends and Issues. In *Pastoral Economies in Africa and Long-Term Responses to Drought*, ed. Jeffrey C. Stone. Proceedings of a Colloquium at the University of Aberdeen, April 1990. African Studies Group. Aberdeen: Aberdeen University.

Doucha,T., E. Mathijs, and J. F. M. Swinnen. 2001. Case Study: Post-Communist Land Reform and Changes in Tenure in the Czech Republic. In *Access to Land, Rural Poverty, and Public Action*, ed. A. de Janvry, G. Gordillo, J. P. Platteau, and E. Sadoulet. A study prepared for the World Institute for Development Economics Research of the United Nations University (UNU/WIDER). Clarendon: Oxford University Press.

Eggertsson, T. 1990. *Economic Behavior and Institutions*. Cambridge Surveys of Economic Literature. New York: Cambridge University Press.

————. 1996. The Economics of Control and the Cost of Property Rights. In *Rights to Nature: Ecologic, Economic, Cultural and Political Principles of Institutions for the Environment*, ed. S. S. Hanna, C. Folke, and K. Maler. Washington, DC: Island Press.

Eliot, C. 1905. *The East Africa Protecorate*. London: Frank Cass and Co.

Ellis, J. E., and D. M. Swift. 1988. Stability of African Pastoral Ecosystems: Alternate Paradigms and Implications for Development. *Journal of Range Management* 41: 450–459.

Ellison, L. 1960. Influence of Grazing on Plant Succession of Rangelands. *Botanical Review* 26: 1–78.

Ensminger, J. 1992. *Making a Market: The Institutional Transformation of an African Society*. New York: Cambridge University Press.

ETC East Africa. 1998. Framework for Natural Resources Use and Management. Arid and Semi-Arid Lands Program, Kajiado District. Final Report. SNV Kenya, Nairobi.

Evangelou, P. 1984. *Livestock Development in Kenya's Maasailand: Pastoralists' Transition to a Market Economy*. Boulder, CO: Westview Press.

Fallon, L. E. 1962. *Masai Range Resources, Kajiado District*. Nairobi: USAID Mission to East Africa.

Feder, G., and D. Feeny. 1991. Land Tenure and Property Rights: Theory and Implications for Development Theory. *World Bank Economic Review* 5(1): 135–153.

Feeny, D. 1993. The Demand for and Supply of Institutional Arrangements. In *Rethinking Institutional Analysis and Development*, ed. Vincent Ostrom, D. Feeny, and Hartmut Picht. San Francisco, CA: ICS Press.

Fernandez-Gimenez. 2002. Spatial and Social Boundaries and the Paradox of Pastoral Land Tenure: A Case Study from Postsocialist Mongolia. *Human Ecology* 30(1): 49–78.

Field, B. C. 1986. Induced Changes in Property Rights Institutions. Research Paper Series 86–1. Department of Agricultural and Resource Economics, University of Massachusetts, Amherst.

Firmin-Sellers, K. 1995. The Politics of Property Rights. *American Political Science Review* 89(4): 867–881.

————. 1996. *The Transformation of Property Rights in the Gold Coast: An Empirical Analysis Applying Rational Choice Theory*. New York: Cambridge University Press.

Fratkin, E. 1994. Problems of Pastoral Land Tenure in Kenya: Demographic, Economic and Political Process among the Maasai, Samburu, Boran and

Rendille, 1950–1990. Working Paper No. 177. African Studies Center, Boston University.

Fratkin, E., and E. A. Roth. 1990. Drought and Economic Differentiation among Ariaal Pastoralists of Kenya. *Human Ecology* 184: 385–402.

Fratkin, E., and K. Smith. 1994. Labor, Livestock and Land: The Organization of Pastoral Production. In *African Pastoralist Systems: An Integrated Approach*, ed. Elliot Fratkin, Kathleen A. Galvin, and Eric Abella Roth. Boulder, CO: Lynne Rienner Publishers.

Fratkin, E., and R. Mearns. 2003. Sustainability and Pastoral Livelihoods: Lessons from East African Maasai and Mongolia. *Human Organization* 62(2): 112–122.

Galaty, J. G. 1981. Book Review. *Age, Generation and Time: Some Features of East-African Age Organizations. Man* 16(4): 702–703.

———. 1989. Seniority and Cyclicity in Maasai Age Organization. Discussion Paper No. 6.

———. 1992. The Land Is Yours: Social and Economic Factors in the Privatization, Subdivision and Sale of Maasai Ranches. *Nomadic Peoples* 30: 26–40.

———. 1993. Maasai Expansion and the New East African Pastoralism. In *Being Maasai: Ethnicity and Identity in East Africa*, ed. Thomas T. Spear and Richard Waller. London: J. Currey; Dar es Salaam: Mkuki na Nyota; Nairobi: EAEP; Athens, OH: Ohio University Press.

———. 1994a. Ha(l)ving Land in Common: The Subdivision of Maasai Group Ranches in Kenya. *Nomadic Peoples* 34/35: 109–121.

———. 1994b. The Pastoralist's Dilemma: Common Property and Enclosure in Kenya's Rangeland. In *Food Systems Under Stress in Africa*, ed. R. Vernooy and K. M. Kealey. Proceedings of a Workshop held in Ottawa, Ontario, Canada, November 7–8, 1993. Ottawa: IDRC.

———. 1999a. Property in the Strict Sense of the Term: The Theory and Rhetoric of Land Tenure in East Africa. ALARM Working Paper, August 1999. Center for Basic Research.

———. 1999b. Grounding Pastoralists: Law, Politics and Dispossession in East Africa. *Nomadic Peoples* 3(2): 56–73.

Galaty, J. G., and D. L. Johnson. 1990. Introduction: Pastoral Systems in a Global Perspective In *The World of Pastoralism: Herding Systems in Comparative Perspective*, ed. J. G. Galaty and D. L. Johnson. New York: Guilford Press.

Gibson, Clark, C. 1999. *Politicians and Poachers: The Political Economy of Wildlife Policy in Africa*. Cambridge: Cambridge University Press.

Goheen, M. 1988. Land Accumulation and Local Control: The Manipulation of Symbols and Power in Nso, Cameroon. In *Land and Society in Contemporary Africa*, ed. R. E. Downs and S. P. Reyna. University of New Hampshire: University Press of New England.

Goldschmidt, W. 1980. The Failure of Pastoral Economic Development Programs in Africa. *Future of Pastoral Peoples*, ed. G. Galaty, D. Aronson, and P. C. Salzman. Proceedings of a Conference Held in Nairobi, Kenya, August 4–8, 1980.

Grandin, B. E. 1986. Land Tenure, Subdivision and Residential Change on a Maasai Group Ranch. Bulletin of the Institute for Development Anthropology 4(2). Development Anthropology Network.

———. 1987a. Pastoral Culture and Range Management: Recent Lessons from Maasailand. ILCA Bulletin 28. International Livestock Center for Africa, Addis Ababa, Ethiopia, September 1987.

————. 1987b. East African Pastoral Land Tenure: Some Reflections from Maasailand. In *Land, Trees and Tenure*, ed. John B. Raintree. Proceedings of an International Workshop on Tenure Issues in Agroforestry, Nairobi, May 27–31. ICRAF (International Center for Research in Agroforestry)and the Land Tenure Center, Nairobi and Madison, WI.

————. 1988. Wealth and Pastoral Dairy Production: A Case Study from Maasailand. *Human Ecology* 16: 1–21.

Greig-Smith, P. 1983. *Quantitative Plant Ecology*. Studies in Ecology, Volume 9. Berkeley, CA: University of California Press.

Guillet, D. 1981. Land Tenure, Ecological Zone, and Agricultural Regime. *American Ethnologist* 8(1): 139–157.

Halderman, J. M. 1972. An Analysis of Continued Semi-Nomadism on the Kaputiei Maasai Group Ranches: Sociological and Ecological Factors. Discussion Paper No. 152. Institute for Development Studies, University of Nairobi.

————. 1985. Problems of Pastoral Development in Eastern Africa. *Agricultural Administration* 18(4): 199–216.

————. 1989. Development and Famine Risk in Kenya Maasailand. Unpublished PhD dissertation. University of California, Berkeley, CA.

Hardin, G. 1968. The Tragedy of the Commons. *Science* 162: 1243–1248.

Harry, I., H. Schwartz, H. C. Pielert, and C. Mosler. 1996. Land Degradation in African Pastoral Ecosystems and the Destocking Controversy. *Ecological Modelling* 86: 227–233.

Hedlund, H. 1971. The Impact of Group Ranches on a Pastoral Society. Staff Paper No. 100. Institute for Development Studies, University of Nairobi.

Helland, J. 1980. *Some Issues in the Study of Pastoralists and the Development of Pastoralism*. Addis Ababa, Ethiopia: International Livestock Center for Africa (ILCA).

Herren, U. 1990. Socio-Economic Stratification and Small Stock Production in Mukogodo Division, Kenya. *Research in Economic Anthropology* 12: 111–148.

Herskovitz, M. J. 1926. The Cattle Complex in East Africa. *American Anthropologist* 28: 230–272.

Hill, M. O. 1991. Patterns of Species Distribution in Britain Elucidated by Canonical Correspondence Analysis. *Journal of Biogeography* 18: 247–255.

Hinde, S. L. 1901. *The Last of the Masai*. London: Heinemann.

Hinga, G., F. N. Muchena, and C. M. Njihia, eds. 1980. *Physical and Chemical Methods of Soil Analysis*. Nairobi: National Agricultural Laboratories, Ministry of Agriculture.

Holland, K. 1989. New Needs and New Maasai Adaptive Strategies. Discussion Paper No. 9. East African Pasture Systems Project, Department of Anthropology, McGill University.

Hopcraft, P. N. 1980. Economic Institutions and Pastoral Resource Management: Consideration for a Development Strategy. In *The Future of Pastoral Peoples*, ed. G. Galaty, D. Aronson, and P. C. Salzman. Proceedings of a Conference Held in Nairobi, Kenya, August 4–8, 1980.

Huntingford, G. W. B. 1953. *The Southern Nilo-Hamites*. Ethnographic Survey of Africa, Part VIII. London: International African Institute.

Huntley, B. J., and B. H. Walker, eds. 1982. *Ecology of Tropical Savannas*. Berlin: Springer-Verlag.

Huxley, E. 1948. *The Sorcerer's Apprentice*. London: Chatto and Windus.

Ibrahim, K., and C. H. Kabuye. 1988. *An Illustrated Manual of Kenya Grasses*. Rome: Food and Agriculture Organization of the United Nations.

Ingule, F. O. 1980. Cultural Change and Communication among the Pastoral Maasai of Kajiado District of Kenya. Unpublished MA thesis. Daystar International Institute, Wheaton College Graduate School, Wheaton, IL.

Jacobs, A. 1965. The Traditional Political Organization of the Pastoral Maasai. Unpublished PhD dissertation. Oxford University, Nuffield College.

————. 1980. The Pastoral Maasai and Tropical Rural Development. In *Agricultural Development in Africa: Issues of Public Policy*, ed. Robert H. Bates and Michael F. Lofchie. New York: Praeger Publishers.

Jahnke, H. 1978. A Historical View of Range Development in Kenya. International Livestock Center for Africa, Nairobi.

Jahnke, H., H. Ruthenberg, and H. U. Thimm. 1972. *Range Development in Kenya: The Kenya Livestock Development Project and Its Impact on Rural Development*. Washington, DC: IBRD Consultation.

James, L. 1939. The Kenya Masa: A Nomadic People Under Modern Administration. *Africa* XII: 49–73.

Jodha, N. S. 1987. A Case Study on the Degradation of Common Property in India. In *Land Degradation and Society*, ed. P. Blaikie and H. Brookfield. London: Methuen.

————. 1992. Common Property Resources: A Missing Dimension of Development Strategies. World Bank Discussion Paper 169. Washington, DC, World Bank, August.

Jongman, R. H. G. , C. J. F. Ter Braak, and O. F. R. Van Tongeren, eds. 1995. *Data Analysis in Community and Landscape Ecology* Cambridge: Cambridge University Press.

Kabubuo-Mariara, J. 2005. Herders Response to Acute Land Pressure under Changing Property Rights: Some Insights from Kajiado District, Kenya. *Environment and Development Economics* 10(1): 67–85.

Kamara, A. B., B. Swallow, and M. Kirk. 2004. Policies, Interventions and Institutional Change in Pastoral Resource Management in Borana, Southern Ethiopia. *Development Policy Review* 22(4): 381–403.

Kanyinga, K. 2000. Redistribution from Above: The Politics of Land Rights and Squatting in Coastal Kenya. Political and Social Context of Structural Adjustment in Africa. Research Report No. 115. Nordiska Afrikainstitutet, Uppsala, Sweden.

Kent, M., and P. Coker. 1992. *Vegetation Description and Analysis: A Practical Approach*. London: Belhaven Press.

Kenya Colony and Protectorate. 1934. *Report of the Kenya Land Commission, September 1933*. His Majesty's Stationery Office, Kenya. Nairobi: Government Printer.

————. 1955. A Plan to Intensify the Development of African Agriculture in Kenya. Nairobi: Government Printer.

Kenya, Government of. 1962. *African Land Development in Kenya, 1946–1962*. Nairobi: Ministry of Agriculture, Animal Husbandry and Water Resources.

————. 1966. *East Africa Royal Commission Report, 1953–1955*. London, Her Majesty's Stationery Office.

Kenya, Republic of. 1966. *Report of the Mission on Land Consolidation and Registration in Kenya, 1965–1966*. Nairobi: Government Printer.

———. 1968a. Group (Land) Representatives Act. Chapter 287 of the Laws of Kenya. Nairobi: Government Printer.

———. 1968b. The Land Adjudication Act. Chapter 284 of the Laws of Kenya. Nairobi: Government Printer.

———. 1981. *Kenya National Population and Housing Report Volume I: Population Distribution in Administrative Areas*. Central Bureau of Statistics. Ministry of Finance and Planning. Nairobi: Government Printer.

———. 1990. *Kajiado District Atlas*. Kajiado: Ministry of Reclamation and Development of Arid, Semi-Arid Areas and Wastelands.

———. 1994. *Kenya National Population and Housing Report Volume I: Population Distribution in Administrative Areas*. Central Bureau of Statistics. Ministry of Finance and Planning. Nairobi: Government Printer.

———. 2001a. *Kajiado District Development Plan, 2001–2008*. Office of the Vice President and Ministry of Planning and National Development. Nairobi: Government Printer.

———. 2001b. *Kenya National Population and Housing Report Volume I: Population Distribution in Administrative Areas*. Central Bureau of Statistics. Ministry of Finance and Planning. Nairobi: Government Printer.

Kenya Times, July 19, 1983.

———. March 9, 1985.

Keohane, R. O., and E. Ostrom. 1995. *Local Commons and Global Interdependence: Heterogeneity in Two Domains*. London: Sage Publications.

Keya, G. A. 1997. Effects of Herbivory on the Production Ecology of the Perennial Grass *Leptothrium senegalense* (kunth.) in the Arid Lands of Northern Kenya. *Agriculture, Ecosytems and Environment* 66: 101–111.

Khazanov, A. 1984. *Nomads and the Outside World*. New York: Cambridge University Press.

Kimani, K., and J. Pickard. 1998. Recent Trends and Implications of Group Ranch Subdivision and Fragmentation in Kajiado District, Kenya. *Geographic Journal* 164(2): 202–213.

Kipury, N. 1989. Maasai Women in Transition: Class and Gender in the Transformation of a Pastoral Society. Unpublished PhD dissertation. Temple University, Philadelphia, PL.

Kirk, M. 1999. *Land Tenure, Technological Change and Resource Use: Transformation Processes in African Agrarian Systems*. Frankfurt: Peter Lang.

Kituyi, M. 1990. *Becoming Kenyans: Socio-Economic Transformation of the Pastoral Maasai*. Nairobi: African Center for Technology Studies Press.

Knight, J. 1992. *Institutions and Social Conflict*. New York: Cambridge University Press.

Kraler, T. 1955. Principles and Structures in the Organization of the Asiatic Steppe Pastoralists. *Southwestern Journal of Anthropology* 11(2): 67–92.

Lastarria-Cornhiel, S. 1997. Impact of Privatization on Gender and Property Rights in Africa. *World Development* 25(8): 1317–1333.

Legendre, P., and L. Legendre. 1998. *Numerical Ecology*. Amsterdam: Elsevier.

Lesorogol, C. K. 2003. Transforming Institutions among Pastoralists: Inequality and Land Privatization. *American Anthropologist* 105: 531–542.

Lesorogol, C. K. 2005. Privatizing Pastoral Lands: Economic and Normative Outcomes in Kenya. *World Development* 33: 1959–1978.

Lewis, R. W. 1965. A Plan for the Development of Maasailand. Kabete: Department of Veterinary Services.

Leys, N. 1923. *Kenya*. London: Frank Cass and Co.

Li, O., R. Ma, and J. R. Simpson. 1993. Changes in the Nomadic Pattern and Its Impact on the Inner Mongolian Steppe Grasslands Ecosystem. *Nomadic Peoples* 33: 63–72.

Libecap, G. D. 1989. *Contracting for Property Rights*. New York: Cambridge University Press.

———. 1998. Distributional and Political Issues Modifying Traditional Common-Property Institutions. In *Law and the Governance of Renewable Resources: Studies from Northern Europe and Africa*, ed. E. Berge and C. Stenseth. Oakland, CA: ICS Press.

Little, P. 1985. Social Differentiation and Pastoralist Sedentarization in Northern Kenya. *Africa* 55: 243–261.

———. 1999. Living in Risky Environments: The Political Ecology of Pastoralism in East Africa. In *African Development in the 21st Century*, ed. S. Taylor, G. White, and E. Fratkin. Rochester, NY: University of Rochester Press.

Livingstone, I. 1977. Economic Irrationality among the Pastoral People in East Africa: Myth or Reality? Discussion Paper No. 25. Institute for Development Studies, University of Nairobi.

———. 1986. The Common Property Problem and Pastoral Behavior. *Journal of Development Studies* 23: 5–19.

Lund, C. 2002. Negotiating Property Institutions: On the Symbiosis of Property and Authority in Africa. In *Negotiating Property in Africa*, ed. K. Juul and C. Lund. Porstmouth, NH: Heineman.

Mahoney, J. 2000. Path Dependence in Historical Sociology. *Theory and Society* 29: 507–548.

———. 2001. *The Legacies of Liberalism: Path Dependence and Political Regimes in Central America*. Baltimore, MD: Johns Hopkins University Press.

McCay, B. J., and J. M. Acheson, eds. 1987. *The Question of the Commons: The Culture and Ecology of Communal Resources*. Tucson, AZ: University of Arizona Press.

McCune, B., and M. J. Mefford. 1999. *PC-ORD: Multivariate Analysis of Ecological Data (Version 4)*. MjM Software Design, Gleneden Beach, OR.

McNaughton, S. J., and F. F. Banyikwa. 1995. Plant Communities and Herbivory. In *Serengeti II. Dynamics, Management and Conservation of an Ecosystem*, ed. A. R. E. Sinclair and P. Arcese. Chicago, IL: University of Chicago Press.

Medina, E. 1996. Biodiversity and Nutrient Relations in Savanna Ecosystems: Interactions between Primary Producers, Soil Microorganisms, and Soils. In *Biodiversity and Savanna Ecosystem Processes*, ed. O. T. Solbrig, E. Medina, and J. F. Silva. Ecological Studies, Volume 121. Berlin: Springer-Verlag.

Meinzen-Dick, R., and R. Pradhan. 2002. Legal Pluralism and Dynamic Property Rights. CAPRi Working Paper 22. IFPRI, Washington DC, January.

Meinzen-Dick, R., L. Brown, H. Feldstein, and A. Quisumbing. 1997. Gender, Property Rights and Natural Resources *World Development* 25(8): 1305–1315.

Mendes, L. 1988. Private and Communal Land Tenure in Morocco's Western High Atlas Mountains: Complements, Not Ideological Opposites. Paper 26a. Pastoral

Development Network, Agricultural Administrative Unit, Overseas Development Institute.

Migot-Adholla, S. E., and P. D. Little. 1980. Evolution of Policy toward the Development of Pastoral Areas in Kenya. In *The Future of Pastoral Peoples*, ed. G. Galaty, D. Aronson, and P. C. Salzman. Proceedings of a Conference Held in Nairobi, Kenya, August 4–8, 1980.

Migot-Adholla, S. E., P. Hazell, B. Blarel, and F. Place. 1991. Indigenous Land Rights Systems in Sub-Saharan Africa: A Constraint on Productivity? *World Bank Economic Review* 5(1): 155–175.

Mingay, G. E. 1968. *Enclosure and the Small Farmer in the Age of the Industrial Revolution*. London: Macmillan.

Mol, F. 1996. *Maasai Language and Culture: Dictionary*. Limuru: Kolbe Press.

Mulder, M. B. 1991. Datoga Pastoralists of Tanzania. *National Geographic Research and Exploration* 72: 166–187.

Mulder, M. B., and Sellen, D. W. 1994. Pastoralist Decision Making: A Behavioral Ecological Approach. In *African Pastoralist Systems: An Integrated Approach*, ed. E. Fratkin, K. A. Galvin, and E. A. Roth. Boulder, CO: Lynne Rienner Publishers.

Munei, K. 1987. Grazing Schemes and Group Ranches as Models for Developing Pastoral Lands in Kenya. In *Property, Poverty and People: Changing Rights in Property and Problems of Pastoral Development*, ed. P. T. W. Baxter and R. Hogg. Manchester, UK: Department of Social Anthropology and International Development.

Munoz-Pina, C., A. de Janvry, and E. Sadoulet. 2003. Recrafting Rights over Common Property Resources in Mexico: Divide, Incorporate and Equalize. *Economic Development and Cultural Change* 52(1): 129–158.

Mwalyosi, R. B. B. 1992. Influence of Livestock Grazing on Range Condition in South-West Maasailand, Northern Tanzania. *Journal of Applied Ecology* 29 (3): 581–588.

Mwangi, E. 2003. Institutional Change and Politics: The Transformation of Property Rights in Kenya's Maasailand. Unpublished PhD dissertation. Indiana University, Bloomington, IN.

Mwendera, E. J., M. A. M. Saleem, and Z. Woldu. 1997. Vegetation Response to Cattle Grazing in the Ethiopian Highlands. *Agriculture, Ecosystems and Environment* 64: 43–51.

Ndagala, D. 1991. Rural Development: The Ilparakuyo Experience. In *Sociological Publications in Honor of Dr. K. Ishwaran. Vol. VIII*. New Delhi: Reliance Publishing House.

Netting, Robert M. C. 1972. Of Mean and Meadows: Strategies of Alpine Land Use. *Anthropological Quarterly* 45: 132–144.

———. 1976. What Alpine Peasants Have in Common: Observations on Communal Tenure in a Swiss Village. *Human Ecology* 4: 135–46.

Ng'ethe, J. C. 1992. *Future of Livetsock Industries in East and Southern Africa*. Proceedings of a Workshop, Kadoma Ranch Hotel, Zimbabwe. Addis Ababa, Ethiopia: International Livestock Center for Africa, July 20–23, 1992.

Niamir-Fuller, M. 1998. The Resilience of Pastoral Herding in Sahelian Africa. In *Linking social and Ecological Systems: Management Practices and Social Mechanisms for Building Resilience*, ed. Fikret Berkes and Carl Folke. Cambridge: Cambridge University Press.

Niamir-Fuller, M. 1999. Managing Mobility in African Rangelands. In *Property Rights, Risk and Livestock Development*, ed. Nancy McCarthy, Brent Swallow, Michael Kirk, and Peter Hazell. Nairobi/Washington, DC: ILRI/IFPRI.

Njoka, T. J. 1979. Ecological and Socio-Cultural Trends of Kaputiei Group Ranches in Kenya. Unpublished PhD dissertation. University of California, Berkeley, CA.

North, D. 1990. *Institutions, Institutional Change and Economic Performance*. New York: Cambridge University Press.

———. 1997. Prologue. In *The Frontiers of the New Institutional Economics*, ed. J. N. Drobak and J. V. C. Nye. San Diego, CA: Academic Press.

North, D., and R. B. Thomas. 1973. *The Rise of the Western World: A New Economic History*. Cambridge: Cambridge University Press.

Noy-Meir, I., M. Gutman, and Y. Kaplan. 1989. Responses of Mediterranean Grassland Plants to Grazing and Protection. *Journal of Ecology* 77: 290–310.

Nugent, J. B., and N. Sanchez. 1991. Tribes, Chiefs and Transhumance: A Comparative Institutional Analysis. Paper presented at the Annual Meeting of the Middle Eastern Economic Association, Washington, DC, December 27–30, 1990.

———. 1998. Common Property Rights as an Endogenous Response to Risk. *American Journal of Agricultural Economics* 80: 651–657.

O'Connor, T. G., and P. W. Roux. 1995. Vegetation Changes (1947–71) in a Semi-Arid, Grassy Dwarf Shrubland in the Karoo, South Africa: Influence of Rainfall Variability and Grazing by Sheep. *Journal of Applied Ecology* 32: 612–626.

Odell, M. 1981. Botswana's First Livestock Development Project: An Experiment in Agricultural Transformation. A Project Completion Report Prepared for SIDA. Synergy International, USA.

Ohman, J. L., and T. A. Spies. 1998. Regional Gradient Analysis and Spatial Pattern of Woody Plant Communities of Oregon Forests. *Ecological Monographs* 68(2): 151–182.

Okoth-Ogendo, H. W. O. 1976. African Land Tenure Reform. In *Agricultural Development in Kenya*, ed. J. Heyer, J. K. Maitha, and W. M. Senga . Nairobi: Oxford University Press.

———. 1989. Some Issues of Theory in the Study of African Land Tenure. *Africa: Journal of the International African Institute* 59(1): 6–17.

———. 1991. *Tenants of the Crown*. Nairobi: African Center for Technology Studies Press.

———. 1993. Agrarian Reform in Sub-Saharan Africa. In *Land in African Agrarian Systems*, ed. T. J. Bassett and D. E. Crummey. Madison, WI: University of Wisconsin Press.

Ole Sadera, P. L. K. 1986. Evolution of Individuation of Group Ranches. In *Range Research and Development in Kenya*, ed. Richard M. Hansen. Morrilton, Ark: Winrock International Institute for Agricultural Development.

Ole Simel, J. 1999. Premature Land Subdivision, Encroachment of Rights and Manipulation in Maasailand—The Keekonyokie Clan Section. Arid Lands and Resource Management Network in Eastern Africa (AlARM). Working Paper No. 8. Center for Basic Research, Kampala, Uganda.

Olson, M. 1965. *The Logic of Collective Action: Public Goods and the Theory of Groups*. Cambridge, MA: Harvard University Press.

Onchoke, S. N. 1986. The Impact of Cooperative, Group and Individual Ranching Systems on Resource Productivity in South Central Kenya. Unpublished MSc thesis. A & M University, College Station, TX.

Osgood, E. S. 1970. *The Day of the Cattleman*. Chicago, IL: University of Chicago Press.

Ostrom, E. 1990. *Governing the Commons: The Evolution of Institutions for Collective Action*. Cambridge: Cambridge University Press.

————. 2001a. Reformulating the Commons. In *Protecting the Commons: A Framework for Resource Management in the Americas*, ed. J. Burger, E. Ostrom, R. B. Norgaard, D. Policansky, and B. D. Goldstein. Washington, DC: Island Press.

————. 2001b. The Puzzle of Counterproductive Property Rights Reforms: A Conceptual Analysis. In *Access to Land, Rural Poverty, and Public Action*, ed. Alain de Janvry, Gustavo Gordillo, Jean-Philippe Platteau, and Elisabeth Sadoulet. A Study Prepared for the World Institute for Development Economics Research of the United Nations University (UNU/WIDER). Clarendon: Oxford University Press.

————. 2005. *Understanding Institutional Diversity*. Princeton, NJ: Princeton University Press.

Ostrom, E., J. Burger, C. Fields, R. B. Norgaard, and D. Policansky. 1999. Revisiting the Commons: Local Lessons, Global Challenges. *Science* 284: 278–282.

Palmer, M. 1993. Putting Things in Even Better Order: The Advantages of Canonical Correspondence Analysis. *Ecology* 74(8): 2215–2230.

Peters, P. E. 1987. Embedded Systems and Rooted Models: The Grazing Lands of Botswana and the Commons Debate. In *The Question of the Commons: The Culture and Ecology of Communal Resources*, ed. B. J. McCay and J. M. Acheson. Tucson, AZ: University of Arizona Press.

————. 2002. The Limits of Negotiability: Security, Equity and Class Formation in Africa's Land Systems. In *Negotiating Property in Africa*, ed. K. Juul and C. Lund. Porstmouth, NH: Heineman.

Picht, C. 1987. Common Property Regimes in Swiss Alpine Meadows. Paper Prepared for the Conference on Advances in Comparative Institutional Analysis, at the Inter-University Center of Postgraduate Studies, Dubrovnik, Yugoslavia, October 19–23, 1987. Initial Draft.

Pierson, P. 2000a. Not Just What, but When: Timing and Sequence in Political Process. *Studies in American Political Development* 14: 72–79.

————. 2000b. The Limits of Design: Explaining Institutional Origins and Change. *Governance* 13: 475–499.

Platteau, J.-P. 1995. Reforming Land Rights in Sub-Saharan Africa: Issues of Efficiency and Equity. Discussion Paper No. 60. United Nations Research Institute for Social Development.

————. 1996. The Evolutionary Theory of Land Rights as Applied to Sub-Saharan Africa: A Critical Assessment. *Development and Change* 27(1): 29–86.

————. 2000. *Institutions, Social Norms and Economic Development: Fundamentals of Development Economics*. Amsterdam: Harwood Academic Publishers.

Pratt, D. J., and M. D. Gwynne. 1977. *Rangeland Management and Ecology in East Africa*. London: Hodder and Stoughton.

Raikes, P. L. 1981. Livestock Development and Policy in East Africa. Center for Development Research. Publication No. 6. Scandinavian Institute of African Studies, Uppsala.

Richards, E. 1982. *A History of the Highland Clearances*. London: Croom Helm.

Rocheleau, D., and D. Edmunds. 1997. Women, Men and Trees: Gender, Power and Property in Forest and Agrarian Landscapes. *World Development* 25(8): 1351–1371.

Rodriguez, C. L., C. S. Galbraith, and C. H. Stiles. 2006. False Myths and Indigenous Entrepreneurial Strategies. In *Self-Determination: The Other Path for Native Americans*, ed. T. L. Anderson, B. Benson, and T. E. Flanagan. Stanford: Stanford University Press.

Roemer, J. E. 1989. A Public Ownership Resolution of the Tragedy of the Commons. *Social Philosophy and Policy* 2(6): 74–92.

Runge, C. F. 1986. Common Property and Collective Action in Economic Development. *World Development* 14(5): 623–635.

Rutten, M. M. E. M. 1992. *Selling Wealth to Buy Poverty: The Process of the Individualization of Landownership among the Maasai Pastoralists of Kajiado District, Kenya, 1890–1900*. Nijmegen Studies in Development and Cultural Change, Volume 10. Breitenbach: Saarbrucken.

———. 1995. The Tragedy of Individualizing the Commons: The Outcome of Subdividing the Maasai Pastoralist Group Ranches in Kajiado District, Kenya. Paper presented at the Fifth Common Property Conference, Reinventing the Commons, Bodo, Norway, International Association for the Study of Common Property, May 24–28, 1995.

Sandberg, A. 1993. Entrenchment of State Property Rights to Northern Forests, Berries and Pastures. Working Paper W93–25. Workshop in Political Theory and Policy Analysis, Indiana University, Bloomington, IN.

Sandford, G. F. 1919. *An Administrative and Political History of the Masai Reserve*. London: Waterlow and Sons.

Sandford, S. 1981. Review of World Bank Livestock Activities in Dry Tropical Africa. Agriculture and Development Department, World Bank, Washington, DC.

———. 1983. *Management of Pastoral Development in the Third World*. Overseas Development Institute. Bath: Pitman Press.

Schlager, E., and E. Ostrom. 1992. Property Rights Regimes and Natural Resources: A Conceptual Analysis. *Land Economics* 68(3): 249–262.

———. 1996. The Formation of Property Rights. In *Rights to Nature: Ecologic, Economic, Cultural and Political Principles of Institutions for the Environment*, ed. S. S. Hanna, C. Folke, and K. Maler. Washington, DC: Island Press.

Scoones, I., ed. 1994. *Living with Uncertainty: New Directions in Pastoral Development in Africa*. London: Intermediate Technology Publications, IIED.

———. 1995. Integrating Social Sciences into Rangeland Management: Chairperson's Summary and Comments. Invited Presentation at the Fifth International Rangeland Congress, Salt Lake City, Utah, July 23–28, 1995.

Seabright, P. 1993. Managing Local Commons: Theoretical Issues in Incentive Design. *Journal of Economic Perspectives* 7(4): 113–134.

Sheehy, D. P. 1993. Grazing Management Strategies as a Factor Influencing Ecological Stability of Mongolian Grasslands. *Nomadic Peoples* 33: 17–30.

Shipton, P., and M. Goheen. 1992. Introduction: Understanding African Land-Holding: Power, Wealth and Meaning. *Africa: Journal of the International African Institute* 62(3): 307–325.

Simpson, M. C. 1973. Alternative Strategies for Range Development in Kenya. Rural Development Study No. 2. Department of Agricultural Economics, University of Leeds, Leeds.

Sneath, D. 1998. State Policy and Pasture Degradation in Inner Asia. *Science* 281: 1147–1148.

SNV/SARDEP. 1999. Poverty, Target Groups and Governance Environment in Kajiado District, Kenya: A District Analysis. Unpublished Report. ETC East Africa.

Solbrig, O. T. 1991. Ecosystems and Global Environmental Change. In *Global Environmental Change*, ed. R. Correll. Berlin: Springer-Verlag.

———. 1993. Ecological Constraints to Savanna Land Use. In *The World's Savannas: Economic Driving Forces, Ecological Constraints and Policy Options for Sustainable Land Use*, ed. M. D. Young and O. T. Solbrig. UNESCO Man and the Biosphere Series, Volume 12. Paris: UNESCO and the Parthenon Publishing Group.

Solbrig, O. T., E. Medina, and J. F. Silva. 1996. Determinants of Tropical Savannas. In *Biodiversity and Savanna Ecosystem Processes*, ed. O. T. Solbrig, E. Medina, and J. F. Silva. Ecological Studies, Volume 121. Berlin: Springer-Verlag.

Sommer, G., and R. Vossen. 1993. Dialects, Sectiolects, or Simply Lects? The Maa Language in Time Perspective. In *Being Maasai: Ethnicity and Identity in East Africa*, ed. T. Spear and R. Waller. London: J. Currey; Dar es Salaam: Mkuki na Nyota; Nairobi: EAEP; Athens, OH: Ohio University Press.

Sorrenson, M. P. K. 1968. *The Origins of European Settlement in Kenya*. London: Oxford University Press.

Southgate, C., and D. Hulme. 2000. Uncommon Property: The Scramble for Wetland in Southern Kenya. In *African Enclosures? The Social Dynamics of Wetlands in Drylands*, ed. Philip Woodhouse, Henry Bernstein, and David Hulme. Oxford: James Curry.

Spear, T. 1993. Introduction. In *Being Maasai: Ethnicity and Identity in East Africa*, ed. Thomas T. Spear and R. Waller. London: J. Currey; Dar es Salaam: Mkuki na Nyota; Nairobi: EAEP; Athens, OH: Ohio University Press.

Spencer, I. R. G. 1983. Pastoralism and Colonial Policy in Kenya, 1895–1929. In *Imperialism, Colonialism and Hunger: East and Central Africa*, ed. R. I. Rotberg. Toronto: D. C. Heath and Company.

Spencer, P. 1988. *The Maasai of Matapato: A Study of Rituals and Rebellions*. Bloomington, IN: Indiana University Press.

———. 1993. "Being Maasai, being in time." In *Being Maasai: Ethnicity and Identity in East Africa*, ed. T. Spear and R. Waller. London: James Currey, 140–156.

———. 1997. *The Pastoral Continuum: The Marginalization of Tradition in East Africa*. Oxford: Clarendon Press.

Stevenson, Glenn, G. 1991. *Common Property Economics: A General Theory and Land Use Applications*. Cambridge, MA: Cambridge University Press.

Stoddart, L. A., A. D. Smith, and T. W. Box. 1975. *Range Management*. New York: McGraw Hill.

Sutton, J. E. G. 1993. Becoming Maasailand. In *Being Maasai: Ethnicity and Identity in East Africa*, ed. Thomas T. Spear and Richard Waller. London: J. Currey; Dar es Salaam: Mkuki na Nyota; Nairobi: EAEP; Athens, OH: Ohio University Press.

Swinnen, J. F. M. 2001. Transition from Collective Farms to Individual Tenures in Central and Eastern Europe. In *Access to Land, Rural Poverty, and Public Action*, ed. A. de Janvry, G. Gordillo, J. P. Platteau, and E. Sadoulet. A study prepared for the World Institute for Development Economics Research of the United Nations University (UNU/WIDER). Clarendon: Oxford University Press.

Talle, A. 1988. *Women at a Loss: Changes in Maasai Pastoralism and Their Effects on Gender Relations*. Stockholm: Department of Social Anthropology, University of Stockholm.

Tapper, R. 1979. *Pasture and Politics: Economics, Conflict and Ritual among Shahsevan Nomads of Northwestern Iran*. London: N. Y. Academic Press.

———. 1985. The Politics of Desertification in Marginal Environments: The Sahelian Case, In *Divesting Nature's Capital: The Political Economy of Environmental Abuse in the Third World*, ed. H. Jeffrey Leonard. New York: Holmes and Meier.

Ter Braak, C. J. F . 1986. Canonical Correspondence Analysis: A New Eigen Vector Analysis for Multivariate Direct Gradient Analysis. *Ecology* 67(5): 1167–1179.

———. 1987. The Analysis of Vegetation-Environment Relationships by Canonical Correspondence Analysis. *Vegetatio* 69: 69–97.

———. 1994. Canonical Community Ordination. Part I: Basic Theory and Linear Methods. *Ecoscience* 1(2): 127–140.

———. 1995. Ordination. In *Data Analysis in Community and Landscape Ecology*, ed. R. H. G. Jongman, C. J. F. Ter Braak, and O. F. R. Van Tongeren. Cambridge: Cambridge University Press.

Thebaud, B., H. Grell, and S. Mieke. 1995. Recognizing the Effectiveness of Traditional Pastoral Practices: Lessons from a Controlled Grazing Experiment in Northern Senegal. International Institute for Environment and Development. Issue Paper No. 55. Drylands Program.

Thelen, K. 1999. Historical Institutionalism in Comparative Politics. *Annual Review of Political Science* 2: 369–404.

———. 2003. How Institutions Evolve: Insights from Comparative Historical Analysis. In *Comparative Historical Analysis in the Social Sciences*, ed. James Mahoney and Dietrich Rueschmeyer. Cambridge: Cambridge University Press.

Thomas, D. S. G., D. Sporton, and J. Perkins. 2000. The Environmental Impact of Livestock Ranches in the Kalahari. Botswana: Natural Resource Use, Ecological Change and Human Response in a Dynamic Dryland System. *Land Degradation and Development* 11(4): 327–341.

Thompson, J. T., D. Feeny, and R. J. Oakerson. 1992. Institutional Dynamics and Dissolution of Common-Property Resource Management. In *Making the Commons Work: Theory, Practice and Policy*, ed. D. W. Bromley. San Francisco, CA: ICS Press.

Thomson, J. T. 1885. *Through Masai Land: A Journey of Exploration among the Snowclad Volcanic Mountains and Strange Tribes of Eastern Equatorial Africa*. London: Frank Cass and Co.

Thurow, T. L., and A. J. Hussein. 1989. Observations on Vegetation Responses to Improved Grazing Systems in Somalia. *Journal of Range Management* 42: 16–19.

Tignor, R. T. 1976. *The Colonial Transformation of Kenya: The Kamba, Kikuyu and Maasai from 1900 to 1939*. Princeton, NJ: Princeton University Press.

Tinley, K. L. 1982. The Influence of Soil Moisture Balance in Ecosystem Pattern in Southern Africa. In *Ecology of Tropical Savannas*, ed. B. J. Huntley and B. H. Walker. Berlin: Springer-Verlag.

Tomikawa, M. 1979. The Migrations and Inter-Tribal Relations of the Pastoral Datoga. *SENRI Ethnological Studies* 5: 1–46.

Toulmin, C., and J. F. Quan, eds. 2000. *Evolving Land Rights, Policy and Tenure in Africa*. London: DFID/IIED/NRI.

Trollope, W. S. W. 1982. Ecological Effects of Fire in South African Savannas. In *Ecology of Tropical Savannas*, ed. B. J. Huntley and B. H. Walker. Ecological Studies, Volume 42. Berlin: Springer-Verlag.

Tserendash, S., and B. Erdenbataar. 1993. Performance and Management of Natural Pasture in Mongolia. *Nomadic Peoples* 33: 9–15.

Turner, M. D. 1999. Spatial and Temporal Scaling of Grazing Impact on the Species Composition and Productivity of Sahelian Annual Grasslands. *Journal of Arid Environments* 41: 277–297.

Van den Brink, Rogier, Daniel W. Bromley, and Jean-Paul Chavas. 1995. "The Economics of Cain and Abel: Agro-pastoral Property Rights in the Sahel." *Journal of Development Studies* 31(3):373–399.

Van Wijngaarden, W. 1985. *Elephants-Grass-Trees-Grazers*. ITC Publications No. 4. Enschede, the Netherlands.

Waller, R. D. 1993. Acceptees and Aliens: Kikuyu Settlement in Maasailand. In *Being Maasai: Ethnicity and Identity in East Africa*, ed. Thomas T. Spear and Richard Waller. London: J. Currey; Dar es Salaam: Mkuki na Nyota; Nairobi: EAEP; Athens, OH: Ohio University Press.

———. 1999. Pastoral Poverty in Historical Perspective. In *The Poor Are Not Us: Poverty and Pastoralism in Eastern Africa*, ed. D. M. Anderson and V. Broch-Due. Oxford: James Curry; Nairobi: East African Publishing House; Athens, OH: Ohio University Press.

Western, D., and T. Dunne. 1979. Environmental Aspects of Settlement and Site Decisions among Pastoral Maasai. *Human Ecology* 7(1): 75–98.

Westoby, M., B. Walker, and I. Noy-Meir. 1989. Oppurtunistic Management of Rangelands Not at Equilibrium. *Journal of Range Management* 42(4): 266–274.

White, J. M., and S. J. Meadows. 1981. *Evaluation of the Contribution of Group and Individual Ranches in Kajiado District, Kenya*. Nairobi: Ministry of Livestock Development.

Wiebe, D. W., and R. Meinzen-Dick. 1998. Property Rights as Policy Tools for Sustainable Development. *Land Use Policy* 15(3): 203–215.

Wily, L. 2002. New Land Policy in Africa: An Overview of Emerging Trends. A presentation to the Land Seminar of the Constitution of Kenya Review Commission, Whitesands Hotel, Mombasa, May 4–5, 2002.

Williams, D. M. 1996. Grassland Enclosures: Catalyst of Land Degradation in Inner Mongolia. *Human Organization* 55(3): 307–313.

Woodhouse, P. 1997. Governance and Local Environmental Management in Africa. *Review of African Political Economy* 74: 537–547.

World Bank. 2003. *Land Policy for Growth and Poverty Reduction*. Oxford: Oxford University Press.

Yelling, J. A. 1977. *Common Field and Enclosure in England, 1450–1850*. Hamden: Archcon Books.

Zaal, F. 1999a. *Pastoralism in a Global Age: Livestock Marketing and Pastoral Commercial Activities in Kenya and Burkina Faso*. Amsterdam: Thela Thesis.

———. 1999b. Economic Integration in Pastoral Areas: Commercialization and Social Change among Kenya's Maasai. *Nomadic Peoples* 3(2): 97–114.

INDEX

Note: *Italic* page numbers refer to figures and tables.